On Being the Church
of Jesus Christ in
Tumultuous Times

On Being the Church
of Jesus Christ in
Tumultuous Times

Joe R. Jones

Cascade Books
A division of *Wipf & Stock Publishers*
199 West 8th Avenue, Suite 3 • Eugene OR 97401

On Being the Church of Jesus Christ in Tumultuous Times

Cascade Books
A Division of Wipf and Stock Publishers
199 West 8th Avenue, Suite 3
Eugene, Oregon 97401

ISBN: 1-59752-276-7

Printed in the United States

In grateful memory of
parents extraordinaire

Idabel Augusta Seitz Jones
Judge Dick Sterling Jones

and for siblings

Judge Charles Redman Jones
Mary Carolyn Jones Ford
Sterling Brown Jones

generous and patient
with a
rambunctious younger brother

Contents

Part Three: Church Discourses and Practices in Tumultuous Times

Acknowledgements

Permission to publish previously copyrighted articles has been granted by *Mid-Stream*, *Encounter*, and *The Journal of Religion* (University of Chicago Press). All previously published articles have been edited for inclusion here.

All biblical quotations and reference formatting style, unless otherwise noted, are from the New Revised Standard Version Bible, copyright 1989, Division of Christian Education of the National Council of Churches of Christ in the United States of America.

Chapter Three published in *Mid-Stream* 33 (1994) 377–89.

Chapter Four published in two parts in *Encounter* 66 (2005) 1–21, 87–105.

Chapter Five published in *The Journal of Religion* 57 (1977) 232–51. © 1977 by the University of Chicago Press.

Chapter Six published in *Encounter* 57 (1989) 232–51.

Chapter Seven published in *Encounter* 56 (1995) 1–18.

Chapter Eight published in *Encounter* 59 (1998) 274–91.

Chapter Nine published in *Encounter* 63 (2002) 129–36. This *Festschrift* issue was in honor of Professor Clark Williamson upon his retirement from Christian Theological Seminary.

Chapter Eleven published in *Encounter* 61 (2000) 439–48.

Chapter Twelve published in *Encounter* 65 (2004) 215–21.

Chapter Sixteen published in *Encounter* 65 (2004) 403–11.

Preface

It is one of the blessed wonders of life that we can accrue debts to folk who have graciously enriched our lives and elicited from us surprising possibilities that might otherwise have been hidden or neglected. My family of origin, to whom I have dedicated this book, formed me in ways that only age and maturity could truly bring to my awareness and appreciation. My parents are now dead, and many are my laments that I missed having this or that conversation with each about important matters of life and death and that I was too often too reticent to express the gratitude that was their due. Hopefully the writings in this book will convey something of what I have made of their abiding influence on my life and my gratitude for their unceasing generosity.

In honoring my parents, I am also honoring siblings, raised in the same household of sturdy love. Brother Charles, an inspirational lay leader in the church, died an untimely death amidst a flourishing career in the federal judiciary. Sister Carolyn and brother Sterling have remained admirably steadfast in conveying a more conservative view than I have been wont to adopt. Even so, bonds of love and patience abound.

My own immediate family—spouse, Sarah, and three extraordinary daughters, Serene, Kindy, and Verity Jones—have similarly tethered me with affectionate threads of respect, critique, hope, and abundant laughter. They have empowered me to bring to fruitful expression the beneficent trajectories of being raised in a Christian family and living in the church as the Body of Christ. And Sarah has been that primordial mate who builds up, shines light, and persuades with grace.

Over three decades ago, Paul A. Crow, Jr, then President of the Council on Christian Unity—the ecumenical office of the Christian Church (Disciples of Christ)—solicited my service on the Commission on Theology, which functioned as the point of reference for theological reports and controversies among the Disciples of Christ. Upon completion of its final report on ecclesiology in 1997, the Commission was disbanded. Its reorganized successor has also since been disbanded as dysfunctional—a development that stands as a sad commentary on the present state of affairs among Disciples. Working on the Commission was a great joy and benefit to me, and I regret its demise. Several of the chapters in this book had their origin in my writings for the Commission. I am grateful to Paul Crow for the wise and energetic leadership he rendered to the Disciples in ecumenical affairs and for the friendship, collegiality, and encouragement he extended to me over these several decades.

Sermons in chapters 10, 16, and 17 and the prayers in chapter 20 were given in the last few years at St. Paul United Methodist Church in Muskogee, Oklahoma. I am grateful to the Reverend M. Kevin Tully for his pastoral friendship and for inviting me to participate with his congregation in these ways.

I am grateful to Stanley Hauerwas—a colleague in graduate school and formed by many of the same questions, concerns, and patterns of thought as I, and a vigorous conversation partner and provocateur in the last decade—for urging me to get more writings into print and for recommending Cascade Books.

Finally, the folk of Cascade Books—Jon Stock, K. C. Hanson, Jim Tedrick, David Root, and Jim Stock—have been immensely kind and helpful in gathering this book together and getting it into publishable form.

Joe R. Jones
Anchor Point
Ft. Gibson Lake, Oklahoma

Introduction

Even a casual acquaintance with the history of the church will disabuse us of the nostalgic notion that the church of the past lived in virtually non-tumultuous times, utterly unmarked by violence, conflict, and disagreement. Instead we know that worldly and churchly turbulence has been with the church throughout the centuries.

This is a collection of essays, sermons, and prayers that have been composed across almost four decades of dramatic conflicts both within the church and between the church and its various American cultures. As I look back over thirty-five years of teaching theology and ethics in universities and seminaries, it appears to me that all of it has been in the midst of severe seismic shifts in church life and in the larger culture. I hope that bringing together the writings in this book will at least provide some evidence as to how one passionate professor and rather minor author struggled with being a theologian for the church during tumultuous times, persisting even into this century.

Believing that the church is the Body of Christ in the world, we must remember that it is also an "earthen vessel," ever in need of grace, reform, and renewal. Precisely as the Body of Christ, comprised of many members, the church must be the sort of community that sustains a vigorous and continuing conversation within itself as to who has called it into being, to whom it is responsible, and what it is called to be and to do.

In the midst of uncertainties and troubling divisions within itself, the church is tempted *either* to look to the world for some clues as to what the world—or the elites of the world—finds credible and worthy of the church's being and doing *or* to turn in upon itself in simple opposition to the world. Neither option will work well for the church. The church has been much too tempted in the last century to discern its calling and defining self-understanding from the voices of the world. Yet, even though it must recover its most basic calling from its founding Scriptures and profound traditions, the church cannot simply be in opposition to the world.

Even though the church—as an earthen vessel—is often also a *broken body*, it must strive, in the midst of its brokenness in tumultuous times, to remember its calling and mission as an *alternative community living an alternative way of life under the Lordship of Jesus Christ*.[1] This collection of writings is bound together by the pursuit of what it means to be such an alternative community in any and all worldly times.

Being so bound together, this collection contains some work from the late 1970s, but most of the writings have come to life since 1988, at which time I began teaching at Christian Theological Seminary. Much of my academic activity as a systematic theologian came to fruition in the publication in 2002 of *A Grammar of Christian Faith: Systematic Explorations in Christian Life and Doctrine*.[2] While I had done considerable writing before this publication, not much of it was well known or widely read. To some it appeared that the systematic theology had sprung to life out of nowhere. In the interest of showing the seeds from which the work sprang, I am including some of the earlier essays, as well as a host of

---

[1] The reader should be aware that I use italicized words to emphasize points and to draw attention to that particular use of the word or words. Also, I will use single and double quotes in special ways. Single quote marks ['. . . .'] are used to indicate one of three signals. (1) It can signal that we are talking *about* a word or sign, as in the sentence 'The word 'language' is used to refer to the natural languages of persons.' (2) It can signal that we are highlighting a special use of a word or locution, as in 'The actions of 'perichoresis' are crucial to church life.' (3) It can signal that we are talking about the meaning of the sentence itself that is included within the single quotes, as in the two sentences used above. Functions one and two of the single quotes can also be accomplished by use of *italic* type. Double quote marks [" . . . "] are used when I am actually quoting from another text or some person's actual speech. These writing practices may seem peculiar, but they are ways in which I am intending to remind the reader that words have varying uses which are often unnoticed in ordinary styles of writing.

[2] 2 vols., Lanham, MD: Rowman and Littlefield, 2002. Hereinafter referred to as GCF.

writings from the 1990s. The sermons and prayers included in this collection all date from the twenty-first century.[3]

It is my hope that the writings are also able to stand on their own, whether or not they illuminate the ruminations that led into and out from *A Grammar of Christian Faith*. In that respect, the collection's availability does not depend on the reader having read the systematic theology.

Church Discourses and Practices

An important early essay was published in 1977, "Some Remarks on Authority and Revelation in Kierkegaard."[4] I had been working on the essay for several years while the concepts in it were brewing steadily. It should be evident that, not only was I working through objections then current to theological discussions of Christian revelation-talk, I was also reaching for a method of writing and thinking that relies heavily on the analysis of language in living, concrete use.

The next early piece is "Christian Illiteracy and Christian Education," given as an address to the General Assembly of the Christian Church (Disciples of Christ) in October 1977.[5] As the title itself suggests, my concern was the incapacity of my own tradition, and by extension most other mainline traditions, to teach the faith with clarity and passion. While much theology being done during these years was emphasizing the need to change Christian language and concepts to fit modern conditions of relevance and intelligibility, my emphasis was that the distinctive language of the church itself must be recovered in order to form the lives of folk otherwise confused about what it means to be a member of the church as the Body of Christ and thereby to be a Christian.

Out of these early works and my teaching during the 1960s and 1970s, three patterns of concepts emerged for me. First, all attempts to elucidate Christian faith require focusing on what I came to call *the discourses and practices*

---

[3] All of these writings have previously been posted on my web site, www.grammaroffaith.com.

[4] *The Journal of Religion*, vol. 57, no. 3, 232–51. Included here as chapter five.

[5] Not previously published, but included here as chapter two. In a similar vein and presented about this time, see "On Doing Church Theology Today," *Encounter*, vol. 41, no. 3 (Summer, 1980), 279–86.

of the church. It is in the language of church—and its grounding in particular practices—that we learn how to engage in an enlivening and nurturing conversation about Christian faith. We must strive to identify and explain the distinctive themes and teachings of the church and identify and describe the distinctive practices that are congruent with those themes and teachings.

Second, from these early years of teaching, a definition of the church was beginning to emerge and eventually took the following shape, which will reappear often in the writings in this book:[6]

> The church is that liberative and redemptive
> community of persons
> called into being
> by the Gospel of Jesus Christ
> through the Holy Spirit
> to witness in word and deed
> to the living triune God
> for the benefit of the world
> to the glory of God.

It is unlikely that the church will ever have a vivid and intellectually cohesive life if there is continual disarray in its own self-understanding about who it is and what its mission is. My definition is offered as an orienting conversation-starter about what it means to be the church of Jesus Christ. By emphasizing that the mission of the church is "to witness in word and deed to the reality of the triune God," I place *witnessing to God* as central to the life of the church. The issues of revelation and Christian doctrines that are explored in the Kierkegaard article are only meaningful in the context of the life of the church with its distinctive discourses and practices.

Third, if the church is that sort of community of persons that is called into being by the Gospel of Jesus Christ, then obviously it is decisively important to have some agreement about that Gospel. Given my already muscular insistence on an incarnational understanding of Jesus and a

---

[6] See in particular chapters 1, 3, and 4 for extended discussions of this definition of the church.

trinitarian understanding of the reality of God, the following definition of the Gospel has long held an anchoring function for my theological work:

The Gospel of Jesus Christ is the Good News
that the God of Israel, the Creator of all creatures,
has in freedom and love become incarnate
in the life, death, and resurrection of Jesus of Nazareth
to enact and reveal God's gracious reconciliation
of humanity to Godself, and
through the Holy Spirit calls and empowers human beings
to participate in God's liberative and redemptive work by
acknowledging God's gracious forgiveness in Jesus,
repenting of human sin,
receiving the gift of freedom, and
embracing authentic community by
loving the neighbor and the enemy,
caring for the whole creation, and
hoping for the final triumph of God's grace
as the triune Ultimate Companion of all creatures.

Among many matters of note in these two proposed definitions, I hope it is apparent that the theological center is in a high christology that is simultaneously incarnationally *kenotic*[7] in character and therefore

---

[7] The Greek word *kenosis* comes into Christian discourse largely through its use in Paul's rightly surprising use in Philippians 2:5-8:

Let the same mind be in you that was in Christ Jesus,
who, though he was in the form of God,
did not regard equality with God
as something to be exploited,
but **emptied** [*ekenosen*] himself,
taking the form of a slave,
being born of a slave.
Being born in human likeness,
and being found in human form,
he humbled himself and became obedient to the point of death—
even death on a cross.

Jesus, then, is the self-emptying of God-coming-in-human-form, indeed in the form of a slave eventually encountering death on the cross.

demanding a trinitarian explication. When a high kenotic christology stands at the center, it requires a reconstructed trinitarian doctrine of a God who is complex and tri-moded.[8] It is not so much that every Christian and all of the church must understand the nuances and fine points of trinitarian doctrine; rather, the need is to understand that God has become human in Jesus of Nazareth without ceasing to be God and that this becoming human is for the salvation of the world. It also follows that if God has become incarnate in a human being, then God must in some sense be conceived as having the power of temporal agency and movement and the power of being-acted-upon by creatures. Most of traditional theology wanted to be incarnational without being kenotic, without having a complex, interrelated God, and without having God subject to being-acted-upon.[9]

These considerations are important for the life of the church, for a church is completely lost if there is not some common understanding in answering these critical questions: 1) Who is God?—or, how is God to be identified? 2) Who are we humans and how are we to live? 3) What is our destiny and for what may humans hope? As will come to the fore repeatedly through this collection of writings, the character and content of the discourses and practices of the church matter greatly to the self-understanding and life of the church.

There is a strong inclination among church folk in our time to suppose that 'beliefs do not really matter; what matters are our actions and feelings.' It is sometimes said 'belief in the divinity of Jesus does not matter; what matters is following Jesus.' Such language presupposes that it is intelligible to *believe* in the divinity of Jesus and *not* follow Jesus. On the contrary, I argue that such is not intelligible in Christian terms. To believe in the divinity of Jesus is impossible—even unintelligible—without following Jesus' pattern of teaching and living. To be sure, some person may *say* 'I believe in the divinity of Jesus' without in any actual way living according to Jesus' pattern. But let us call this what it is: *lip-service-chatter*

---

[8] The further rationale for understanding God as triune is explored in some detail in chapters four and eight.

[9] These are difficult notions, I must admit, but their implications are astonishingly important because Christian theology pivots around a divine/human Jesus and a triune God. The full explication of these concepts takes up much of the space in GCF, but pages 149–232 can be consulted.

disconnected from any discipleship to Jesus. People, even people within the church, often speak shallowly and live superficially. It takes passion and commitment to *say and mean* 'I confess Jesus as Lord and Savior.'[10]

Of course, one might 'follow after Jesus' in some ways and not believe in Jesus' divinity, but it would be a Jesus detached from the incarnate life of God graciously enacting the reconciliation of the world. Remember, folk have to *learn how* to call Jesus divine, and that cannot be done in separation from following after him. I worry that there are too many earnest folk who suppose the divinity of Jesus is dispensable for Christian speaking and living. Further, this emphasis on a non-divine Jesus fails, in my judgment, to grasp how radically Jesus—as incarnate God—alters and intensifies our understanding of the reality of God. Yet, there is much confusion and discord about what it means to be the *church of Jesus Christ*.

This theme will be constant in this collection of writings: *the church is the necessary context for becoming and being a Christian.* However, it has been common in the American liberal tradition to suppose that one could be a Christian individually without any connection to the church. Chapter four, "The Church as Ark of Salvation," is largely conceived as a critique of this supposition. Being Christian and being in the church are inherently and necessarily bound together. It is in the discourses and practices of the church that one *learns how* to be a Christian and to live in Christian community.

Hence, *ecclesiology*—the consideration of what sort of community is the church of Jesus Christ—is present in all my theologizing efforts. The church, as the context for becoming a Christian, is also the context for Christian theologizing. In fact, I propose that all of the church's distinctive discourses are *theological*—intending in a variety of ways to say who God is and what God has done and is doing and what we humans are to become. Theology is not something performed first or supremely in the academy by professors of theology. Theologizing is being done any time the people of the church speak in their distinctive language. It is, of course, another question as to whether the theology being done, in particular or in general,

---

[10] Paul Holmer, a former professor and mentor of mine, made a similar point when he said in class one day that an old man had once confessed to Holmer that it had taken him years "to know how to say and mean 'I know my Redeemer liveth.'" That is what I call the 'depth grammar' of Christian discourse.

is faithful and true. But the church is first and last that *place* where the conversation about what is faithful and true to God is carried on and sustained in self-critical dialogues. There is such a thing as *being-learned* in the speaking and enacting of Christian discourse. We should be wary of supposing that academic professors are always *learned* in that peculiar way.[11]

I should also note that I am proposing an understanding of Christian faith that eventuates in what I call "Universal Redemption." This is a long-standing conviction, especially given my radically Reformed understanding of God's grace. I stand with Augustine and Calvin in affirming that no one is saved in any other way than by the grace of God, thereby denying that any of us save ourselves by our own righteous living. Unfortunately, Augustine and Calvin both believed that an *ultimate dual destiny* is a theological necessity for the church. This belief required each to ground both salvation and damnation in God's presumably eternal pre-destination of folk from the foundations of the creation.[12]

Chapter seven, "Schematic Reflections on Salvation in Jesus Christ," was the first published attempt to bring these convictions about salvation to the light of public scrutiny, though several earlier versions were present in my courses and in presentations to the Faculty Colloquium at Christian Theological Seminary. To discuss salvation issues with clarity requires making some distinctions among various meanings of the word 'salvation' in biblical and traditional discourses. What are simply labeled "Salvation I," "Salvation II," and "Salvation III" in this schematic discussion, are later in GCF named respectively "Justification and Reconciliation," "Historic Redemption," and "Ultimate Redemption."[13] It is my hope that the nuanced and multi-dimensional analysis being proposed about God's ultimate redemption will find its way more explicitly into the liturgical, prayer, and educational discourses of the church.

By the time a reader has read the whole of this collection of writings, I hope she will no longer think it odd that a radically orthodox christology

---

[11] As an academic professor of theology and ethics, I have myself often been called up short by my continual readings in the works of Søren Kierkegaard. Chapter eleven, "Kierkegaard: Spy, Judge, and Friend," contains some relevant musings on the perils of professorship.

[12] The concept of dual destiny is rigorously examined in GCF, 709–24.

[13] See further discussion of salvation concepts in GCF, 503–09, 712–17, 741–48.

of incarnate grace and a radically orthodox doctrine of Trinity imply irrevocably a radically inclusive ultimate redemption by the triune God who is the merciful Ultimate Companion of all creatures.

Tumultuous Times in Politics, Terror, and War

These present times are tumultuous because we are daily reminded that a so-called "War on Terror" is the defining movement and cause around which all other contemporary movements and causes are to be understood and evaluated. Were the discourses of the church sturdy, lucid, and deep, we would be empowered to worry whether this 'war' has become an idol undermining Christian construals of—ways of thinking about—God and neighbors and strangers and enemies. As it is, this war deeply divides Christians and is wreaking havoc in the world.

On September 24, 2001, following what we have come to refer to simply as "9/11," I wrote a letter to the churches, included here as chapter one, struggling to sort through the overwhelming feelings and fears that seemed to be stalking all of us—Americans certainly but even many beyond America. In this letter I was struggling with a centuries-old dilemma of the church's relation to the world in which it lives. That dilemma is especially acute in the modern world characterized by the rise of nation-states that organize and provide identity to humans in their various social locations. I did not want to repudiate all meaningful patriotic feelings for the nation-states in which persons live, but neither did I want to presume those feelings should be uncritically and automatically endorsed by the church.

Certainly throughout the church's life it has been a constant temptation to Christians to regard their national/cultural identity as more basic than their Christian identity. Hence, many in the church in our time are confused about their most basic self-understanding and identity: am I first and last an American who *happens* also to be a Christian, or am I first and last a Christian who *happens* also to be an American? Which identity is the most powerful in shaping how one lives and thinks? I contend that one symptom of the disarray in the church today is that most of its actual members are more decisively formed and informed by their national identity than by their identity as disciples of Jesus Christ.

But I propose that the decisive identity for the church—and therefore for the Christian—is an identity grounded in affirming Jesus Christ as Lord and Savior. Without some clarity about the priority among our various socially-conferred and socially-constructed identities, the church—and therefore the presumed Christian—will be utterly incapacitated to think pertinently about war and peace, and therefore about this war and the claim to pursue peace and freedom by means of war. In the absence of a vigorous self-understanding grounded in the Gospel of Jesus Christ, the church devolves into being no more than a *mirror image* of the values—the discourses and practices—that shape the world in which it lives. Hence, being the church of Jesus Christ in tumultuous times at least involves understanding what it means simply in all times and places to be that community that is the Body of Christ in the world.

This problem is most acute for the so-called 'liberals' and the so-called 'conservatives' among the church, for both seem determined to think about the war and terror simply according to the their liberal or conservative political dispositions. Completely lost in this is how to think and act, first and foremost, from the perspective of being a confessing and disciplined member of the Body of Christ in the world. Put another way: the discourses of the church should be the means by which Christians come to construe the world of the nation-states, with their internal and external politics, as the world over which Jesus Christ reigns.

In this connection, in debt to the writings of John Howard Yoder and Stanley Hauerwas, I am beginning to think of the discourses and practices of the church as constructing a *politics* that is to be distinguished from the politics of the nation-states.[14] In contrast to the political theories and practices of the worldly nation-states, the church is that sort of *polis*—that sort of visibly identifiable community—that is summoned into existence by the Gospel of Jesus Christ and given the salvific task of

---

[14] John Howard Yoder's book, *The Politics of Jesus*, 2d ed. (Grand Rapids, MI: Eerdmans, 1994), with original edition appearing in 1972, can be seen as the principal text initiating a new understanding of the church as a political community. See Stanley Hauerwas, *In Good Company: The Church as Polis* (Notre Dame: University of Notre Dame Press, 1995) for a felicitous statement of these concerns. An excellent study of Hauerwas and the understanding of the church as *polis*, see Arne Rasmusson, *The Church as Polis: From Political Theology to Theological Politics as Exemplified by Jürgen Moltmann and Stanley Hauerwas* (Notre Dame, IN: University of Notre Dame Press, 1995).

witnessing in all of its words and deeds to the redemptive activities of the triune God. Its politics—its ways of organizing itself and witnessing—has its own construals of human good and flourishing, even as it disarmingly construes the human penchant for sinning against God through pride, domination, violence against others, and unrestrained greed. A person's decisions and actions are mostly guided by her powers of construal. When the nation-state and its attendant cultures are the source of all the basic construals—the patterns of thinking and valuing—of its inhabitants as to what it means to be human and to whom we are to be obedient, we see just how seductive the politics of the state can be for the individual Christian and for the church. The summons of the Gospel must never be confused with the summons of the nation-state and its supporting cultures.

To elaborate this notion of the *church as polis*, I want to say that the politics of the church is a social ethics construing a way of life, including life-in-relationship, life-together, and life-in-community. Politics—all politics—are simply the practices, conversations, and processes of forming and sustaining a particular community. While politics as practices are concrete and particular, they are also guided by a *vision*—a construal—of what the community is to be and become. This vision construes those goods the community aims to achieve and whose goods it aims to serve and how it aims to distribute those goods. Hence, the church, in its politics, has a vision conformed to that Kingdom of God that we see in the preaching and action of Jesus and in the witness of the New Testament to Jesus. But there is no vision of the Kingdom in separation or detachment from the life—the teachings and enactments—and the death and the resurrection of Jesus of Nazareth.[15]

In contrast to all nation-states, the church, as the Body of Christ, has no defining geographic boundaries that it must defend at all costs. It does

---

[15] Especially helpful in formulating this statement has been Stanley Hauerwas' *The Peaceable Kingdom: A Primer in Christian Ethics* (Notre Dame, IN: University of Notre Dame Press, 1983, esp. 96–115.

There are complexities to this vision of the church as a polis that yet elude my clear grasp and discernment, as well as elude my practical living. It is my hope that I will be able in the future to bring something fuller to print about *The Church as Polis in Dialectic with the World as Polis*. The foretaste of that project is everywhere evident in this collection of writings and in GCF, 47–52, 648–53.

have boundaries of Gospel-summons, truth-telling, and faithful-witnessing that are essential to its political life together and in relation to the world. This is the fundamental reason the church is *catholic* in character and calling: it has no land to defend, it is not bound to any particular ethnic group over against any other, and it is summoned to bring reconciliation and peace to the world. Wherever Jesus' body—the one crucified and raised from the dead—lives in the world, there the church is a political entity with a distinct theology and ethics. But the church's political witness, as indicated in the definition of the church, is for the *benefit of the world*. It is this tumultuous world—and any other world that has gone before and will yet come to be—that God is determined to reconcile and redeem.

This account of the church as *polis* clearly means that the church's political skills and practices must be vital and available as the church and the individual Christian engage the politics of the world. A church whose members are largely illiterate about the patterns of language and practices of a Christ-centered faith is a church that will repeatedly be overwhelmed and held hostage by the nation-state and its political discourses and practices.

While many of the writings in this collection are appropriate for other times of being the church, some of the writings and prayers are preoccupied with being the church in these tumultuous times of war and terror. I do not have any easy answers to how to live in these days, though it will become evident in this book that I am a confessing pacifist, with many questions about how to be a *pacifist*.[16] But I am not a pacifist because I think there are better ways to settle disputes than by war—though I do believe that as well—rather I am a pacifist because I think that pattern of life is how Christians are summoned to think and to live in conformity to the God we know in Jesus Christ and in expression of the hope we have in the triune God.[17]

---

[16] The writings of Yoder and Hauerwas have been nudging me toward pacifism for the past twenty years. It has been a difficult path to follow, as in my earlier years of teaching I seem to fall naturally into that sort of politics and thereby ethics that calls itself "political realism" under the guidance of the writings of Reinhold Niebuhr. That is a hard and powerful menu of ideas to relinquish in a time when one is engulfed in the unexamined givenness of the practices of being a liberal Democrat.

[17] In addition to "A Letter to the Churches After 9/11," I am wrestling with these issues in chapter twelve, "Is Jesus Lord in Time of War?" and in many of the other chapters including the sermons and prayers.

On Being a Disciples of Christ

To further contextualize some of these writings, the reader should understand that I am a third generation member of the Christian Church (Disciples of Christ), and I have spent a considerable portion of my academic career teaching in Disciples-related institutions. I have been deeply formed by this tradition, often in ways beyond my easy comprehension. Several of the writings in this collection were written under special assignments for Disciples churches and organizations, and this will be evident in those writings. One might assume, therefore, that these writings are irrelevant to other church traditions. There is a measure of truth in this assumption, for my tradition has developed discourses and practices that have resulted in conundrums peculiar to the Disciples tradition. We are a quintessential American church tradition, with all the promises and problems that such an inheritance brings in its train. But it is also my conviction that many of the miasmas of the Disciples tradition are also present in other church traditions.

My tradition began as part of what is called 'the Stone-Campbell movement' of the early decades of the nineteenth century here in America. The movement itself primarily emerged out of Presbyterian and Baptist traditions and traded heavily on the frontier individualism and religious freedom that were indigenous to American religious practices. We often said our lodestar was "Christian unity," and it was thought that such unity could be achieved—or at least encouraged and enhanced—by embracing such normative phrases as "No creed but Christ," "Where the Bible speaks, we speak, and where the Bible is silent, we are silent." In keeping with our emphasis on "believer's baptism," persons were asked whether they could affirm "that Jesus is the Christ, the Son of the living God, and my personal Savior and Lord." It was fervently believed that creeds were the cause of Christian discord. Along with this came the firm belief and practice of minimizing the distinction between clergy and laity, with a strong accent on the practice of independent congregations being governed by laity.[18]

---

[18] See *The Encyclopedia of the Stone-Campbell Movement*, eds. Douglas A. Foster, Paul M. Blowers, Anthony L. Dunnavant, D. Newell Williams (Grand Rapids: Eerdmans, 2004) for a wide range of entries on this movement. The movement eventuated in three branches

One might have thought this tradition would have led to a strongly Christ-centered theology and practice. But that was not to be. The suspicion of creeds was too easily translated into suspicion of any *binding beliefs*, and we lacked the means whereby there could be any common authoritative teachings of the faith. Of course, authoritative teachings of all sorts did flourish among the congregations, but they were largely a function of the idiosyncratic inclinations of individual pastors. Powerful journal editors did teach and publishing houses did produce literature full of teachings; but the elusive center of much of the church's life remained the unexamined American dogma: *no one can tell me what I have to believe; I am free to believe what I please.*

I have heard folk unfamiliar with Disciples ask 'What does your church believe?' and just as often I have heard others respond: 'We do not have any dogmatic beliefs, so you are free to believe whatever seems compelling to you; we do not have creeds.' I have argued that the Disciples tradition might never have come into existence if the early dissenters from the Presbyterians had believed that any creed or confession is *reformable*. We were frightened by presumably irreformable doctrines into believing that all creeds and doctrines are somehow corrupting of the faith and the prime sources of Christian disunity. The bitter irony is that a tradition that came into being pursuing Christian unity, developed discourses and practices that in fact perpetuated even more disunity by engaging in the practice of reducing theological belief to private, individual preferences. Hence, a tradition that began by saying "No creed but Christ" ended up with a Christ who disintegrates into no more than whatever the individual believer might think.[19]

---

that exist today: Christian Church (Disciples of Christ), the Church of Christ, and the Independent Christian Churches. The standard history for the Christian Church (Disciples of Christ) is Lester G. McAllister and William E. Tucker, *Journey in Faith* (St. Louis: The Bethany Press, 1975). An extraordinary conference was held in 1987 at Christian Theological Seminary to explore what it might mean to be Disciples in the twenty-first century. See *Disciples of Christ in the 21st Century*, ed. Michael Kinnamon (St. Louis: CBP Press, 1988); my presentation, "Earthen Ambassadors," is on 45–49. See also the fine research about Disciples in *A Case Study of Mainstream Protestantism: The Disciples Relation to American Culture, 1880–1989*, ed. D. Newell Williams (St. Louis: Chalice Press and Grand Rapids: Eerdmans, 1991).

[19] Nevertheless, we Disciples have practically felt the need for a common confession that could be used in worship. Accordingly the widespread use in worship of the Preamble to

While our practicing ecclesiology disallowed any authoritative teachings, over the years our tradition came to reflect the various educational backgrounds of its ministers. Hence, ministers educated at the University of Chicago Divinity School reflected the views of that faculty; so too with Yale Divinity School, Phillips Theological Seminary, Brite Divinity School, Lexington Theological Seminary, Christian Theological Seminary, and so forth. I am sure that the influence of the divinity school in which the pastor is educated is also reflected in other traditions, but our tradition had no ecclesial means to counter or attenuate the dominating and defining influence of the seminaries.

The Commission on Theology, on which I served for a couple of decades, composed and published numerous theological reports and studies for the denomination, many of which expressed careful, insightful, and sound theological reflection and understanding.[20] But these reports, though "received" by our General Assemblies, were still-born from the printer. Except for the Council on Christian Unity, I could not detect any concerted effort by the general leadership of the Disciples to distribute and encourage the study of the reports among the congregations and regions. In short, the Disciples are ecclesiologically incapable of developing and teaching a common theological understanding of the Gospel and the mission of the church that might give it the sort of cohesion I have discussed above concerning the discourses and practices of the church.

Hence, however distressed I am with my own tradition, I continue to engage it with as much loving criticism as I can muster. Yet it is also true that the church about which I continually write and teach is that church largely evident in the *ecumenical traditions* of the Christian faith. I have not taught in a Methodist seminary, nor taught the many other church traditions represented in the student bodies of the Disciples seminaries, without an abiding concern for Christian unity.

---

the Design for the Christian Church (Disciples of Christ) arose in many congregations and at regional and general meetings. See my essay, written for the Commission on Theology, "A Theological Analysis of the Design," *Mid-Stream*, vol. xix, no. 3 (July 1980), 309–321. For my most recent discussion of doctrine and confessional theology, see GCF, 24–25, 30–42, 141–48.

[20] These reports, from 1979 to 1997, are contained in *The Church for the Disciples of Christ: Seeking to Be Truly Church Today*, eds. Paul A. Crow Jr. and James O. Duke (St. Louis: Christian Board of Publication, 1998).

It now appears, however, that this ecumenical theology, about which I have been writing and teaching, with its high christology and explicit trinitarian character and its resultant pacifism, is not so welcome among Disciples.[21] While this apparent disinterest in these theological themes among Disciples saddens me, I have not given up hope that we might recover a common theological base from which to be renewed in a cohesive life of mission and conversation.

The reader will discover in this book that I am mounting a running, critical commentary on what I regard as the infelicities of contemporary church life. Be assured that I do not believe these infelicities are simply and only at home in the Disciples tradition; they are present in the actual lives of congregations in most of the traditions today. I do hope, however, that in all of these writings I am understood as being a theologian who lives and writes for the church. The academy, of course, lurks in there somewhere, but it is the practical formation of Christian life and witness that is foremost in my mind.

Sermons and Prayers in Tumultuous Times

I am grateful that some of my sermons, all of which have been preached since my retirement from Christian Theological Seminary in 2000, are included in this book. The sermon is always a venturesome exercise in a particular context of the church's life. The reader will quickly discover that the sermons contain few stories, and little humor, apart from some irony. Nevertheless, they aim to speak clearly from the scriptural text to the gathered congregation. The sermon is the prime teaching tool for the congregation, and it pains me that many sermons I hear do not engage the grand themes of the faith. I struggle to keep these grand themes explicitly before the congregation in the sermon itself.

While some may think these sermons more suitable for the seminary chapel, I want to assure you that they are constructed with the laity in mind. I worry that some preaching today seeks out the lowest theological and imaginative threshold among the gathered and thereby mostly speaks

---

[21] This sort of christology, while fully discussed in GCF, 365–482, is also firmly sketched in chapters nine and ten herein.

down to them. It has been my overwhelming experience in working with laity over many years in several different traditions that they have an appetite for earnest and probing theological discussion and understanding. I have consistently been mindful of that appetite and have tried to engage it. That I might often fail to engage all of the gathered in a particular exercise of preaching goes without saying, but not without regret.

The prayers included here are all from my occasional duties as a liturgical assistant in worship praying what is traditionally called 'the pastoral prayer.' It has been a blessing to be given such a responsibility, which I understand is the summons to pray *with* and *for* the congregation as it gathers before God. In order to keep me and the congregation aware that the *prayer is to God* and not a sermon to the congregation, I use— perhaps inelegantly—some *thees* and *thys* that might seem archaic and inappropriate to others. *Thous* are of a more unhappy and awkward diction, so I also use *you* when appropriate. However, the use of these words is a reminder that we are praying to a God who is a personal presence and agent and who has invited us to pray and has promised to hear our prayers.

Hence, praying is not intended to be an indirect, veiled message to the congregants; but insofar as I am praying *with* the congregation, I am intending to reach into their innermost hearts and honestly pray just those concerns, anxieties, fears, and hopes that lurk there in virtual unutterability. Yet, to pray in this way might be an indirect message to some as to what is worth praying for and about. I am not sure I pray well in such worship settings, but I do know that the easy-going assumption among pastors and laity alike that 'Anyone can pray to God if they just try' is gravely misleading. It often seems not to have dawned on us that Luke represents the disciples—all of whom we may be sure were devout Jews—asking Jesus to "teach us to pray" (Luke 11:4). We may hope our public prayers will help teach us both what to pray for and how to pray for or about that which seems important to us as we gather before God.[22]

As the church prays in tumultuous times, the church stands under the guidance of many of the Psalms, prayed as they were in hours of desperation, fear, uncertainty, and dismay. I hope that my prayers empower us to engage and pray on behalf of this contemporary world in its agony and violence and conflict and to reach towards those possibilities that

---

[22] See further my extended discussion of the practices of prayer in GCF, 676–88.

only the Holy Spirit can inspire in us, even girding us with the courage to act in hope. Indeed, my overarching prayer throughout this collection of writings is that God will continue to reform and renew the church, granting it wisdom and courage in times tumultuous in dangers but redolent in redemptive possibilities.

Part One

On Being the Church
of Jesus Christ

1

A Letter to the Churches After 9/11

This letter was written after 9/11 and was sent by e-mail to many friends and relatives. It was widely circulated and was posted on several web sites.

September 24, 2001

Dear Friends:

Something crushingly new happened to our nation two weeks ago. Not only have we all been shocked by the faceless character of these evil acts and the sheer hatred that seems to have engendered them, we have grieved deeply for the many persons and families that have experienced brutal deaths. We are angry, and we are afraid. Our presumed safety and invulnerability have been shattered and wrenched from us. I am wrung out emotionally, as I know you are too. The future seems so uncertain and threatening.

But I write to say a few words about the nature and role of the church in the midst of our nation and culture in the coming months and years. I write to clarify my own thinking and to be in conversation with you my dear friends. Most of us are imbued with an undying affection for our nation, even though we may be earnestly critical of it at many points in its life and history. Our democratic institutions are indeed beacons of hope in a world still filled with despots and tyrants.

Yet it is this very affection for things 'American' that causes me alarm for the future of the church in North America. All of us are both citizens of the national culture and members of the church of Jesus Christ. And sometimes the distinction between these different realities blurs in our minds and profoundly affects our passions and our actions. Then things American and patriotic receive unhesitating endorsement from Christians and the church. The distinction is overwhelmed and laid aside, and the church becomes the 'chaplain' for the nation and performs in ways demanded by the nation. It then becomes possible to preach a Jesus who endorses and sanctifies whatever the nation—or the leaders of the nation— say is necessary to our national security and future and the cause of 'justice and freedom.' Jesus the sanctifier of righteous violence!

This situation is not new, but this time of crisis brings it to the fore with startling clarity: the empirical church in America, with few exceptions, exists under the lordship of the culture and does the bidding of the culture. The basic attitudes and values of the empirical church are at heart what Americans want, and the church is not happy to be reminded that it serves another Lord and is summoned into existence to be conformed to an alternative way of life from that which serves the self-interests of the culture. That alternative way is the way of discipleship to Jesus Christ.

What might it mean in the days ahead for each of us to be firmly aware of the summons by Jesus to discipleship? It will certainly mean a ministry of service in which the wounds and fears of our people are confronted by inaugurating processes of healing. It will certainly mean praying for the families of the victims and for the leaders of our nation. But it will not mean praying for the deaths of the terrorists and dealers in death. There is no doubt that the terrorists are swordwielders for the kingdom of death and hate. But, for the disciple, they are also the *enemy/ neighbor* we are commanded to love and toward whom we are not to return evil for evil. They are the ones who are also children of God and therefore ones for whom Christ died. Just as Christ carried the sins of the world with him to the cross, which includes our sins, so too he carried the sins of the enemy.

The disciple of Jesus is called to a cross-bearing existence, which will often conflict with the principalities and powers that reign in the world.

It is not easy to be a disciple of Christ and to witness to a Lord who renounces violence as the legitimate means to any realization of that kingdom God is intent on bringing. If we do not openly acknowledge this is in the life of the church, then the church will simply be the chaplain appendage to the national 'war' against terrorism, blessing whatever means our leaders might choose to employ. Our discourses and practices, which were meant to witness to the Gospel of Jesus Christ, can easily be infiltrated and subverted by the categories and concepts of a just war against the enemies of 'our way of life.'

To be a community of Christian disciples means to be that place in a culture in which the faithful inquire about why our brothers and sisters in other lands and religions find American life and governmental policies so offensive and hateful, why they regard America as the enemy, the very Devil himself. It means to be a community that is not intent on justifying one against another, being aware that all sinful humanity has been graciously justified in Christ Jesus. It means to be that community that is so given to peace-making that it cannot pick up the gun in the name of Jesus and his peace. It means to be that place where the works of love are the first order of business. It means to be that place where people honestly believe—and live as though they believe—that Christ is Lord, not only of the church, but also of the whole of human history and the cosmos. It means to be that place in which the Creator of the world is not understood as the vengeful enemy ready to destroy the world in the blink of an eye, but is instead worshipped as the One who gives life and became incarnate in order to reconcile lives, to welcome sinners, and to summon folk to a new way of existence. That is the sort of community that was launched in history by the life, death, and resurrection of Jesus the Jew. Needless to say, history is full of *pretenders* to be the community Jesus launched into space and time.

When the church is truly a community of disciples of Jesus, it is an open community of faith seeking understanding. It promotes practices of inquiry, questioning, and seeking, of honesty and truth-telling, even in the face of fear, dread, and threat. Such a community, through the empowerment of the Holy Spirit, is capacitated with an uncommon courage.

It will be excruciating—cross-bearing—to be the church of Jesus Christ in the days ahead. Many of you are pastors, and your 'servant leadership' will be sorely taxed as to whose servant you are. To be the church of Jesus Christ will require courage and a 'supernatural' hopefulness. I will be praying for you as you find your courageous and discerning ways to be a servant of Jesus Christ.

As many of you know, I have been using the following definition of the church, which you might find helpful:

> The church is that liberative and redemptive
> community of persons
> called into being
> by the Gospel of Jesus Christ
> through the Holy Spirit
> to witness in word and deed
> to the living triune God
> for the benefit of the world
> to the glory of God.

This definition at least means that the church is not called into existence by the American way of life, not called into existence in order to punish evildoers, not called into existence to endorse any given political regime, and not called into existence to protect Christians and wreak vengeance on nonchristians. But it does exist for the 'benefit of the world,' though not on the world's own terms regarding what it finds beneficial as an endorsement of the way it prefers to live.

But, as many of you have heard me say in less troubling times, if you do not find this definition helpful, at least these questions are crucial for each of us:

1. What is the mission of the church?
2. What is the Gospel of Jesus Christ?
3. Who is God and what are God's ways with the world?
4. Who are our brothers and sisters?
5. Who then is Lord of the church and the Christian?

When the church—either ecumenically or as a particular congregation—in its practical everyday life is unclear about how to answer these questions, then its life will be a miasma of disarray and confusion.

So do not let anyone say that theology does not matter here. It desperately matters who we think God is and how we are called to live. Of course, real theology is inseparable from the practices that shape the lives of folk. But I fear that more church folk in America are willing to die for America than to die for the sake of the peaceable Lordship of Jesus Christ. Make no mistake about it, that sense for 'America first' is a theological belief; it is just that it is a pagan theology as old as humankind and the protection of the clan from the dangerous stranger and outsider.

Let us put our Christian theological caps on and think about how pervasive the passion of hatred is in our world, and not just among terrorists. Hatred arises in the hearts of folk who think that they are victims of another's violence, and hatred typically thinks its passion is a justified response to the harm and wounds done by the enemy. In that guise, hatred is one of the great engines perpetuating sin in human history. Hatred wants revenge, wants retaliation, wants 'justice,' for only that which 'repays' the evildoer is adequate to the harm done to the hater. When we stand in dismay at these terrorist haters, we have only to look in the mirror to see the structure of thinking that generates such passionate hate. The vicious cycle of harm, hatred, violent revenge, presumed justice, harm, hatred . . . goes on until it is broken. Violence itself can never break that cycle. The kingdom about which Jesus talked and the cross he bore intend the breaking of that cycle and the coming of a new day of peace. So too, the disciple of Jesus intends a way of life that breaks that cycle of violence and seeks alternative ways of resolving human conflict and defusing the sources of hatred within us and among us. In the context of the disciple church, the justice God seeks is not unremitting retribution and just deserts but the forgiving and merciful pursuit of human flourishing in peace.

A word now even for those among us who are confirmed 'just war' advocates and ready to retaliate with a sense of justice on our side: consider carefully the sort of world in which we now live and the possible consequences of retaliating with too much force. First, 'we' run the risk of killing many nonterrorist innocent folk. Second, 'we' run the risk of galvanizing a restless, resentful mass of transnational Arabs into a fierce and unyielding militancy under the banner of Islam. Islam itself does not require that, but the enemies of America will use it that way. A world war pitting Arabic Islam against the West would be a demonic war that would darken and poison life for generations—for centuries—around the whole world.

When I realize that this past century witnessed the greatest numerical slaughter of persons in human history and that much of that slaughter was carried out for the sake of some *cause* that appealed to justice—justified violence against those who do not deserve to live and whose lives can be sacrificed for the sake of some 'righteous' historical future—I want to put the word 'justice' in the cupboard so that we might have a respite from its vagaries of usage.

This letter is not intended as an indictment against those in our churches who are serving or will be called to service in the military. We must pray for them and their safe keeping and that they come home intact and not ravaged by the acts of violence they will be asked to perform. But we, as the church of Jesus Christ, *dare not pray* that whatever harm they are commanded to inflict on the 'terrorists infidels' be blessed in the name of Jesus.

In conclusion, I simply ask the church to be the church of Jesus Christ. Refuse to be the servant of any other lord. Pray for guidance by the Holy Spirit. Love generously, do not be overcome with fear, and remember who you are and who those who hate you are: you are both the ones for whom Jesus died and rose from the grave. But do not fall into being just another ideological critique of America's ideology. You do not need to be grounded and proficient in the discourses of democratic liberal pluralism or in those of conservative republicanism in order to have a pertinent theological witness to the nation and the world. Just be the church of Jesus Christ! Be the church and let your witness be faithful, truthful, and peaceable.

I trust all of you have thought these thoughts prior to my mentioning them. I write to clarify my own thinking and in the hope that my words might be upbuilding to the church during this time of fear, confusion, grief, and passionate avowals of retaliation. I welcome your responses extending this conversation beyond the confines of this mailing.

Finally, let us remember that we Christians believe that there is a Sovereign and Almighty power already at work in the world for whom things impossible for humans become possible. That Almighty power is the Alpha and Omega Lover of the world, the Wisdom and Word at the source of all things good, and the crucified Lamb who has taken the sins of the whole world into an everlasting tabernacle of forgiveness and hope.

May the peace of our Lord Jesus Christ be among you.

2

Christian Illiteracy and Christian Education

This is an address given to a plenary session of the General Assembly of the Christian Church (Disciples of Christ) in October 1977. At the time I was Dean of the Phillips University Graduate Seminary. The address has never before been published.

As a seminary educator in the context of the church it has certainly been my repeated task to face squarely a variety of questions and complaints by the people of the church concerning Christian education. It is surely one of the most discussed fields in the life of the church, and we can safely acknowledge that providence has made it a timely and urgent question for us today. As we have witnessed decreasing membership, disinterested youth, and somnambulant services of worship, many church folk have become aware that somehow the crisis in the church is related to Christian education. And I candidly admit that I too am one of those persuaded that the disarray in the church, its lack of focus, its discordant voices, its complacent captivity to cultural dispositions, its negligence, its clumsiness, and its sloth are all related to some basic failures in Christian education.

In my judgment the church has fallen on ill times because it has gradually but definitely become *illiterate in the faith*. Through an almost imperceptible succession of compromises the church seems to have lost its roots, its bearing, and its hope. Instead of a sprightliness grounded in a literate faith, we find a sluggishness, a recalcitrance, and a hard-heartedness bred and born in the darkness of illiteracy. And it is an illiteracy that infests the church at every level of its existence. Decisions collective and individual are regularly made with only the flimsiest sense of being truly enjoined by the faith. Instead they seem to be more like decisions evoked and rationalized from within some aspect of our preferred cultural reference point.

But what more precisely do I mean when I speak of illiteracy in the faith? Just as illiteracy in general has to do with one's inability to read, write, and aptly speak, so too illiteracy in the faith has to do with one's inability to read, write, and speak aptly with respect to the faith. We are illiterate in relation to Holy Scripture in that we are quite unacquainted with the biblical literature, with the stories and larger narratives; and when we do read such literature it is often with the most wooden and superficial understanding. When we do have occasions explicitly to write and speak the *language of faith*, we stumble clumsily and ungrammatically. Worst of all, the language of faith has too often become hollow and empty sounds on our lips.

If it is the case that there is widespread illiteracy of this sort among the people of the church, then is it any wonder that confusion and failure of nerve characterize the lives of individual congregations and individual church members? Doesn't it, therefore, make some sense to say that—from the standpoint of faith—we are an uneducated church, that we are not grounded in and informed by the Gospel of Jesus Christ? To be sure, such judgments as these are generalizations, and there are no doubt significant exceptions scattered among the churches. But I leave it to you individually to identify and celebrate the exceptions. I want to move from these general diagnostic statements to a consideration of why education is essential to the church.

No claim is being made here, however, to provide a complete picture of the rationale for the practices of education in the church. Learning is not a general phenomenon with an identical set of traits in every instance. Learning is various and multi-dimensional, and there are no simple recipes for teaching and learning successfully. But there are some elemental points to be pondered concerning Christian education, its special rationale and purpose, and I dare to propose that a grasp of these points may represent a step toward correcting a dreadful malaise in the church.

First, I want to make a proposal concerning the basic nature and purpose of the church. There are, of course, numerous definitions that have been and can be advanced concerning the church. In proposing yet another, I invite discussion with differing conceptions, and I assume that such discussion is healthy for the church. It should make us more cognizant of how loose and varied are the meanings of the term "church." We are accustomed to use "church" to refer to a building or a congregation as an identifiable social unit or institution. And we are accustomed to speaking of membership in the church in terms quite similar to our talk of membership in voluntary organizations: service clubs, fraternities, country clubs, professional societies, political parties, etc. It is tempting to assimilate the logic of talk about the church to the logic of talk about other voluntary social organizations. When we do this, however, we inevitably miss something in the concept of church that seems crucial to me. Therefore, it requires a conscientious effort on our part to avoid the temptation and to remind ourselves that speaking of the church of Jesus Christ is not finally the characterization of one more social institution. Social institution it certainly is; it is at least the flesh and blood of voluntary human acts and organized activities. But the proper intentionality of those acts and activities is missed if we do not discern and speak of something else. To speak of this something else is to speak normatively and theologically.

As a summary formulation of the basic nature and purpose of the church, I propose the following: The church is that community of persons called into being by the Gospel of Jesus Christ to witness in word and deed to the living God for the benefit of the world.[1]

Let us now unfold and elaborate this summary statement. Whatever else we might say about the community of persons who comprise the

---

[1] This definition of the church was an early formulation that was later to become, showing the later words inserted in italics: The church is that *liberative and redemptive* community of persons called into being by the Gospel of Jesus Christ *through the Holy Spirit* to witness in word and deed to the living *triune* God for the benefit of the world *to the glory of God.* Even though these italicized words were later included in the definition, in my own mind they only made more explicit what was already implicit.

church, we must first say that it is called into being by the Gospel of Jesus Christ. Properly understood it is not a community that calls itself together by voluntary decisions to organize and cooperate. Certainly the tradition of the Free Church, and of Disciples of Christ in particular, has often yielded to the temptation to think of the church as first the community of persons who decide to join together. Too often the accent has fallen on these decisions and implied the normative view that the church is a self-determining democratic organization. This accent, however, misses the mark and fails to express the essential point that the church is called into being by the Gospel of Jesus Christ.

The church is called forth, and the right initial response is the acknowledgement of the definiteness of this call as the call of the Gospel of Jesus Christ. There is an historical particularity to this call that cannot be removed. There is church because there was first the specific life of an individual person, and in that person it is revealed that God is Emmanuel, that God is with us and for us. *The Gospel of Jesus Christ is first and last the story of this man Jesus as the revelation of God's eternal resolve and disposition towards humanity and the creation.* It is the good news that the ultimate creative power is the power of the free and loving God who rejoices in the multitude of God's creatures and seeks to bring them to fullness of life in response to God's presence. The church is that community of persons who have heard the call of that Gospel.

From having heard the call of the Gospel, the church is incontestably given the task of *witnessing in word and deed* to the living God for the benefit of the world. The call to the church is the call to witness, and here we must understand that church and witness are inseparable. No Gospel call has been heard where the community is not obediently engaged in witnessing to the God who has called. The apparent community may be busy about many matters, but if that busyness is not a form of witness to the living God, then that community is not the church of Jesus Christ. Literally, all that the church does has its center of gravity in bearing witness to the living God.

The concept of witness, of Christian witness, has not been in clear focus in the recent life of the church. Some disputes over so-called evangelism and so-called social action might have been avoided—or more sharply and deeply grasped—if we had been clearer about the centrality of witness to the life of the church. The news that is the Gospel is meant to be shared; it must be shared. But its being shared means confronting the world with the presence of the living God. The witness of the church can no more be restricted to the conversion of individual persons than it can be reduced to deeds in pursuit of justice and liberation.

It is in the elaboration of the concepts of the *called church* and the *witnessing church* that we find the essential foundation for education in the church. It is here that education emerges as a continuing obligation of the church. The call of God in the Gospel of Jesus Christ is not a simple event that can be precisely isolated and exhaustively described. The call is always mediated through creaturely bearers, and for most of us that means that we have heard the call indirectly through the witness of some previous or contemporary Christians. The call comes in and through other witnesses and in turn charges the hearers with the task of becoming witnesses to others—others both as contemporaries and as future possibilities.

This response to the call and its fulfillment in witness requires a *literacy in the Gospel*. The Gospel is not willy-nilly whatever people choose it to be. It is not just any presumably good or comforting news. But to be able to hear well and to witness well, the church must incessantly cultivate an understanding of the Gospel and the light it throws on the world. Whenever the church has neglected this cultivation, this education, it has itself become a wandering nomad, bedeviled by the mirages of passing fancies and fads.

This point can also be considered by noting some significant negations. In being called by the Gospel of Jesus Christ to witness in word and deed to the living God, the church is not being called by the various lords and reigning powers of the world. The church is not called by a noble idea, a worthy cause, a self-evident principle, or a fetching configuration of satisfying feelings. It is not being called by presumed intimations of divine beneficence in general human experience, or by a sense of the holy, or by the depths of ultimate concern, or by the morality of world justice and liberation. In being called by the Gospel and called to bear the Gospel, it will also find itself addressing and tending to many of these matters as well. But it will address and tend these matters because they are implied in hearing the Gospel and witnessing to the living God. To understand one's involvement otherwise is to risk losing the heart of the Gospel.

It is also important to note that neither the church nor the individual Christian is called to bear witness to itself or to himself or herself. The

14

object of the witness is the living God as known in the Gospel of Jesus Christ. And the witnessing of the community of faith is not self-advertising; it is not proud and presumptuous.

The church must candidly recognize that its bearing witness is a charge—an imperative or a behest—for which it is responsible. As a responsible witness—as an accountable witness—the church should properly acknowledge that its witness, in all its forms, is confronted by an *ineradicable question*—that is, by a question that cannot finally be answered and eradicated by the witness. This question is whether the witness of the church is an adequate and truthful witness to the living God. In its heart and mind the church knows that God has placed this question before it; indeed, it is the divine interrogation of the church. And the church must ceaselessly be disturbed and prompted by this question. It can never take for granted or assume that what it says and does in witness is adequate and truthful. Hence, it is a measure of how earnestly the church accepts its responsibility that it be continually engaged in reflective self-tests of its witness.

Every Christian and every generation of Christians must also be disturbed by this ineradicable question. Each must bear a responsible witness, which involves expressing the Gospel in word and deed for one's contemporaries. Sometimes we are misled into thinking that we can escape this responsibility and that we can thoughtlessly proceed on our way witnessing without disturbance or enjoying a private relationship to God. In fact, we are sometimes—laity and clergy alike—tempted to think that our witness need not undergo such interrogations and that questions only confuse. But this is a devilish temptation to be overcome. The education, which the church requires in order to be responsibly ready to be the church, is one that involves the full range of *handing on* the past witness of faith, of listening to Holy Scripture as norm for the church, of appropriating the Gospel and conveying it in words and deeds that will be luminous and pertinent to this world, namely, this contemporary world in which we all live.

The educational activities and dimensions of the church spring most properly from this sense of responsibility to witness in word and deed to the living God. Let us look at what I mean by *witness in word*. Certainly we are necessarily a people of the word. It is through the word that we understand and that we have heard the story of Jesus Christ. But word is not here some magical formula to be thoughtlessly recited. Word well-wrought, well-thought, and well-spoken is an intellective exercise, at least. We must learn again to speak an intelligent word that expresses the Gospel and is illuminating to the world.

But to speak an articulate word of witness will involve a recovery of the Bible as Holy Scripture. We need to be re-educated to read the Bible *as* Holy Scripture. Certainly the actual church in our time is quite lost in reading and interpreting Scripture. One explanation for the popularity of resurgent brands of fundamentalism is that they appear to take the Bible seriously. And many folk of more liberal persuasion wring their hands in dismay and virtually concede the Bible to the fundamentalists. This must cease. The *Bible is the church's book*, and we ought not to concede that the fundamentalist view is the most appropriate view of the Bible as Holy Scripture. But how can one contend against such misleading views when the community is so unacquainted with Scripture itself?

The Scripture is decisive for the church because it contains the witness of the early Christians to the Gospel of Jesus Christ. It is that source to which we must return again and again to test our understanding of the Gospel. Yet we must take what we hear and express it in ways that stir passions, enliven imaginations, and command earnest and intelligent grappling in the world today. In a longer discourse I might explore suggestions as to how this can be done. But for now it should be sufficient to emphasize that such a discourse would itself be an educational exercise: it would represent a striving to understand and hand on the Gospel.

Is it not appalling that so many leaders of the church are so unprepared for such discussions and have no appetite for it? Whatever else an *elder* might be in the New Testament, he or she is at least a teacher, and that means at least being one who can express the Gospel in word and track its bearing on the ways of everyday life. The elder is not a secularly successful businessperson or professional who now extends or confers his or her secular respect on the churchly office.

Thus far it is obvious that I am emphasizing what some might call the *content* of the Gospel. And surely some would protest that we do not need more "head knowledge," that we need instead to get our affections untied and reoriented. But this is a needless dispute. I do not reckon vain and empty chatter filled with Christian terms to be thereby expressive of Christian faith. Call it what it is: people speaking words that they no longer mean or understand. But don't call it 'head knowledge'—as though we truly had many folk shifting about who understand the Gospel and yet stand unrepentant and hard-hearted. I should like to find a few such persons, but I hardly think they would be symptoms of past mistakes in Christian education, namely the mistake of knowing the content of the Gospel and yet not knowing how to live it. I suggest we let that whipping boy pass into the recesses of time and fancy. The real whipping boy is the one who thought everything was obvious and therefore thought little about it and thereby had little thoughtful to say and finally forgot what the question was.

The educational work of the church is, of course, not just the cultivation of an articulate understanding; it also involves the cultivation and encouragement of acts of obedience to the divine presence. We do learn through doing, through engaging in those deeds that seem commanded by the Gospel. Properly, word and deed cannot be separated in the living witness of the church. Yet we must acknowledge a condition in the church today that undoubtedly vitiates many of our ostensible educational endeavors; it is the condition of *hypocrisy*, of the lie, in which the actual life of the churchly group stands in contradiction to the apparent meaning of the words it uses in worship. Surely the *language of faith* has for many of our contemporaries been rendered empty and pointless by routine and mindless repetitions that have nothing to do with *how* the speakers actually live.

In contrast to this, the understanding, which we need to teach in the church, should express itself not only in articulate word but in intentional acts of obedience to God. Such intentional obedience is not the by-product of dumb passivity; it is the fruition of deliberation, discernment, and prayer. It is at this juncture, however, that some would request a discussion of the nuances of that hoary debate concerning the priorities of theory and practice. While I think much of that discussion in our day has been misleading, I will limit my remarks to two brief suggestions.

First, our actions are often what they are because our understanding is unduly constricted or mistaken; consequently, enlarging, sharpening, and deepening the understanding do provide opportunities for newly conceived acts. Second, our actions surely may be occasions for learning; and hence, we may not have fully grasped some behest of the Gospel until we have invested ourselves in specific courses of actions. Yet, it is as false to claim that it is always better to act than to abstain or postpone as it is to claim that we should never act until we have achieved complete clarity about why we are to act and the possible consequences of the act. But in repudiating these two extremes, we ought also to admit that the church today could scarcely be charged with the sin of neglecting duties and actions because it is unduly preoccupied with thoughtful clarification of the issues and the marshalling of sound arguments!

I hope it is not inappropriate to pause at this point and consider the prospects that are before us in the next few days. Who of us has not grimaced upon reading some of the resolutions for action that are coming before this assembly? Deep and complex questions being reduced to the simplicities of a resolution can be a chilling development. We may well wonder how an illiterate church could ever decide such matters when it is so unaccustomed to sustained reflection and thoughtful conversation! In the days ahead we will hear many pronouncements, some arguments, the spewing of some hot air, and such should be no surprise considering the present state of the church. Certainly we should pray that our discussing, resolving, and voting will be educational for us all. It is a positive sign that we do gather in assembly for such discussion and such striving for a common mind, for this is a form of our witness to one another and to the world. But I urge us not to be misled by a vain sense of the significance of voting. And that vanity is a possibility for us, both as we see our pet resolutions adopted and as we see them rejected. Our votes are not eschatological. They are fallible and corrigible. Yet all of our discussing and voting should challenge us to further inquiry and to actions that are wrought in the context of the firm conviction that God is finally Lord of creation and history and that God seeks our best thoughts and our most earnest commitments.

Returning now to the teleological point of my initial statement on the church, we must see that the witnessing of the church is *for the benefit of the world*. The world in this sense is our contemporary world and the future rising before it. We are not called to witness to some past world and to clutch it in our memories or fantasies as the beloved object. Instead it is this sprawling, buzzing, tempestuous, and confused contemporary world that is the context and focus of our witness. Hence, our education in the Gospel must have this world in view—which means that we must strive to understand this world better than it understands itself.

Let me now indicate some specific implications of the view developed thus far for the life of the church today. First, we must recover a sense for those educational processes that accentuate learning the content of the Gospel and giving it intelligent expression for the world. The reign of fascination with techniques and gimmicks must cease, for they are repeatedly subject to misuse. By their nature they depend on serving the lords of the worldly 'interesting' and the 'relevant,' wherein we expend great effort in getting the world's attention but are mute and incompetent in conveying the Gospel.

Second, we need to recognize that *doing theology* is not a luxury for the few. Theology is done whenever someone speaks or acts in the context of witness. The question is not whether we do theology or whether each is a theologian. The question is whether the theology we do is an adequate and truthful representation of the Gospel for the world. To be literate in the faith is essential to being Christian. How can one be a Christian if one's life is not informed and shaped by the Gospel, and how can one be shaped and formed by a Gospel about which one is illiterate?

Third, we must recover a sense for the *pastor as teacher and theologian for the community*. It is not that he or she does it alone for the community or instead of the community. But it must be that at least he or she does it self-consciously, explicitly, and persistently in and with the community. There is literally no other task more important than this for the congregational pastor. Preaching, counseling, and social criticism will become empty exercises apart from a keen sense of being teacher and theologian, of being energetically engaged in striving for an adequate and truthful witness to the living God as known in the Gospel of Jesus Christ.

Fourth, we need a massive effort to educate adults who are already in the institution called church and even serving as leaders of the church. Adults who abstain or refuse this engagement with the articulate witnessing of the Gospel have simply broken with the church's basic call and mission. In short, we need to ground ourselves in the Gospel with an articulate understanding and committed life. To say this is but to call for a *conversion* of the institution called church that it might hear afresh the call of the Gospel and find itself responsibly involved in bearing witness to the world.

In conclusion, I want to emphasize that I am urging us to open our eyes and ears to the Gospel and to recover a sense of the priority of the Gospel's call. But in and with that recovered sense we are set on a process of witness, and it will often be the case that our words and deeds are confused and inadequate. We need each other to help us understand more clearly, more deeply, and more passionately how God lives among us as loving presence. In and with a renewed vigor in our articulated common life, I trust it will also become and be evident that we are empowered to love God, our neighbor, and this world.

3

Signs of the Church's Identity

This essay was written for the Commission on Theology of the Council of Christian Unity of the Christian Church (Disciples of Christ) in 1993.

Presupposing the traditional marks of the church, I contend there is also a theological need today to think more concretely and complexly about the signs of the church's identity. To facilitate this discussion, I propose the following working, normative, theological definition of the church:

> The church is that liberative and redemptive
> community of persons
> called into being
> by the Gospel of Jesus Christ
> through the Holy Spirit
> to witness in word and deed
> to the living triune God
> for the benefit of the world
> to the glory of God.

When we ask about the signs of the church's identity, we are asking a distinctively *theological question*. It is always the case that wherever the church truly exists it exists as some concrete, empirical, historic group of persons in some social location and world. Yet we are confronted with the fact that the term 'church' is not just something the church of Jesus Christ has under its control. It is also part of the nomenclature of cultures, and therewith is under the control of cultures. The powers of the world are always ready to identify what they call 'church' according to their interests. Legislatures, law courts, tax codes, news media, telephone directories, and many other principalities and powers name some empirical groups 'church' and allocate them a designated place among other social institutions. Hence, this theological definition of the church aims at being normative, offering a contrast to many of the contemporary culture-bound and culture-conferred identifications of church. Theologically, it is an *ineradicable question* whether any empirical group called 'church' by whomever is truly the church of Jesus Christ.

In asking now about the signs of identity of the true church, we are seeking those *characteristics* that are theologically *essential* for some community of persons actually to be the church. Our working definition of the church has already made it clear that the church is essentially a liberative and redemptive community of persons that is called into being by the Gospel of Jesus Christ through the Holy Spirit. It is the type of community or *koinonia* that is called into life and given definition by the Gospel of Jesus Christ. This being called out and assembled (*ekklesia*) by God's work in Jesus of Nazareth is foundational for the church. Empirical churches of even noble demeanor are continually tempted to be called out, identified, sanctioned, and justified by the various reigning spirits of the world and hence to serve other lords than Jesus Christ. Being called by the self-revealing, gracious and reconciling presence of God in Jesus Christ through the movement of the Holy Spirit is the constitutive sign of the church's true identity. Where this call is not heard and heeded there is no church.

Our definition goes on to say that the church is given a *defining mission*: *to witness in word and deed to the living triune God*. This mission of witness is the most comprehensive context in which to characterize and understand the other signs or traits of the church. Everywhere in the New Testament, the sense of being called to give witness to the wondrous and gracious mystery of God's self-communicating and redemptive acts in the history of Israel and in Jesus of Nazareth is either explicit or presupposed. Where this witness is absent today there is no church of Jesus Christ.

To explicate fully the witness of the church requires an understanding of the trinitarian essence and actuality of God, emphasizing that *God is self-identifying* in the history of Israel, in Jesus Christ, and in the calling of the church. In this history of acts God discloses God's own actuality, and the church witnesses to God on the basis of these self-disclosures. Hence, God's being or reality is not hidden behind these acts but is revealed in them. We can say that God has God's own living actuality precisely in the triune being-in-acts as *Creator, Reconciler, and Redeemer* of the world.

So too the church is only truly the church when it is engaged in the concrete being-in-acts of witnessing to the full actuality of God's triune life. Where these being-in-acts of witness do not exist, there is no actual church; the church has its actuality, its real life, only in the complex richness of its life of witness. So, where these being-in-acts happen, which are only possible as empowered by and in conformity with the being-in-acts of the triune God, there the church truly exists. *The fundamental signs of the church's identity will be found in the characteristic being-in-acts of the church as witness to God.*

Before moving on to further specifications of the appropriate signs of the church's living witness, we should note plainly that the church exists and witnesses to God *for the benefit of the world*. It is this contemporary world and its future that God loves with an unfathomably gracious love and intends to redeem. Therefore, the church does not exist simply for itself or as an end in itself; it exists for and moves towards the world as witness to God's loving life for the world.

It should be helpful here to note and distinguish three different but interrelated meanings of the term *world* in the church's discourse:

1. the world as the cosmos created by God;
2. the world as any human culture with its structures, relations and relationships, powers, values, meanings, and languages;
3. the world as human culture infected and skewed by human sin.

The *church exists for the world in all three senses of the word*. And the church itself is always some empirically locatable community of persons in some world in all three senses. In these senses, then, the world is in the church and the church is in the world. This means that the church is irremovably an *earthen vessel*, a worldly reality in all three senses of *world*, and therefore is itself always in need of *reform, renewal, and God's grace*. The critical and enduring question is *how* the church exists in the world without losing itself, without losing its fundamental identity. How does the church have a distinctive identity in the world, such that it is in the world but not of the world? The church only embodies its distinctive identity when it actually becomes a living witness to God for the benefit of the world in which it lives. The church is that liberative and redemptive community that lives for the transformation and redeeming of the world by the triune God.

It is now in the witnessing of the church that we seek those further signs of the church's authentic identity. The church witnesses in *word and deed*. While we cannot separate word and deed, and while we must even say that the witness in word is also a doing, an activity, a deed, we can distinguish between the linguistic and nonlinguistic practices of the church's witness. To be sure, word separated from deed is hypocritical, vain, deadly, and a lie, and deed separated from word loses its defining context, intention, and luminosity. But by calling these being-in-acts of witness *practices*, we draw attention to their concreteness as human acts in their historical and communal traditions and locations. It is in the distinctive practices of the church as a liberative community of witness that we find the further identifying signs of the church's essential reality.

To unfold these signs in an orderly fashion, we should also distinguish between the *nurturing practices* and the *outreach practices* of the church. The nurturing practices are those activities of the church that primarily focus on the support and care of the community of faith itself. The outreach practices are those activities of the church that aim toward the transformation of the world. Clearly the distinguishing of these practices does not imply any sharp boundaries between them. Many concrete practices have dual faces: one toward the community of faith and the other toward the world. The church lives in the dynamic interaction between nurturing itself for witness and engaging the world in the concrete works of love for the benefit of the world. Put simply, in its nurturing practices the church is an important symbol of witness to the world, and in its outreach practices the church finds itself nurtured by the Spirit.

24

Looking now at the *nurturing practices of the church*, we can discern the spheres of inner church life in *worship*, in *education*, in *communal care,* and in *administration*.[1] These spheres cannot be segmented and separated sharply, but we can speak of them as overlapping moments in the life of the church. And these spheres of practice lead continually to and are shaped by the outreach practices of the church and of the individual Christian in and for the world.

In describing the *signs of worship*, we see vividly how word and deed are intertwined in the life of the church. The community called into life by the Gospel of Jesus Christ is a community of peculiar and distinctive discourses and self-understanding. The call it hears is a call of the Word of God, of God self-communicating with the church in the history of Israel and in Jesus Christ. The call of the Gospel is inseparable from the narratives of Israel, of the life, death, and resurrection of Jesus Christ, and of the Spirit's call to the early church as embodied in the Old and New Testaments. From these narratives and teachings the church is given a distinctive language of concepts, images, beliefs, and practices that both engender and critique the church's own life in word and deed. Therefore, among the distinctive identifying signs of the church are the multiplex practices of listening to Scripture as the Word of God and being called, authorized, shaped, and critiqued by this listening.

It is around the Scriptural witness that the church's worship is crucially formed. Fundamentally *worship is the act or activity of praising God as the Creator, Reconciler, and Redeemer of the human world and the creation.* In communal worship the church enacts further identifying signs of its reality: it *proclaims* the Word heard in Scripture, it *confesses* its sin and embraces the forgiving grace of God, it *celebrates* God's gracious life in sacramental acts of Baptism and Holy Communion, and it communicates in *prayer* with the self-communicating life of God. In essence, worship is the multi-dimensional practices of praising and conforming to the triune life of God.

In the Protestant traditions the emphasis has been on the signs of Word and Sacrament as not only essential to worship but to the whole

---

[1] At the time of writing this article I included the administrative practices among the nurturing practices of the church. Later in my theologizing I made administration on a par with nurturing and outreach practices as a third sphere of church practices. See my discussion in GCF, 621–23, 634–44.

being of the church. We too affirm their essential character for the living church. But there is also a tendency to claim that Word and Sacrament are the only essential signs of the church. This we do dispute, for this tends to focus only on the nurturing practices of the church and thereby minimizes the outreach practices of the church as essential signs of identity.

Of course, the proclamation of the Word, given in Israel, in Jesus Christ, and in the early church as attested in Holy Scripture, is critical to the church's life of witness. Yet such proclamation is not only in the sermon in worship, but also in the myriad ways in which the Scriptural word shapes the life of the church. Below we will attend to how the witness in word to the Word is elemental to the educational practices of the church.

Understanding the word 'sacrament' to mean 'sign,' we regard the sacraments of baptism and the Lord's Supper as visible, regular practices of conforming the church's life to the gracious life of God. In *baptism*, the sign of the free human acknowledgement of God's grace in Jesus Christ and the human promise to live faithfully from that grace, the church acts as community to recognize a person's entry into the life of faith as a life of witness in the church for the world. The baptismal act is not the purchasing of forgiveness of sin but is, instead, the open, public acknowledgment of the person's acceptance of forgiveness and justification in Christ. In baptizing the new believer, the church confirms the believer's commitment to Christ and the church promises to nurture the person in a life of faith.

In the regular celebration of the *Lord's Supper* (or Holy Communion or Eucharist), the church remembers God's specific, historic act of reconciliation in the life, death, and resurrection of Jesus of Nazareth and it encounters through the Spirit the living grace of the resurrected Christ. In this sacrament, as a sign of Jesus Christ's prior grace and atonement on behalf of all humans, the church finds its worshipping center. But this sacrament neither repeats the sacrifice of Christ nor adds to that sacrifice; it celebrates what Jesus Christ has already done and his continuing life in the Spirit for the church. In the common, creaturely realities of the bread and the fruit of the vine, the church knows itself sustained by the body and blood of Jesus Christ's eternal life.

That the church prays incessantly is a decisive being-in-act of the church. Prayer is the individual and communal practice of intentional communication with God's self-communicating life. Such practice is undertaken in the name of Jesus Christ and expresses the belief that God is a living Subject who solicits, hears, is affected by, and responds to human prayer. In the many moments of praying, the church gives thanks to God, praises God, confesses its sin, lifts petitions and supplications to God, seeks God's guidance and Word, makes intercession for the world, listens silently in reverent openness, cries out in pained lamentation, and groans in "sighs too deep for words" (Rom 8:26). In these signs of prayer the church has its sustaining identity.

Hence, in the practices of worship the church finds its life nurtured by the triune life of God in all God's concreteness and richness. Without the practice of reading Scripture and proclaiming the Word heard therein, the church inevitably becomes ruled and authorized by some other supposedly life-conferring and life-directing 'good news.' Without the confession of sin and reception of grace, the church is tempted to become presumptuous and self-righteous in its life. Without the celebration of baptism, the church forgets how radically renewing and converting the Gospel is and how it calls persons to a new way of living and self-understanding and to a resurrecting destiny. Without the regular celebration of the Lord's Supper, the church becomes forgetful of its being grounded in the reconciling life, death, and resurrection of Jesus of Nazareth, the incarnate Son of God. Without prayer, the church pretends to give itself its own guidance day by day and neglects to live intentionally before the loving Spirit who calls and directs the church into a redeeming future. In all these being-in-acts of worship the church truly happens, but it never happens in isolation from the being in-acts of the outreach practices in which the church exists for the world.

The *practices of educating and being educated* pervade the life of the church. As a community of persons called into new creation by the Gospel and sent on a mission of witness, all the members of the community are called to being conformed in the totality of their lives to the triune life of God. Such conformity is the conformity of faith. It is intrinsic to faith to seek in all ways and in all times and ages to understand God, and therewith also to understand itself and the world more deeply and richly. *Faith seeks understanding* both in the individual Christian and in the whole community. Hence, the church cannot live in faith without the multitude of practices in which it teaches both the *what* and the *how* of faith: what the church most fundamentally believes and understands about God, human life and destiny, and the world; and how persons live concretely a sanctified life of understanding and action under the call of the *ethics of grace*. The what and the how cannot be separated in vital faith, but there is no simple recipe as to their living togetherness. The how is aimless without the what, and the what is vacuous without the how. No member of the church is ever beyond the imperative of grace to seek to learn more profoundly how to live before the Holy Triune God. Therefore, no member can ever dispense with or vacate the educating practices of the church. And the church can never assume that educating-in-faith is ever finished and completed short of the eschaton.

However true it may be that much Christian educating comes indirectly through loving relationships, it is essential to the identity of the church that it engage intentionally in explicit practices of *teaching the faith*. Such teaching is necessarily theological in character and is itself a witness to the triune God. *From* the enlightening and upbuilding power of preaching in explicating Scripture and engaging concrete human living *to* the intentionally designed classes and conversations *to* the silent but acute observations of saintly examples in its midst, the church educates and is educated by the Spirit. But distinctively Christian education would be rendered impossible without the church being a *community of theological discourse*—a discourse in which all things are referred to and discerned in the light of self-communicating life of God. When this discourse becomes vacuous or vain or unfocused or dissipated by counterfeit substitutes, then the church loses its capacity to educate persons in the faith that lives from the Gospel of Jesus Christ.

The educative signs of the identity of the church are also evident in the discursive practices of being critically responsible for the church's witness. Such responsibility arises from the awareness that the church is called by the Gospel of Jesus Christ and thereby responsible to God and even questioned in its witnessing by the life of God. Herein the church confesses that it is put to *ineradicable questioning* by God as to whether its witness in word and deed is:

1. adequate and faithful to the Gospel of Jesus Christ, and
2. luminous, truthful, and transformative for the world.

This questioning and answering can never finally be put to rest in the time of the church. Meanwhile, in the life of the church, this responsible, theological questioning is a *sign* that the church is called, sent, disturbed, and enlivened by the Spirit of the living God.

Worshipping and educating are inseparable from the totality of ways in which the community is itself a *community of mutual love.* Here love is that peculiar openness and self-giving to another that wills the good of the other as one's neighbor before God. Christian love, and the practices of care that go with it, is always loving in particular, loving this person and that person. Called as it surely is to perform *works of love* in and for the world, the church can hardly intend such works in the absence of works of love within the community. In loving one another through mutual self-giving and care, the church is truly a *koinonia,* a fellowship and communion of mutual upbuilding. Such loving—empowered as it is by the self-giving Spirit of God—is what empowers love for the world of neighbors and strangers. This communal love is never exclusive or restricted, and in being open to the neighbor-in-the-church, it becomes the *school* in which one learns how to love the neighbor-in-the-world. In all these ways this communal love is an ethics of grace made possible by God's self-giving life in Jesus Christ who calls the church into being and life. The ethics of grace is Christian living that springs from the forgiveness of sin and the justification by grace in Jesus Christ and that lives in freedom for the neighbor and for God.

As a historical social group locatable somewhere, the church cannot avoid some organizational economy (*oikonomia*) in the pursuit of its mission. This *administering* of the household of the church is in general necessary, but it is always subordinate to mission. Historically the churches have disagreed as to the proper administration of church life. While selecting leaders and assigning duties and functions will always happen, the church is not constituted as church by any particular arrangement of offices, officers, or process of selection or election. Whatever administering relationships and structures may obtain in the church, they are all subject to the critical criterion of whether they facilitate concretely the mission of the church in its various social and historical locations. *Organization and administration are always subordinate to the mission of witness.*

The whole church—as the people (*laos*) of God—is organizationally involved in the ministry of witness to the reality of God for the benefit of the world. For the sake of this whole ministry, and in conformity to the servanthood of Jesus Christ, the Spirit of God calls out particular persons to functions and tasks of *servant leadership*. Some of these servant leaders are formally ordained by the church to provide specific functions and assume ongoing leadership responsibilities. It is in the practices of ordaining-by-the-church and the practices of persons providing servant-leadership that we see true signs of the identity of the church. But the *signs are in the servant practices* and are not static traits of persons or of persons' occupation of offices.

These ordained leaders, variously called 'pastors,' 'elders,' 'bishops,' and 'deacons,' or simply 'ministers,' by Scripture and tradition, are entrusted by the church with leadership responsibilities that involve preparatory and continuing theological education, regular disciplines of spirituality, and bold and timely initiative in and with the people of the church. Since they are ordained to ministry for the whole people of God, there are no criteria of exclusion by virtue of race, class, or sex.[2] Called by the Spirit and examined and ordained by the church, these ministers are typically assigned servant-leadership roles in relation to many of the essential being-in-acts of the church's witness: leadership in worship, in education, in pastoral care, and in administering the organized life of the church.

They lead best by serving—serving first the Lord Jesus Christ and his Gospel and then serving the church in its witness to the Gospel. In this serving, the ministerial leader is responsible also to the whole *laos* of the church. But such leaders must always resist the temptation to regard themselves as the head of the church and the controller of its life. They are servants of Jesus Christ, who is the Head of the church and who has the church as his body.

But the formally ordained leaders of the church are not the only leaders called out and necessary to the administering of the church's life. The Spirit from time to time calls others of the *laos* to short-term and long-term tasks and functions for the sake of the church's witness in nurturing and outreach practices. These other real leaders, in their work and ministry, are signs of the identity of the church as people called to witness. The

---

[2] I have come later to include sexual orientation in this list. This is a profound and divisive issue for the church today. I regard unfaithfulness and promiscuity as the basic sexual disorders that undermine agapic love. Agapic love, therefore, should be the controlling concept in how we evaluate so-called 'same-sex relationships.'

distinction between the formally ordained and the non-ordained but called and selected leaders should remain fluid, open, and nonhierarchical in the life of the church. Pragmatic servant hierarchies may from time to time serve the interests of the church's mission, but none is necessary to that mission as such.

The church must remember—as a sign of its theological faithfulness—that its structures created for mission are not eternal or essential but are subject to continuous review and reform by reference to their adequacy to and fitness for witness.

It must always be clear that the internal administering of the life of the church moves incessantly towards the administering of the church's *outreach practices* in the world. Obviously, these practices are not first the practices of ordained ministers: they must be the practices of the whole church and every member of the church. Before looking at the general shape of these practices, we must recall that the church is a *liberative community*. This sense of liberation has two distinct but interrelated meanings. First, the church is the community that is called by the liberating Gospel of Jesus Christ and this liberating in Christ is rooted in the acknowledgement of God's reconciliation and justification of the sinners in Christ, which is God's judgment that sin will not have the last word in determining the meaning and destiny of humanity. Christians, the church, are the persons who say 'yes' to this liberation in Christ and who experience by the Spirit the newness of life and direction: they are free from the slavery of sin and its consequences. As the church celebrates this gracious liberation of God, it also is called and sent to take this liberating good news to the world. Hence, in the second sense of liberation, the church is the bearer of a liberative witness in word and deed for the world. In all its life the church is engaged in the ethics of grace: ethics that live from God's grace and justification, do not seek just reward, and take shape as the works of love on behalf of the neighbor. What are the general spheres of these outreach works of love on behalf of the world?[3]

The first sphere is that of *evangelism*. Evangelism is simply the whole of those activities in which the church conveys to the world the good

---

[3] In GCF I came to identify four spheres of outreach practices as 1) evangelism, 2) prophecy, 3) emancipating works of agapic love for justice and peace, and 4) vocation. See GCF, 627–34.

news of Jesus Christ and invites the world to respond to this news with a renewal of life and a change of direction. While it is appalling that some practices of empirical churches have sullied and obscured the proper practices of evangelism, it would be an abdication of responsibility and theological identity if the church were ever to abandon or renounce the multiple practices of inviting, interpreting, and applying the Gospel of Jesus Christ on behalf of the world. Evangelism is not restricted to practices of Gospel declaration but also involves practices of persuasive interpretation of the Gospel in conversation with the world. The church dialogues with the world that God loves and calls into a redemptive relationship with God's own life. At the least, the church has to speak a language that the world can understand, even as the church retains its own peculiar content and message.

All the evangelistic practices of the church must continually be critiqued for their possible infection by the values and causes of a particular, hegemonic nation, class, race, or sex. Further, it is a healthy reminder to the church that the practices of evangelism, while often heavily weighted in linguistic practices, can never be separated from many nonlinguistic works of love on behalf of the world. However ashamed the church may be of past and present practices of an infected and distorted evangelism, the church can never be ashamed of the Gospel itself, and this Gospel beckons the church to share the news of God's saving grace in Jesus Christ with the world that God loves. The church confesses and announces the Good News of Jesus Christ to the world and is not ashamed, and the church enacts the Good News in humble service to the world.

The second sphere of outreach practice is the way in which the individual Christian exists in the world on a daily basis and is called to witness to the reality of God in word and deed for the particular neighbors met day by day and for the particular social institutions in which we live in the world. Here we are talking about particular care for individual persons through practices of words and practices of caring presence. Here, in the call to these outreach practices, the Christian is most vulnerable to being engulfed and dictated to by the practices and norms of the world, and then the church member is in the world only on the world's terms. These concrete practices of Christian life in the world are essential to the church existing in witness for the world. Here the Christian meets every

32

person in his or her concrete otherness and knows and relates to this other as one created and loved by God.

The third sphere of outreach practices includes those communal and collaborative practices of pursuing in and for the world the love, justice, and peace envisaged in the Kingdom of God. These *projects of social justice* may not be the leveraging of the Kingdom by human acts. But these projects are provoked and called forth by the Kingdom as the realization of historical human well-being before God in which mutuality and openness obtain, which are the signs of *shalom*. In collaboration with many others beyond the church, the church must pursue, in its various concrete locations, those projects that feed the hungry and empower the poor for full social participation in life's goods, that bring to the center of life those who are pushed to the margins by the principalities and powers of the world, and that capacitate persons to be nonviolent neighbor-keepers. While these practices cannot commandeer the Kingdom of God, they are *signals* of the God's reign, and they are *signs* of the identity of the church. Communities that omit these outreach practices are hardly the witnessing community of Jesus Christ.

It should be clear, then, that the pitting against each other of nurturing practices and outreach practices and of evangelizing practices and social justice practices are inimical and confusing to the life of the church. These are no more mutually excluding alternatives than are witness in word and witness in deed. Ecclesiology, as the doctrine of the fullness of the church's life and being, cannot simply be about the nurturing practices of the church or merely about the administering practices in nurture. Ecclesiology is about the fullness of the church's life in the richness and complexity of the being-in-acts in which it witnesses to the richness of God's love for the world. It would not be misleading to say that ecclesiology properly comes to include all the other doctrinal topics of the church's theology and all the practices whereby the church enacts its witness for the benefit of the world.

Here we can emphasize what has been allowed to remain in the background in the preceding discussion: namely, the church witnesses to God for the benefit of the world *to the glory of God*. In that odd Christian sense, the world's true benefit, and therefore also its glory, is first and last prefigured and contained in God's glory. The glory of God—which the church knows and towards which it moves—is a glory that includes the glory of the world of sinners reconciled. God's glory is not God's selfish possession but is a glory shared with the world by the triune Subject who uniquely creates, reconciles, and redeems all things. Hence, it is not a glory on the world's terms, nor is it always a benefit on the world's terms. But God's glory is finally the only eternal benefit that can save and redeem the world. It is a sign of the church's identity that it witness to the glory of God as that reality from which and towards which all things move. In the absence of such witness, the empirical church is drawn to its own transient and worldly glory, or it becomes subservient to the glory of some other creaturely reality.

4

The Church as Ark of Salvation

This essay was prepared for and presented to a seminar in the Dallas/Ft. Worth area of the Christian Church (Disciples of Christ) at the Community Christian Church in Richardson, Texas, February 22, 2004.

This essay is guided by two undergirding presuppositions. The first presupposition is that the right context for Christian theology is the church itself, with its given discourses and practices. It is here that Christian theological reflection has its anchor and defining context. This means that ecclesiology—the doctrine of the church—is itself fundamental to any theological project. I propose the following theological definition of the church as a guide to our further reflections in this paper:

> The church is that liberative and redemptive
> community of persons
> called into being
> by the Gospel of Jesus Christ
> through the Holy Spirit
> to witness in word and deed
> to the living triune God

for the benefit of the world
to the glory of God.[1]

The second presupposition of this essay is that the church itself, in its discourses and practices, is in wild disarray today in North America concerning what it means to be the church of Jesus Christ. Not only is my definition of the church intended to guide us through the morass of confusion about the church today, but I hope the whole of this essay will clarify some of the issues surrounding the identity and necessity of the church for the living of the Christian life. It is not uncommon in our American culture these days to say, both from within the church and beyond the church, that a person can be a good Christian, or at least authentically 'religious,' without any involvement in the life of the church. That conviction can be quite misleading about the connection between the church and the Christian life, and I intend to critique and dismantle that conviction.

Here at the outset of this essay, I propose that we should not assume that every group that calls itself the church of Jesus Christ is in actuality the church that is embodied in the definition I have just stated. While admitting that the church itself often lives amidst brokenness and disagreement within itself, I am weary of being called upon to defend—or even interpret—the discourses and practices of some groups that claim to be the church. Some groups are so profoundly antithetical to what I understand the Gospel of Jesus Christ to be and how the church is called into being by that Gospel that I am ready to raise the question of their heretical status. I will not directly address the question of how we decide matters of orthodoxy and heresy, but I do contend that any ecclesiology that is incapacitated from discussing these matters is hardly an ecclesiology that could be called 'Christian' (See GCF, 33–42, 645–58).

I am more than a little worried that the tradition in which I stand— the Christian Church (Disciples of Christ)—is so wishy-washy on issues of heresy that it allows its discourses and practices to be skewed by theological commitments that are deleterious to a faithful and truthful witness to the Gospel. Sometimes it seems that the real center of its theology

---

[1] I have been massaging this definition of the church since my first years of teaching at Perkins School of Theology. It is explicitly developed in my *A Grammar of Christian Faith: Systematic Explorations in Christian Life and Doctrine*, 2 vols. (Lanham, Md: Rowman and Littlefield, 2002), 25–35, 609–54. Further references to this work will be in parentheses within the text in the form of (GCF).

is the dogma that we are a church in which anyone can believe anything he or she pleases and that any diversity is a welcome participant in the church's life and witness. For a church tradition that seems hesitant about 'doctrine,' that *dogma* of free belief and diversity is rather paradoxical in its occupying so central a place in the discourses and practices of Disciples.[2]

I am proposing, then, that by discussing the topic of the church as ark of salvation we will be plunging into and clarifying some aspects of what it means to be the church of Jesus Christ and how such a church might talk about human salvation. I will proceed according to this outline. First, I will construct a traditional model of the church as the ark of salvation, outside of which there is no salvation. Second, I will construct a model of the liberal church that thinks of itself as in serious disagreement with the traditional model. Third, I will then construct a revised model of the church as ark of salvation that critiques some aspects of both the traditional model and the liberal model. It is this revised model that I am proposing to the church as a way of reclaiming its distinctive identity and mission.

A Traditional Model of the Church as Ark of Salvation

It was a common conviction of the church in its first centuries that there was no salvation outside the church: *extra ecclesiam nulla salus.*[3] This is

---

[2] For almost a quarter of a century I was a member of the Commission on Theology of the Council on Christian Unity of the Christian Church (Disciples of Christ). The Commission made regular reports to the church over this period concerning basic issues of ecclesiology, culminating in a final report to the church on ecclesiology in 1997. This report, and other previous reports dating back to 1979, are helpfully contained in *The Church for Disciples of Christ: Seeking to be Truly Church Today*, eds. Paul A. Crow Jr. and James O. Duke (St. Louis: Christian Board of Publication, 1998). While I regard these reports as theologically sound for the most part and thoughtfully construed to encourage further study by the church, I am not aware of any sustained attempt by the officers of the General Church to see to the distribution of this book to the local and regional churches for serious study. Many of my remarks about the Disciples of Christ are diagnostic summaries of how I have heard and observed laity and clergy talk and act and make decisions at all levels of the church over a lifetime of being a member of the Disciples.

[3] See J. N. D. Kelly, *Early Christian Doctrines*, rev. ed., (San Francisco: HarperSanFrancisco, 1978), 206–7, 403, and Jaroslav Pelikan, *The Christian Tradition: A History of the Development of Doctrine*, vol. 1, *The Emergence of the Catholic Tradition (100–600)* (Chicago: University of Chicago Press, 1971), 157–59.

vividly expressed in the image of the church as the ark of salvation, harkening back to Noah's ark. Relative to Noah's ark, we find a reference joining the ark to salvation in 1 Peter 3:18-21:

> For Christ also suffered for sins once for all, the righteous for the unrighteous, in order to bring you to God. He was put to death in the flesh, but made alive in the spirit, in which he also went and made proclamation to the spirits in prison, who in former times did not obey, when God waited patiently in the days of Noah, during the building of the ark, in which a few, that is, eight persons, were saved through water. And baptism, which this prefigured, now saves you . . . through the resurrection of Jesus Christ . . .

Just as Noah's ark saved the eight persons from drowning and death during the flood, so too baptism by the church saves one from the perils and destiny of sin. Cyprian, a third century bishop, citing this passage in 1 Peter, said: "In saying this, he [viz. Peter] proves with his testimony that the one ark of Noah was a type of the one church."[4] This facilitates Cyprian saying later, "there is no salvation outside the Church . . . " (*salus extra ecclesiam non est*).[5] The clear implication of this interpretation of the church is that only the members of the church are or will be saved, wherein one becomes a member of the church, as the body of Christ, through baptism.

This image of the church as ark of salvation retains a firm grip on the doctrines of ecclesiology and soteriology—the doctrine of salvation— throughout much of the church's history. It plays into what Avery Dulles calls the "institutional" model of the church in which the emphasis falls on the priesthood and episcopacy and definitive sacramental practices that determine what counts as church and how one comes to be a member of the church and by virtue of that becomes a recipient of salvation.[6] As an institutional society, the church must be an identifiable and distinct society in the midst of the many other societies, both large and small, that

---

[4] *The Library of Christian Classics*, vol. 5, *Early Latin Theology*, ed. and trans. S. L. Greenslade (Philadelphia: Westminster, 1956), 151 (Letter 73.2).

[5] Ibid., 169 (Letter 73.21).

[6] Avery Dulles, *Models of the Church*, expanded edition (New York: Doubleday, 1987), 34–46. See Dulles' further discussions of other models of the church. In the long run, however, Dulles never repudiates the conviction of *extra ecclesiam nulla salus*.

make up the human world. There should be no obscurity as to whether some group is truly the church of Jesus Christ, for if there is, then persons will be confused as to the group to which they must belong in order to enjoy the gracious and saving benefits of Christ's life, death, and resurrection. Not every group that might claim to be the church of Jesus Christ is in fact that church that is the ark of salvation. Hence, the *visibility* of the church becomes the focus of this model. The visible church exists where certain identifiable discourses and practices take place in public view.

The Roman Catholic Church has been most insistent on an ecclesiology that pivots around this institutional model. In its harshest moments, we can see that there really is no salvation outside of the church: the church is itself the necessary *means of grace* by virtue of which salvation is conferred. Hence, outside the church these means of grace—such as baptism, Eucharist, truthful teachings based on God's revelation—are simply not available. Those who are without these means are thereby also without the saving grace of God. Indeed, at Vatican I Council in 1870 it was declared that "It is an article of faith that outside the Church no one can be saved . . . Who is not in this ark will perish in the flood."[7]

There are ways to soften this understanding of the church, and Vatican II strives mightily to open possibilities of salvation to those who are visibly outside the boundaries of the church.[8] One can, for example, distinguish with Augustine between the church-visible and the church-invisible. While the church, at least in its invisibility, is necessary for salvation and outside of which no salvation occurs, membership in the church-visible does not guarantee ultimate salvation. The visible church can include both wheat and tares, a mixture of the good and the bad, which will be sorted out in God's consummating and ultimate judgment. The difficult question is whether the invisible church includes more than those who are members of the visible church. If it does not so include others, then the visible church is a necessary means of salvation, even if it is not a sufficient means.

---

[7] Quoted in Dulles, 41.

[8] See *The Dogmatic Constitution on the Church* (*Lumen Pentium*), articles 14–16 in *The Documents of Vatican II*, ed. Walter M, Abbott (New York: Guild Press, 1966), 32–35. See also the succinct discussion of "Outside the Church No Salvation" in *Encyclopedia of Theology: The Concise Sacramento Mundi*, ed. Karl Rahner (New York: Seabury, n.d.), 220–21.

If it does include others outside the visible church, then membership in the visible church is neither a necessary nor a sufficient condition for being saved.[9]

At the heart of this traditional understanding of the church as ark of salvation stand some basic theological convictions that should be noted. First, the church itself is founded in and by God's self-revelation in Israel and in Jesus Christ. It is in the church that humans are taught who God is. This leads to the second conviction, namely, that God is triune as Father, Son, and Holy Spirit. Third, it is in the church that humans learn about the depths of their sin and the grace of God to overcome that sin. Without God's revelation humans might not know that they are sinful and will not know how that sin can be defeated. Fourth, the church is the bearer of the knowledge of God as triune, the knowledge of human creatureliness and sin, and knowledge of the means of grace to overcome sin and its destiny-determining consequences.

Fifth, the church has basic theological convictions about salvation. While there are many uses of salvation language in the Bible and tradition, the most fundamental sense is that salvation stands in contrast to the condition of sin and the consequences of sin. Essentially sin is rebellion against the rule of God, and its consequences include humans being alienated from their own created nature, alienated from God, and alienated from other humans. One consequence of sin is that humans are propelled into a destiny of conflict and alienation in this life and a destiny of death and hell in the next life as the just deserts of sin.

Salvation, then, refers to deliverance from these destiny-determining consequences, and this deliverance is available by the grace of God acting in Christ and in the founding of the church. Salvation, however, includes two different but related spheres of actuality: 1) being-saved in this temporal life, and 2) being-saved to eternal life as life-beyond-death. The church carries the keys to being saved in this life as its discourses and practices are the means of grace that can transform human life now, or at least begin the process of transformation.

In this traditional grammar,[10] it is assumed that there is an intrinsic and necessary connection between how life is lived now in the context of

---

[9] See Kelly, 412–16.

[10] For this use of 'grammar,' see GCF, 4–19. To plot the grammar of basic concepts is to see how they relate to other concepts and are embedded in distinctively human practices.

the church and the life-beyond-death. The further assumption is that there is a *dual destiny*: a destiny of the saved and a destiny of the damned. The church is the necessary means of grace by virtue of which a person gains the destiny of being-saved. For the sake of some linguistic consistency, I propose that we label the temporal process by which God's grace transforms human lives in the church as *historic redemption*. The blessed life-beyond-death we will label *ultimate redemption*. In this context, then, the model of the church as ark of salvation asserts that the church is the necessary condition for achieving both historic redemption and ultimate redemption.

Before leaving this model, I must underscore that this model emphasizes the respects in which the church is a *unique* social group, with a distinct and visible identity in differentiation from other social groups in the world. Hence, it is important that we are able to identify just what the marks or criteria are for identifying the church. If this cannot be done, then Christians and the world will be confused about the *unity*, the *holiness*, the *catholicity*, and *apostolicity* of the church. These are the traditional 'marks' of the church, even though it may not always be clear just which 'Christian' group possesses these marks.[11]

While there are many nuances that can be made to this model of church and salvation, I hope I have identified the grammar of its basic convictions and practices. We will now examine a modern model of church and salvation that I will label 'a liberal model of church and salvation.'

A Liberal Model of Church and Salvation

While I have relied on some Roman Catholic texts to get us started on a traditional model of the church as ark of salvation, this liberal model is so

---

[11] See CGF, 604–5 for a brief discussion of the classical marks. One of the ongoing disputes among churches pivots around the meaning of apostolicity. In ecumenical Protestantism the preferred definition is 'the faith of apostles,' as that faith is contained in the New Testament. But Roman Catholic tradition, along with some Protestant traditions, worry about how that apostolic faith is to be preserved and guarded from distortion and corruption, i.e. from heresy. It answers that it is the ordained office of the priesthood culminating in the office of the bishop that has the authority to teach and determine what the true faith is. The bishops and the priests bear the office of successors to the apostles. In this development we can see how the 'institutional' character of the church, in the office of the bishop, is decisive for determining also where the church exists.

widespread and so deep in the habits of mind and heart of Protestant America that I am not interested in trying to document exhaustively just who advocates this model. Its advocacy is all around us and perhaps in us. I surely grant the word 'liberal' has many other uses than the way I am using it here. There are folk in the church who would call themselves 'liberal' but would not concede to all the points I will attribute to this model. But notice, I am saying "a" liberal model, and thereby I allow that there might be other models of church and salvation that might claim the title 'liberal.'[12]

Before elaborating the particulars of this model, I can specify two of its basic assumptions. First, it assumes that the traditional model of the church as the unique ark of salvation is almost completely misleading about the true nature and mission of the church and the nature of salvation. Second, it assumes that the church functions best under the conditions of liberal democratic theoretical discourses and practices. It should be obvious that this model of church and salvation has arisen primarily in the West under the influence of theories of the function of religious language and the nature of moral and political discourse as rational enterprises developed by Enlightenment philosophies of the eighteenth and nineteenth centuries.

Let us look first at the reinterpretation of the primary discourses of the church. Instead of seeing those discourses pivoting around truth-claims thought to be grounded in divine revelation, this liberal model sees the discourses as 'religious language' participating in a universal form of human understanding and practice. George Lindbeck has called this reinterpretation the "experiential-expressive" understanding of religious discourse.[13] The liberal proposal is that all religions are rooted in a common core experience of the divine that is pre-linguistic and comes to expression in symbolic language. As symbolic language, a particular religion employs a range of images to express itself in ways conducive to social cohesion. As

---

[12] It is well to note that the words 'liberal' and 'conservative' are always relative to some particular discussion of contrasts. There is no one abstract meaning of 'liberal' or 'conservative' that fits all uses of these words. So let us beware: these words often get up and walk around on us. But I can stipulate how I am using this word 'liberal' and expect thereby that the reader will allow me to so stipulate without objecting that my use is not the 'real' meaning of the word.

[13] See George A. Lindbeck, *The Nature of Doctrine: Religion and Theology in a Postliberal Age*, (Philadelphia: Westminster, 1984), esp. 31–32.

symbolic, religious language is not reducible to literal language. Literal language repeatedly misses the symbolic meaning of religious language and its deep resonance in the experiential and existential lives of persons.

It is in this context of understanding that we often hear folk say, "I do not read the Bible literally."[14] Apparently they read it symbolically, and especially when the symbolic rendering matches some of the putative universal themes of human literature about life and death. The odd point about this theory of religion is that in practice a religion will spend much time trying to interpret the symbols of its life, which means translating the symbols into other nonsymbolic language.[15]

Let us consider a couple of examples of this sort of liberal interpretation of the cross and resurrection of Jesus. The cross, while it happened to Jesus, is a symbol for Christians of the crucifying powers of the world that often brutally defeat and kill good and righteous people. The resurrection of Jesus is not really about something that happened to Jesus himself, rather it is a symbol of how the divine is always inviting folk to start over after an apparent defeat, to not give up in the face of one's own culpable, destructive living but realize that tomorrow one can turn around and live differently. In calling these things symbols, we are affirming that the meaning complexes of the symbols are universal in scope, even if a symbol arises in the context of the life and death of Jesus. The symbols, independent of any particular beliefs about Jesus, express something universally available to any individual, and therein lay the real religious significance of that sort of language.

Consider also the word 'God,' which we are implored to regard as a symbol for that which is ultimate, unconditioned, or divine. By appealing to a common core experience of the divine, this model proposes that somehow everyone already has an intuitive sense for what the divine is and therefore to what the word 'God' refers. The various religions, in

---

[14] This locution is so awful conceptually that one hardly knows where to get a hold on it. No sentence of the Bible is literal? Or, even if some sentences are literal, their religious meaning is only symbolic? Notice that when you buy into this sort of thinking, then all the particularities of Christian rootedness in history become relatively unimportant in relation to what is of universal symbolic significance.

[15] Throughout his book Lindbeck critiques the essentialist-expressive model of religion and contrasts it with what he calls a "cultural-linguistic" approach. With some significant qualifications, I am sympathetic to Lindbeck's position.

their symbolic language about the divine, might have different and even disagreeable ways of talking, but these differences are not decisive. We are still entitled to say we all worship the same God, and we will thereby relativize and diminish the significance of the differences.

As a comprehensive way of understanding Christian discourse and the church, we can appreciate that this model construes the Christian church as one among many religions of the world but not one that is particularly more truthful or grounded in a more authoritative revelation than any of the other religions. Christians just happen to be Christians by historical accident of location and inheritance—though confirmed by personal decision. If they do not literalize the discourses of the church, they can get along just fine in this modern or postmodern world.

This view fits nicely with the other presupposition of the liberal model, namely, that liberal democratic political theory and practice are the contextual givens—even the intrinsic desiderata—of the church's life. Before unraveling these, I must admit that contemporary American political discourse is so rife with disputes about 'religion and politics,' 'the separation of church and state,' and 'keep God out of politics,' that I cannot hope to sort through and untangle these conceptual knots in this essay. I can say that I have admired the work of Stanley Hauerwas, who has over three decades challenged the easy assumptions and alliances between the mainline churches and liberal democratic political theory.[16]

When I speak of 'liberal democratic political theory,' I do not mean the Democratic Party as liberal in opposition to the Republican Party as conservative. Rather, I am referring to those foundational beliefs that seem to undergird contemporary political theory and practice, whether it is Democratic or Republican. The following beliefs are what I have in mind as this political theory and its associated practices. First, human beings are *autonomous persons equipped with reason* in terms of which they morally

---

[16] Hauerwas is a prolific author and his critique of liberalism arises in most of his writings. A good place to start is his *A Community of Character: Toward a Constructive Christian Social Ethic*, (Notre Dame: University of Notre Dame Press, 1981). *Resident Aliens: Life in the Christian Colony*, written with William H. Willimon, (Nashville: Abingdon, 1989) is a lively and sustained critique of the liberal presuppositions of the mainline churches. *The Hauerwas Reader*, eds. John Berkman and Michael Cartwright (Durham: Duke University Press, 2002) is an excellent collection of his writings over a long period of time, with a useful index.

should govern their lives by universal ethical principles grounded in rational self-interest. Only if a person stands in rational critique of all traditions and authorities will she be able to understand her rational autonomy and thereby be equipped to deal rationally and morally with other persons. Second, such autonomous persons' rational self-interest compels them to enter into *social contracts* with other autonomous persons in which universal moral principles will apply. This rational covenant will confer rights and responsibilities on all who enter it and maintain it, and such necessarily will issue into democratic laws and procedures for the civic body. Third, religion may provide some emotional and cultural support for the engagement in public politics aimed at governing and ordering the civic community, but no distinctively religious argument is acceptable in the arena of public politics. Consequently, *religious beliefs are 'private' matters,* and it is open to each autonomous person to be or not to be religious in any way he or she desires. Fourth, no vision of human good and flourishing is to be allowed to occupy the center of political discourse and practice. There can be a plurality of religious and metaphysical views of human life, but the fulcrum of democratic politics is the freedom of autonomous individuals to make up their own minds, so long as they do not publicly subvert the principles of rational morality. It is precisely here that the liberal church can embrace the notion that America's public polity and ethics should remain steadfastly 'secular' in distinction from favoring any particular religious view.

When these principles get transported into the discourses and practices of Christian churches, and when they are combined with a symbolic understanding of Christian discourse, we can see why the church becomes a dispensable community, why persons easily think they can be Christian— if they want to be—without any affiliation with a Christian community, why salvation itself gets translated into 'whatever an individual finds meaningful for herself,' and why a traditional understanding of sin and its consequences gets dropped from the discourse of the church—or simply interpreted as 'whatever impedes or frustrates my self-determined self-fulfillment.' For this model of church, then, the whole of Christian faith gets translated into either individual satisfaction or into what is defensible morally in rational public discourse.

Let us now put the implications—and the actual practices—of this model of church and salvation in *contrast to the model of the church as ark of salvation.* 1) The church is not a unique community, founded in divine revelation and necessary for salvation. Rather, the church is itself only one among many religious possibilities. Among religions there is not much sense to the distinction between the true and the false. 2) The liberal church is designed for a liberal political society in which there is a marketplace of religions and ideas, and the autonomous individual is encouraged to shop around to find that religion that is most suitable to his predilections. 3) The discourses and practices of any religion are expected to not violate the universal rational principles of morality that are the linchpins of a democratic society. 4) The liberal church, therefore, can minister to those persons who want to be consumers of religion. However, whatever critique it might undertake of American culture and/ or governmental policies must be in accordance with rationally defensible moral principles, such as justice.[17] 5) It can now be easily seen that the liberal church will construct its fundamental mission in terms of underwriting liberal democracy as the best hope for managing the future of humanity in rational and just ways. By so underwriting liberal democracy, the church will protect its own private and preferential symbolic discourses and practices from government interference. 6) Hence, the ethics of the liberal church becomes indistinguishable from the ethics of liberal democratic theory and practice. 7) Furthermore, this model of church neutralizes the apparent conflict among religions, reducing them all to preferential and experiential discourses that are humanly helpful and should not lead to violence or conflict or arrogant claims to possess 'absolute truth.'

As should be obvious, this model sharply collides with the model of the church as ark of salvation. 1) The church is only accidentally unique as that community that shares certain symbols and practices. It is not unique as the bearer of salvation, as there are many other communities

---

[17] It is one of the great ironies of democratic theory and practice that justice is repeatedly appealed to and is the primary paradigm of secular politics and morality, but it remains so vague and malleable in the hands of various persons, parties, and ideologies. It is a further irony that this last century, which experienced the worst and most extensive slaughter of humans in history, found most of this slaughter being justified by appeal to some idea of justice. For an acute discussion of the vagaries of views of justice, see Alasdair MacIntyre, *Whose Justice? Which Rationality?* (Notre Dame: University of Notre Dame Press, 1988).

and religions that might be bearers of salvation. 2) The church itself is not necessary to human fulfillment and meaning; anyone can mold together a personal recipe of diverse religious symbols without being a member of the church. 3) The primary sense of salvation refers to those processes in human life and history in which persons are being liberated from social oppression, whether that oppression is brought about by socio-economic powers or by personal enslavements and incapacities. Hence, *freedom* and *self-realization*, as being free from unjustified oppression, is the basic salvific aim of the church's life. 4) Salvation as ultimate redemption in life beyond death is a permissible but not an essential belief. It is in the living moment now that folk either do or do not find life meaningful and good or at least endurable.

Whether or not anyone of the readers of this essay would identify with all the points I have attributed to this model, I propose that the constellation of ideas and practices that comprise this model are deeply influential within the actual discourses and practices of the mainline churches in America.

A Revised Model of Church as Ark of Salvation

The revision of the traditional mode of the church as ark of salvation that I am proposing is similar to that view sometimes called *postliberal.* The concept of postliberal is generally associated with George Lindbeck[18] and his colleague at Yale, Hans Frei.[19] I deliberately refrained from using the word 'postliberal' to describe the position I developed in my recent systematic theology. While I have learned much from Frei and Lindbeck, I am not a whole-hearted follower of either, and therefore I did not want, in my systematic theology, to be saddled with having to explicate and defend their positions. It seemed

---

[18] See Lindbeck.

[19] A good place to start on Hans W. Frei's work is his posthumously published essays, *Theology and Narrative*, eds. George Hunsinger and William C. Placher (New York: Oxford University Press, 1993) and *Types of Christian Theology*, eds. George Hunsinger and William C. Placher (New Haven: Yale University Press, 1992). In a spirited way with his own creative voice, William Placher's *Unapologetic Theology: A Christian Voice in a Pluralistic Conversation* (Louisville: Westminster John Knox, 1989) discerningly displays some of the main themes of a postliberal theology.

less complicated to avoid the term and proceed on to discuss theological issues without the burden of that label. The explication of this revised model is my own construction, and I do not assume any responsibility for having accurately interpreted Frei and Lindbeck.

While I develop the concept of 'grammar of discourses and practices' a bit differently than Lindbeck, I do agree with his basic point that Christian faith and the church are more appropriately understood as a distinct "cultural-linguistic" social reality in the midst of many other social realities.[20] I affirm that *the church only exists within its own distinctive discourses and practices*, and when these are in disarray or become neglected or are repudiated, then the church itself falls into brokenness and unfaithfulness.

Further, I am affirming that the church should be moving beyond its liberal phase, which has dominated much of its intellectual life for two centuries, into a new phase that avoids some of the pitfalls of the traditional model of the church and salvation and that positively appreciates some of the contributions of the liberal model. I am proposing that the church move beyond liberalism and pursue a revised traditional ecclesiology that might recover for us the truth of the claim that the church is the ark of salvation. What I develop in miniature in this section takes two volumes to develop more fully in my *Grammar*. However, I am convinced that the wholeness of those two volumes requires an understanding of the church as ark of salvation, even though I will recommend some emendations in what we might mean by salvation and how it is conferred.

Consider now the following theses about language that bring together my discussion of language, as comprised of discourses and practices, in the *Grammar* (17–18):[21]

1. *The uses of words and locutions to make sense are embedded in traditions of usage.* We can't speak language without some community of users

---

[20] See Lindbeck, 32–41, for a brief explication of what he means by a "cultural-linguistic" approach.

[21] I urge my readers and listeners not to despair when they run into some technical words in these theses. I trust the gist of my characterization of language and human understanding and experience will come through nevertheless. But I am indeed teaching some new concepts, and it will, in line with my theses, take some practice to learn how to use them.

bound together through social conventions and rules of practice. These communal practices may be stretched, revised, or flouted, but they cannot be completely omitted and still make sense. Note: *making sense* is a communal activity as well as an individual activity.

2. *Language has to be learned and such learning involves learning skills in using words in social settings and communal games.* Mastering signs is learning how to use the requisite words in determinate social settings, to be able to engage in particular social practices. Mastering signs is like learning how to use *tools* for making sense in life, for working intelligibly in one's life in the world. Think, for example, of *learning how to sing praises to God.*

3. *Language provides the structure of our experience, understanding, and perspectives.* We experience the world and have a world in and through language, through signs, speech acts, and practices. Our *discourses and practices* are how we have a world, or worlds.

4. *In learning particular language networks, we are learning the discourses and practices that comprise having the world in that way.* Think of learning the language of physics: one *sees and understands* the world differently, and one acquires skills in investigating and explaining the world. What we are empowered to see, discern, and describe is dependent on the language we possess.

5. *The limits of our language are in some ways the limits of our understanding and therefore of our world.*

6. *Language is thus a human construct and construal.* It is produced by human interactions, agreements, and social practices. Hence, words do not have eternal and necessary meanings independent of their locations and usages in human communities and traditions.

7. *It is only within some language that we can test our construal of the world: we cannot completely abandon and step outside all language and look simply at the world.*

8. *Our humanity is shaped by our language and the communities of discourses and practices in which we participate.* Our living discourses and practices shape human self-understanding.

9. *The description of the grammar of language is a description of how language makes sense in its syntactic, semantic, and pragmatic dimensions.* The *depth grammar* of a particular set of linguistic practices will show how these dimensions of language hang together to make sense. For example, the depth grammar of trinitarian talk will show how embedded such talk is in self-involving, communal practices of identifying, praising, and witnessing to God in the church.

10. *Learning how to experience Christian faith is learning how to construe the world and oneself through the discourses and practices of the church with its peculiar language, its peculiar ways of being-in-the-world and having-a-world.*

From these theses you can understand why I worry about the church's discourses and practices in these times. The American culture, as a culture that is clearly dependent on many aspects of Christian tradition, uses many of the words of Christian tradition, such as, 'church,' 'sin,' 'grace,' and 'Jesus is Lord and Savior,' without any sense for the distinctive Christian usage that is intended to shape human life and understanding. Even some folk ostensibly in the church no longer use distinctive Christian language to shape their lives. While mouthing the Christian words on repeated occasions, they are concretely shaped by the many discourses and practices of their larger culture. Or, as I have said on other occasions, they do not *inhabit* the discourses and practices of Christian faith. This tension between the discourses and practices of the church and those of the world is inherent in being the church.[22]

In line with these theses about the inescapability of discourses and practices in actual human living, the central proposals for my understanding of the church are: 1) The church is necessarily a distinctive language rooted in the traditions of usage that go back to the Bible and

---

[22] See CGF, 47–52, for a discussion of what I call the 'dialectic between the church and the world.'

come over the centuries through the discourses and practices that are handed on by the church. 2) To be a Christian is to *learn how* to be a Christian by learning how to construe the world in and through the discourses and practices of the church. 3) Since these discourses and practices do convey the faith of the church, they are themselves the *means of grace* by virtue of which Christian understanding and life have content and vitality. 4) Outside these discourses and practices a person simply does not have the means by which to understand himself and God in ways that are salvific. It is in this sense that the church is the ark of salvation, outside of which folk simply do not have salvation because they do not know who God is and what God has done for the salvation of the world. 5) However, in line with some of the primary doctrines of the church, I will propose a revised way of understanding salvation. 6) It is almost as if folk in our time in America have forgotten how to say and mean, and thereby occupy, the distinctive discourses and practices of Christian faith.

In short, I will be proposing some normative understandings of Christian faith, which are surely arguable; but I will not be able in this essay to display all the justifications that others in the church might require. I will start with the normative claims by recalling and explicating my opening definition of the church:

> The church is that liberative and redemptive
> community of persons
> called into being
> by the Gospel of Jesus Christ
> through the Holy Spirit
> to witness in word and deed
> to the living triune God
> for the benefit of the world
> to the glory of God.

By identifying the church as *liberative and redemptive*, I am immediately saying the church has to do with human salvation. This, of course, poses the question of what 'salvation' means here. Earlier in this paper I proposed that most of the salvation language in the Bible and traditions pivots around a contrast between *what one is saved from* and *what one is saved to*.

At the heart of this contrast is sin: one is saved from sin and its consequences and is saved to a life and destiny not determined by sin.

The root of all the forms of sin is human unbelief: the practical refusal to live obediently before God. This primitive unbelief issues 1) into sin as *pride*: living a life in which the self is the center of all valuing and seeks to have life on its own terms; 2) into sin as *sloth*: the refusal to be a responsible self before God and the inclination to permit the powers of the world to tell us who we are and what we are worth; 3) into sin as *concupiscence*: a life of disordered desires driven to and fro by a quest to find fulfillment and satisfaction, yet not understanding that God should be the supreme desire of human life; 4) into sin as *falsehood and lies*: a life given to lies about others and one's situation in the world and to self-deception and its attendant falsehoods.

The consequences of sin are that human life is corrupted and lost, in alienation from God, from one's own created nature and from one's neighbors and enemies. This corruption of life falls into envy, suspicion, anger, hatred, and much violence, culminating in a dominating fear of death. These corruptions also corrupt human societies, and they too suffer from and perpetuate human sinning, resulting in terrible rivalry, fear of the strange others—the stranger and the enemies—and perpetual violence (see GCF, 343–64).

But all this language about sin is unavailable to us without understanding who God is and who God is in Jesus Christ (see GCF, 345–52). The judgment of God—as we shall see in Jesus Christ—is that sin and its consequences, which include both our sinning and our being sinned against by others, produce the sort of life that cannot of itself achieve human flourishing and well-being. God says 'no' to sin as that which leads only to the kingdom of death and death-dealing and therefore to no-life. Hence, left to our own sinful living and therefore to our own devices and stratagems, human life leads only to alienation, conflict, enmity, defeat, despair, and death.

The church, therefore, is a *community of persons* that is involved in the salvation of human beings from their own sinful living and its consequences for their destiny. The church is a community of persons, and this is not some vague social group. It is a community of persons, living in formative interaction with each other. I cannot emphasize too much that the church is not an abstract ideal but is a community of persons who live, think, converse, and act together in the actual formation of how they live in the world. There is a social physicality and concrete interaction that is essential to the church. The church is a visible social body always located somewhere and involving specific persons in interaction with each other.

But even more importantly, it is a community of persons *called into being by the Gospel of Jesus Christ.* When we place an emphasis on the church as called by the Gospel of Jesus Christ, we are immediately denying that the church is primarily a voluntary society of folk who have similar interests and who get together to pursue those interests. It should also be obvious that the church is not a community formed by the free choices of *autonomous* individuals who regard the church as in their rational self-interest. Rather, the church is called or summoned into existence by the Gospel. It is comprised of folk who have heard something from God in Christ and are pulled into the community in the midst of their sinful brokenness as a matter of life and death. Persons may indeed saunter in and take up a place in the community of the church, but they only truly enter the vitalities of the church through the passion of baptism. Without the baptism and passionate confession of faith, persons, who may interact with the community from time to time but in avoidance of baptism, are tempted to become spectators rather than believers.

Over the years of teaching in seminaries, I have repeatedly asked my students in theology to tell me in a short form just what they think the Gospel is. It is a chastening and necessary exercise and experience for the students, for they have presumably come to seminary because they think there is an actual Gospel revealed by God. While it is everywhere evident in the NT that there is some good news that calls the church into existence, the church sometimes forgets what that good news is. When that happens, the church forgets what its founding calling is. Similarly, if the church—in its denominational form or in its particular congregational form—does not have a shared sense for what the Gospel is, then it follows logically and practically that the church will find its actual discourses and practices in disarray. This disarray will result in confusion about its own identity and mission. Put another way, when the actual discourses and practices of the church make it conceptually and practically impossible to determine and discern heretical understandings of the Gospel, then the church falls easily into allowing almost any whim of the moment to occupy the center of its life.

This does raise, then, the question of what that Gospel is. Because its very heart and health are at stake, I believe that every generation of the church must struggle to identify and state clearly just what it regards as the Gospel that is basic to the church's identity and mission. The church is that community that sustains a continuing conversation within itself and in relation to Scripture and traditions concerning the Gospel. It is useless, however, for a congregation to construct a mission statement when there is no shared consensus as to what the Gospel is that calls it into existence. Such an exercise in finding a mission will only reveal the sad extent to which that congregation has lost its identity and is trying to find some way to pretend its fragile life together is really meaningful and perhaps Christian.

A critical question that the church must solve in formulating its understanding of the Gospel is whether 1) Jesus is merely the *bearer* of the Gospel but is not essential to its content, or 2) Jesus is essential to the content of the Gospel and it cannot be truthfully articulated without affirming that he is not only the *bearer* but also the constitutive *heart* of the Gospel. I will argue that Jesus is essential to the Gospel, and I judge that the liberal model of church would contend that the Gospel is independent of Jesus. Hence, it is important in my ecclesiology that 'Gospel' always means 'Gospel of Jesus Christ.'

In my *Grammar* I propose the following statement of the Gospel: (see GCF, 27)

The Gospel of Jesus Christ is the Good News
that the God of Israel, the Creator of all creatures,
has in freedom and love become incarnate
in the life, death, and resurrection of Jesus of Nazareth
to enact and reveal God's gracious reconciliation
of humanity to Godself, and
through the Holy Spirit calls and empowers human beings
to participate in God's liberative and redemptive work by
acknowledging God's gracious forgiveness in Jesus,
repenting of human sin,
receiving the gift of freedom, and
embracing authentic community by

loving the neighbor and the enemy,
caring for the whole creation, and
hoping for the final triumph of God's grace
as the triune Ultimate Companion of all creatures.

Notice that this statement of the Gospel almost has a creedal character to it, as it aims to identify for us just what truly constitutes the essential good news that calls the church into being from its very beginnings in time. Further, notice that there are two outstanding and decisive historical particularities in the statement: *Israel* and *Jesus of Nazareth*. These two particularities, God's electing and covenanting with the people of Israel over a period of time in human history and God's becoming incarnate in a Palestinian Jew who lived at a particular time in history, are the deep anchor points of the Gospel. These particularities are not accidents of history that provide a mix for good symbols; these particularities are at the heart of the Gospel, and without them there is no distinctively Christian Gospel.

It is in this sense that we have a *narrative* framework that is essential to the Gospel. It is a large narrative that is rooted in the biblical testimony in which God identifies Godself to the people of Israel as the one who elects and covenants with them and, therefore, as the only God there is. As such, the God of Israel is the Creator of the whole world. Hence, we have a distinction between the Creator and all creatures who, in being creatures, are not divine.

But human beings created by God and Israel elected by God fall into repeated rebellion against God and want to be divine themselves and have life on their own terms. They do not like being creaturely and finite, and they do not like having to live peacefully with other humans. Their fear of others goads them into violence and wars. It is in this narrative context that God comes to the rescue of Israel and all humanity in a Jew, Jesus of Nazareth. The church arises out of Jesus' proclamation and enactment of the impinging Kingdom of God, his brutal death on the cross by the reigning principalities and powers in his historical world, and his resurrection from the dead as the vindication of his life and as hope for the world in a redemption that is eternal. Those who emerge out of these events as followers of Jesus come to realize they cannot properly narrate the course and significance of his life without regarding his life, death, and resurrection as the revelation of the being and reality of God. Indeed, *Jesus is God's own self-revelation*: the very incarnate presence of God in the events of this man's life and death and resurrection from the dead.

The good news about this is *that God was in Christ reconciling the world to Godself* and thereby not counting human sins against them and thereby giving them grace and forgiveness and hope of life and destiny utterly and completely conferred and sustained by God's grace (2 Cor 5:16-21). This forgiving grace comes into the lives of the followers of Jesus through the Holy Spirit. This Holy Spirit is not some vague spirit flitting here and there, but is the very Spirit of the God of Israel and of Jesus the Son of God. It is this Spirit that provides the empowerment for folk to acknowledge God's gracious forgiveness in Jesus and to repent of their sin and therewith to receive the gift of freedom to live away from sin.

But this living in a new freedom cannot be done without embracing other folk and forming that sort of *authentic community* in which agapic love is manifested. Strangely, this authentic community cannot truly be the community of the faithful without being open to the stranger and the enemy as persons for whom Jesus lived and died and was raised.

Hence, the church is called into existence to be the *Body of Christ* in the world in order that the whole world might hear the Gospel and have their lives transformed as well. It is here that we can return to our definition of the church: *the church is called into existence by the Gospel to witness in word and deed to the living triune God for the benefit of the world.* Witnessing to God and God's gracious good news is then the purpose and mission of the followers of Jesus. Precisely in their *words or discourses* and in their *deeds or practices* they are witnessing to God so that the world might know God, might know themselves as loved and forgiven by God, and might know themselves as beneficiaries of a hope in life and death that is the supreme good of human life. In all these respects, then, the life of the church—precisely in and through its distinctive discourses and practices—bears and conveys the *means of grace* by way of which God's gracious Gospel becomes good news to the world.

Hence, these narrative particulars are essential to the Christian life and witness, and while they do have universal significance, the particulars are not accidental and dispensable. Rather, there is no Gospel message apart from these particulars. Hauntingly, then, where this Gospel-formed narrative is tattered or obscured or even subverted, then the life of the church has lost its vital center and reason for being.

So, in its discourses and practices the church is to witness to the triune God for the *benefit of the world*. It is the world, with all its violence, malevolence, selfishness, and greed, that God loves and has already forgiven and reconciled in Christ. But the world knows neither Christ nor that reconciling forgiveness, and therefore the world does not really know how deeply it is riven with sin. The discourses of the world vacillate between 1) that tragic despair in the unhappy and conflictual nature of human life that is overwhelmed by the fear of death and suffering, and 2) that heroic optimism that just one more war or one more program will make the world safe and hospitable to human flourishing. The world repeatedly invokes divine authorities to buttress their own claims to be the decisive agents in history, but these are the no-gods that perpetuate human enmity and violence under the illusion of pursuing peace and justice.

But the church cannot witness to that world in words separated from deeds of faithfulness in living and being the body of Christ in the world. "Word separated from deed is hypocritical, vain, deadly, and a lie. Deed separated from word loses its proper context, intentionality, and luminosity" (GCF, 164). Hence, the church can only live in faithfulness when it is shaped and formed by the distinct narrative of God's life with the world, which we have been discussing in outline.

The definition of the church speaks of 'the triune God,' and it is fair to ask why I refer to God as triune. Of course, the triuneness of God simply is the language of the ecumenical traditions of the church. It arises in the grammar of the church as it sorts through what it means to say "Jesus is Lord," which is uttered throughout the NT. While Jesus is undeniably human, it would certainly appear to most Jews that he could not be Lord, for there is only one Lord and his name is Yahweh, the God of Israel. But if Jesus, precisely in his life and in his death and in his resurrection, is the self-revelation of the God of Israel, then he is not only the bearer of the Gospel but is himself the Gospel.[23] He is what God is doing on behalf of human salvation. It is because Jesus was finally considered to be divine that trinitarian language emerges in the life of the

---

[23] See the stunning transformation of meanings taking place within Jewish language in Phil 2:5-11.

church's witness. Were one to believe that Jesus is not divine and that his divinity is not crucial to understanding who God is, then trinitarian language would become symbolically optional and even negligible and would not be essential to the statement of the Gospel. Jesus may then be the bearer of good news but he is not himself essential to that news. That I affirm with the ecumenical church that the human Jesus is God incarnate and that God is triune goes to the marrow of what I regard as heretical in the liberal model of church I constructed earlier.

I have tried to make the case for the appropriateness of trinitarian language in the church throughout my *Grammar*. But rooted in the narrative I have outlined above, trinitarian grammar intends to say God has three internally related ways of being one God: as the One who creates all things and elected Israel—*God the ground of all that is*; as the One who became incarnate in Jesus of Nazareth for salvation of the world—*God the One who salvifically encounters us in life*; as the One who is the Spirit that endows life and transforms life—*God the One who is the dynamism that works within creaturely life to bring it to redemption*. The point: we cannot adequately speak the narrative and identify God without speaking in these three different but interrelated ways of God being God.[24]

I want now to propose some distinctions in how we use *salvation language*. These distinctions all presuppose the contrast between sin and its consequences and the grace of God. I affirm that there are three spheres in the use of salvation language in the church. First, there is the sphere of salvation in what God has done for humans in Jesus Christ, which I call the objective sphere of *Reconciliation and Justification*. Second, there is the sphere in which persons say 'yes' to what God has done in Jesus Christ, which is what I call the sphere of *Historic Redemption*. Third, there is the sphere of salvation that pertains to the final destiny of persons in relation to death and to God's final consummation of all things. I call this the sphere of *Ultimate Redemption*. To keep our discussion of salvation straight it is helpful to remember these distinctions, explore their interconnections, and to see that we may be asking different questions in each sphere.[25]

---

[24] See the full statement of trinitarian rationale in GCF, 167–215. My claim is that the Gospel itself cannot be fully conveyed as to who God is without trinitarian language, however difficult and perplexing it might from time to time be. See also chapter eight below.

[25] See CGF, 503–9 for a brief schema of salvation grammar. See also chapter seven below.

This gets us into the interpretation of the first sphere of salvation as *Reconciliation and Justification*. I interpret what happens in Jesus Christ as God-acting and being-acted-upon and as human-acting and being-acted-upon for the salvation of the world. Apart from Jesus Christ the situation of humanity is life in sin, suffering those consequences I have enumerated earlier. God's wrath is God's 'no' to sin as that which is not intended by God as part of the good creation, even though it is permitted by God in conferring finite freedom on humans. But God's wrath is not something God externally imposes on human beings. Rather, God's wrath is God's permitting sin and its consequences to unravel and thwart human well-being. The ways of sin are not the ways to human flourishing. Evil is writ large and small in the ways in which the world organizes itself and distributes goods and powers.

These powers of human sinfulness, who pretend they are the real powers of meaning, life, and death, brutally slay Jesus on a cross of shame. Little do they realize they are slaying the divine Life in the form and presence of this man Jesus. Jesus the eternal Son of God dies a human death on the cross. This is God taking the sins of the world upon and into the divine Life, and thereby disarming the powers of their pretense that they are in control of human life and death. It is God who is in charge of human life and destiny, and, in taking these powers of sin and death into and upon God's own Life, God is graciously forgiving humans their sin, reconciling them to Godself, and refusing to treat them as sinners who are doomed to despair and death.

Further, without the resurrection of Jesus, as something that happened to Jesus and involves his self-manifestation to others, the powers of the world might still be apprehended as the real makers and rulers of the world. The raising of Jesus is the vindication, through redemptive and healing power overcoming death, that the life and death of Jesus is truly the revelation of the Life of God (see CGF, 458–73 on the resurrection of Jesus).

Hence, in this *first meaning of salvation*, in Jesus Christ it objectively happens that God graciously forgives sinners and invites them to new life without suffering the consequences of sin. In the New Testament and the traditions of the church this is variously talked about as atonement, reconciliation, and justification. God's wrath is revealed as only a preliminary word and judgment, but not as God's final judgment. That final judgment is manifested in the cross as God's loving humanity with a love that will not leave us to our devices and self-wrought destiny. In this first sense of salvation, then, all persons are in Christ, whether they know it or not, and whether they live it or not (see CGF, 443–57 on the cross, and 473–80 on the salvific benefits of Christ).

Given, then, what God has done in Jesus Christ for the salvation of the world, we come now to the second sphere of salvation I have called *Historic Redemption*. It is, of course, God's desire that human beings should know and rejoice in what God has done on their behalf in Christ Jesus. The church in its simplest and most primitive form is comprised of those persons who have encountered Christ—living, crucified, and raised from the dead—and have said 'yes' to him as salvific good news. These are the ones who acknowledge Christ as sheer grace, who are caught up in the process of living in conformity with Christ, who are learning how to be loving and forgiving to others, even enemies. These are the ones who worship God as the One who has come among us as a human being and has acted on our behalf and who will continue to act on our behalf. In short, these folk are new creations and a new community that God has launched into human history to witness to God and thereby to witness to a new way of being human and being together with other humans. In other words, these folk form a new community as an *alternative way of life* compared to how they used to live and how the communities of the world actually live.

The Christian life and the church are thus rooted in what God has already done in Christ. We can put it this way: what God has done in Jesus Christ is the *indicative foundation* of the Christian life, and it gives rise to those imperatives for living that I characterize as the *ethics of grace*. This ethics asks: given what God has done for us in Israel and in Jesus Christ, how are we called to live? It is, therefore, not an ethics that seeks the reward of grace and forgiveness. Rather, it is an ethics that is rooted in forgiveness and empowered by the grace of the Spirit, and it seeks to conform human life to God's life in loving God and loving the neighbor, which now includes the stranger and the enemy. This ethics, of course, is to be differentiated from that liberal, presumably rational, ethics that presupposes rational self-interest and calculates obligations according to a utilitarian, cost/benefit analysis (CGF, 511–28).

This life-together in the church can be schematized as *liberation, sanctification, and emancipation.* The church is comprised of those who know they have been given in Jesus Christ liberation or freedom from sin and its consequences. They are forgiven and now called to live that freedom. The full living out of that new freedom intrinsically involves being caught up in the process of sanctification: to live into that holiness that has been given in Christ and now is appropriated in holy living.[26] Further, the Christian and the church are the ones who are committed to the nonviolent emancipation of their neighbors from the domination and subjugation of the powers of the world. The church cannot live its life in ignorance or forgetfulness of the consequences of sin that still stalk life in the world. At the heart of its emancipating works is modeling peace within itself for the world and working in the world to bring about peace in nonviolent ways.

Thus far I think I have shown that this historic redemption is unique, grounded in what God has done in Israel and in Jesus Christ for the whole world. The narrative that captures these activities of God is not a general symbol available wherever people might look or whatever tradition they might live. They need to hear the narrative and learn how to live in the light of it, and that narrative is available only in the church of Jesus Christ. Put another way, the church itself only truly exists where that narrative is recited and lived in the discourses and practices of a community. That is why the actual discourses and practices of the church must be continually critiqued lest they fall into disarray and falsehood. These discourses and practices—in their precious specificity, faithfulness, and truthfulness—are wonderfully the *means of grace* by way of which persons come to know God, have a relationship with God, and come to know themselves as sinners who have been forgiven and called to a new way of living. Here is the heart of what it means to say the church is the ark of salvation, outside of which these means of grace do not exist.

We can now deal with two important questions often asked by the liberal church. First, it asks whether the church, even in my revised model, is presumptuous in thinking it knows God truly. However, notice that

---

[26] I believe it is urgently the case that the Protestant traditions need to rediscover the meaning of sanctification as that disciplined way of living and growing into relationship with God. It is in relation to sanctification that the current popular talk of 'spirituality' should be developed. See my extended discussion of sanctification and spirituality in CGF, 537–45. See also how it relates to Discipleship, 545–53.

this question presupposes that there might be some other context or some other concept of deity that will show us just how presumptuous our discourse about God is. But what is this other context or concept of divinity and where does it come from and what is its privileged status? I suspect it is formed from other premises than those that affirm that God has revealed Godself in the history of Israel and in Jesus Christ and called the church into existence. While it is intrinsic to the grammar of deity in the church that God is incomprehensible, this primarily means that God is not simply characterizable as an object in the world. It does not mean that God is utterly unknown and that Christians and others alike are just 'gassing and guessing' when they speak of deity (see CGF, 31–32, 152–54, 178).

I pray that the church will have the courage to recognize that this liberal critique and my rejoinder represent a clash between two radically different ways of construing God and the world. And I pray and have written this essay in the hope that the church will then have the courage to go about its witness to the God known in the narrative. Either the rough outlines of the narrative are bedrock for Christians and the church or they are not. When it becomes apparent that they are not for some folk, then that church is subverting its biblical and traditional witness. Whatever the subverting group might claim to be, it is difficult to acknowledge them as the church of Jesus Christ.

Second, the liberal model asks whether my revised model of the church implies that folk outside the church, in other religions or not, simply do not know God and thereby do not know 'salvation' in historic redemption. Isn't it arrogant to condemn non-Christians to hell? Well, whatever then does the word 'salvation' mean in this question? Surely we must admit that, outside the church, folk in the world in other communities do often perform, for example, acts of kindness, charity, loyalty, justice, self-giving, and truth-telling. So the question being raised requires a complex answer that I will give here in a shortened version.

According to the narrative of Christian faith I have proposed, all persons, even those who are not actively engaged in saying 'yes' to God's grace in Christ, are in theological fact 'in Christ.' They are included in those for whom Christ lived and died and was raised. Hence, before God they stand forgiven and graced. But surely our saying that, as devout utterances of faith, may make no sense to them. Yet the point is, from the church's perspective, whether that language makes any sense to those outside the church, it does make sense within the church. This means immediately that for the church these others beyond the church are our brothers and sisters before God's grace and are the ones we are summoned to love and to whom we are to witness. And because we believe God has not and will not leave the church to its own devices, so too we can and should believe *that the God who is the Creator, Reconciler, and Redeemer will not finally forsake those beyond the church.* Unfolding this point will take us into the sphere of ultimate redemption, which will be forthcoming below.

We can also affirm that intrinsic to trinitarian theology is the belief that the three ways of God being God—the three persons of the Trinity, Father, Son, and Holy Spirit—are dynamically interrelated such that each way is implicated in what the other ways do. Accordingly, in the New Testament it comes to be said that Jesus Christ was there at the beginning of all things as the Logos that it is at the heart of all things creaturely. Now if the Logos, through whom all things creaturely were made, is Jesus Christ, then the life, death, and resurrection of Jesus must further define for us just what is at the heart of the creation: namely, suffering and self-giving love that is the final redemptive Word in all things.[27] So, we might admit that there are 'signals' of this Logos/Christ in other places and traditions in forms that are now hidden from us. But having said that, we must also say that Christ could not be revealed in other places and forms that 'contradict' what we know of Jesus Christ. God is not duplicitous and in self-contradiction to Godself.

Likewise, the Holy Spirit as the Spirit of Christ is at work in the world wherever redemptive healings and transformations are taking place in the world. The Spirit's work—like Christ's work—is not restricted to the boundaries of the church. Yet, in the construal power of its discourses, the church is that specially gifted community that can discern, name, and rejoice in the Spirit redemptively at work in the world. In the church, through its ways of talking and understanding, we are given the *grace of conceptual lens* through which to identify the work of Christ and the Spirit, which are paradigmatically at work in the church (see CGF, 483–502 on the Spirit).

---

[27] See John 1:1-14; Col 1:19-20; Heb 1:2-3.

We come now to discuss the third sphere of salvation, which I have called *Ultimate Redemption*. Under this rubric I especially include those matters of human ultimate destiny in relation to death and God's final consummation of all things. I have spent a long chapter in my *Grammar* trying to develop a way of talking about these matters that is in significant conflict with many of the ways in which church traditions have talked. I cannot recapitulate here the fullness of that discussion (see CGF, 709–48). But there should be no surprises here, given what I have said to this point.

I have repeatedly emphasized the sovereignty and power of God's love and forgiveness as we know them in Jesus Christ. This is about God's graciousness to humanity that is not given as the just deserts of humans. It is not a reward for being and living righteously. Rather, it is given in spite of the fact that humans deserve condemnation for the sinful ways in which they live in relation to others and to God, and are thereby destructive even of their own good. When we are justified in Christ, we are not being justified as a reward or as what we deserve. We are being justified by an act of God that is prior to any response of ours, but it is, when we acknowledge the justification, evocative of our gratitude and repentance. Put simply: God justifies and forgives us even before we ask for forgiveness. Among ordinary humans, forgiveness is usually given to another only after the other has repented, sincerely apologized, and asked for forgiveness. God works otherwise and by a different logic (see CGF, 513–19).

I propose that this basic and irremovable theme of Christian faith flies in the face of another traditional theme of the church's discourses. That is the theme, expressed at points in the Bible and dominant in the tradition, that ultimately there must be *dual destiny*: a destiny for the saved and a destiny for the damned. When we ask how this destiny is decided, the church ineluctably has moved to say either 1) persons are saved by their own righteous living or 2) persons are saved by the grace of God.

The first alternative comes dangerously close to saying that we *earn* ultimate salvation by how we live. Herein, then, ultimate salvation is a *reward* for holy living. Precisely what that holy is has been hard to pin down in the tradition. But it may look as though one could say that only those in the church, as the ark of salvation, are those who will be ultimately saved.[28] But if the community of the church is comprised of folk who are struggling to learn how to live under the grace of God in Christ and who may not yet be 'perfect' in all of their living, then by what criterion do they earn ultimate salvation? My point is that reward and *just deserts* language in any of its forms is dramatically misleading about the Christian life itself and is therefore also dramatically misleading about ultimate salvation.

If the church is that unique place in which we learn who God is and how gracious God is to sinners and how inexhaustibly God is committed to human redemption, then we ought to talk about ultimate redemption in a way that keeps its focus on God's grace and not on human just deserts. Accordingly, Christians should not be thinking of a life beyond death in which they will meet God as the kindly bestower of what they have properly earned. Christians should not be thinking and saying that we are to trust in our own righteousness as we die and encounter God. Rather, in the church Christians should learn—as they encounter death in others and as their own imminent possibility—that they are to trust in the forgiving graciousness of God rather than their own presumed righteousness. If that is so about Christians in their extremities of dying and death, then must it not also be the case that Christians and the church should teach that we trust and hope in the ultimate triumph of God's grace as the *Ultimate Redeeming Companion* who meets every person in death and transforms him or her into God's own eternal companions (see CGF, 722–24, 724–36)?

What about hell, then? Surely hell primarily refers to the ways of human living in which destruction and retribution and wrath subvert and destroy human flourishing. Hell and thereby the Devil do indeed occupy the hearts and minds of the human family when they live adamantly and indifferently in sin. But hell as an ultimate residence for erstwhile sinners?

---

[28] It is interesting to note that in our earlier discussion of the traditional model of the church as ark we saw that the church had to admit that it was itself comprised of both saints and tares. Hence, it is not a sufficient condition of being saved that one is a member of the church through baptism. Something more is required in order to be ultimately saved. When Augustine gets his mind around this dilemma, he finally affirms that anyone ultimately saved is saved only by the grace of God and not in any sense by their own righteous living and its deserts. When the crunch really comes, salvation is finally by the grace of God only.

I think the church should begin to say that such *an ultimate hell is empty*, for it has been emptied as the final and just judgment on any person by the life, death, and resurrection of Jesus Christ. As the Apostles' Creed says of Christ, "he descended into hell" as he suffered the death-dealing hatred and enmity of his crucifiers. Are we to suppose that Christ left a fully occupied hell as the just deserts of folks? Or are we rather to believe that hell, as that place of extreme and horrendous separation from God, is also a place into which the Son, in his extremities of dying a brutal and forsaken death, plunged deeply and freely and lovingly and gathered up its occupants as the ones who are embraced even in their extremities as persons finally to be redeemed by God?

But if the church does decide to talk and act in the way I have proposed, then its discourses and practices will *modify but not delete the image of the church as the ark of salvation* that contains the saved, both in historic redemption and in ultimate redemption, outside of which there is no salvation. We should say, and say joyfully, that it is in the church that humans are led to encounter God's gracious ways with humanity. Outside the church it is certainly not evident that persons know who God is and how God loves and know therewith how to live as folk who earnestly trust in the grace of God and earnestly desire to live in conformity to God's life. The church, however, is the unique place in which people learn to be transformed by the grace of God in Christ Jesus. The uniqueness resides in the narrative definiteness, the truthfulness, the faithfulness, and the vitality of the church's distinctive discourses and practices.

Yet it is not that we are in the church in order to earn our ultimate salvation. Rather, it is in the church that we find the means of grace to live in the hope of an ultimate salvation that is also the hope for the world. The church might then dare to proclaim that hope, even though it may not be understood and embraced apart from being in the church and learning profoundly and lovingly that God is ultimately gracious.

Let me draw these points together about the church and salvation in my revised model of the church. I am urging that the *church is properly the ark of salvation as the means of grace—in and through its distinctive discourses and practices—in God's historic redemption.* However, I am proposing that these very means of grace—as the mediators of God's saving grace in discourses and practices—empower the hope for ultimate salvation that should lead to and ground the hope for the ultimate salvation of all God's children. In this sense, then, *the church itself is a living witness to the ultimacy of God's grace as we know it in Jesus Christ.*

Some Concluding Remarks

I hope I have been able to persuade folk of the necessity and dignity of the church as the ark of salvation—as that visible community that teaches and witnesses to a gracious God who has come among us in Jesus of Nazareth. It should be clear, I hope, that *being a Christian is impossible without being in the church.* Being a Christian is not possible as the lonely person relying on her own powers of discernment and her own powers of will. Being a Christian is necessarily a matter of *learning how to be a Christian.* To pursue that involves being a member of a community that has characteristic discourses and practices about the narrative of God's grace. When the discourses and practices of the church are alive, vibrant, specific, and Gospel-grounded, then the church is the *Body of Christ* in and for the world.

Let me now specify more nearly what those practices are that one should learn in the church.[29] First, there are the *practices of nurture.* This is especially evident in the many-sided practices of worship in which we learn how to identify God and are thereby empowered to praise God. Not all purported 'praises of God' are praises to the triune God who has come to us in Israel and in Jesus Christ. To praise God depends on knowing who God is. In gathering for worship, as a defining practice of the Christian life, we engage in the regular practices of praising God, praying to God, singing hymns to God, receiving nourishment at God's Table of Communion, reading Scripture, listening to Scripture as the Word of God, and hearing the Gospel proclaimed by wise and saintly persons. These are all practices that we have to learn how to perform. They are not innate in us.

Under nurturing practices are also the practices of communal care in which we learn how to be a community that upbuilds its members in the

---

[29] For a fuller discussion of the church as the Body of Christ in and through its distinctive discourses and practices, see CGF, 617–44.

faith. These include practices of loving others in the church, of praying for others, of tending to the care of others in distress, of educating others in faithful and truthful discourses, of forgiving others, of seeking forgiveness from others. How can Christians love the neighbors in the world if they cannot, do not, and perhaps know not how to love the folk who are their neighbors in the church? When these practices are not occurring regularly and devoutly in the life of a congregation, then it is difficult to know the liveliness of the Spirit.

Second, there are the *practices of outreach to the world*. If the church is called to witness to the triune God for the benefit of the world, then the church is always aimed at the salvation of the world. Briefly, there are 1) the practices of *evangelization* in which the church invites the world to hear the good news of Jesus Christ, 2) the practices of *prophecy* in which the church identifies those powers in the world that are demonic and destructive of human good, 3) the practices of *emancipating works of love* for the neighbors in the world, and 4) practices of *vocation* in which the individual Christian lives faithfully in places of home, of economic work, of citizenship, and of recreation at no other's detrimental expense.

Third, there are the constitutive practices of the church in *administration*. It is in these practices that the church organizes itself for its mission in nurture and outreach, and they are profoundly theological practices. I will refer my reader to my long discussion of these practices (CGF, 634–44). But I want briefly to express my worry when the institutional character of the church becomes dominant, because it begins emphasizing that the church's very reality depends on the offices of an apostolic priesthood and episcopacy. These two offices then emerge as the critical defining signs of where the church exists. Rather, I would emphasize that the church only truly exists where its discourses and practices are in conformity to the Gospel of Jesus Christ and effectively witness to the triune God for the benefit of the world. But it nevertheless is the case that the church, in whatever institutional shape it might exist, will need to have some *magisterial authority*—that is, a teaching and decision-making authority about matters of faith—invested in some communal form. Here I prefer a *consensual body*, comprised of laity and ordained ministers, that is prepared to decide urgent matters of orthodoxy and heresy and to identify areas in which disagreement is permitted and often needed. But churches with a polity that inhibits such a magisterial form from emerging are dangerously inclined to being ruled by the discourses and practices of the larger social worlds in which they exist.

When these distinctive practices are not alive and well in a congregation, then we can easily be overwhelmed by the brokenness of the church. The key, however, to overcoming this brokenness is to proclaim the Gospel repeatedly in the hope that it might be heard as good news to folk disheartened and in disarray.

In conclusion, let it be affirmed that, when the church is called and formed by the Gospel of Jesus Christ, it will also contain folk who are having their lives continually transformed by the gracious works of God. Persons in the world and outside the church need the community of the church as that place where the Gospel is proclaimed and lived. The world needs the church as the ark that carries within itself the *means of grace* that transform human life and give hope for the world. Are these means of grace still available when the community is itself shattered and broken and in conflict? Such brokenness certainly confuses folk and corrupts the language and undermines the efficacy of the practices. But there remains hope as the church still reads the Bible in worship and at least gives lip service to the practice of claiming there is a Gospel. However emptily those practices might be performed from time to time, the very form of their repetition keeps alive the hope that the church might once again hear the words of the Gospel of Jesus Christ as good news for themselves and therewith transformative of how they actually live in the world.

Part Two

Theological Baselines for Doing Church Theology

5

Some Remarks on Authority and Revelation in Kierkegaard

I. The background of these remarks is the contemporary scene in philosophy and theology, strewn as it has been in recent years with such epithets as "God is dead," "the post-Christian age," "the age of secularization," "the meaninglessness of religious language," and "the secular meaning of the Gospel." It is as though profound cultural change and new philosophical discoveries have placed an unbearable burden upon Christian discourse. In the face of such a burden some Christian intellectuals have been engaged in a massive salvage operation of reinterpreting the Christian concepts in such a way as to secure their relevance to the modern, secular mind. And as this salvage operation is being carried out, it should not be surprising that the terms of Christian discourse have become, to use an expression of Kierkegaard's, "volatilized," that is, unsteady and mercurial.

It is this volatilizing of terms that concerns me, especially as regards Christian talk of revelation. However, rather than directly confronting some of the forms of volatilization in our contemporary situation, I want to investigate some features of Kierkegaard's discussion of authority and revelation. Kierkegaard considered his literature to be something of a corrective to the disarray and confusion that was plaguing the discourse of Christians in his time. I hope that attention to how Kierkegaard diagnoses and corrects his contemporaries will be of some benefit in understanding some of the present difficulties in Christian talk of revelation.

Kierkegaard was persuaded that Christian discourse had become corrupted in at least two respects. On the one hand, there was the assimilation of the discourse to the framework and categories of philosophical idealism, with the consequent loss of the decisive concepts of Christian faith. Such assimilation had taken place under the guise of rescuing the "real meaning" of Christian faith from the outmoded language in which it had historically risen. On the other hand, there was the practical domestication of Christian discourse that prevailed in the midst of that notorious arrangement called state religion. In such a situation the terms of Christian discourse had become so overtaken by the conventional practices and attitudes of the people that they no longer had the power to convey the distinctive content of Christian faith. Rather than conveying, for example, a word of judgment and grace, a challenge to worldly interests, the terms of Christian discourse had become largely subservient to those interests. People might still utter the words "sin," "Jesus, Lord and Savior," and "faith," but without a sense of sin, of needing a savior, of striving for faith. The folk who, in one way or another, considered themselves Christian no longer had a Christian understanding, no longer lived within the distinctive concepts of Christian faith: "If it is factual that the language of Christian concepts has become in a volatilized sense the conversational language of the whole of Europe, it follows quite simply that the holiest and most decisive definitions are used again and again without being united with the decisive thought. One hears indeed often enough Christian predicates used by Christian priests where the names of God and of Christ constantly appear and passages of Scripture . . . in discourses which nevertheless as a whole contain pagan views of life without either the priest or the hearers being aware of it."[1] Given such volatilizing of terms by philosophical reinterpretation and by practical domestication,

---

[1] Søren Kierkegaard, *On Authority and Revelation*, trans. Walter Lowrie (Princeton: Princeton University Press, 1955), 166. (Since the writing of this essay, in which I use the texts available at that time, a new translation of those texts is now available in *Kierkegaard's Writings*, vol. 24: *The Book on Adler*, edited and translated by Howard V. Hong and Edna H. Hong (Princeton: Princeton University Press, 1998). It is extensively annotated and contains many related passages from Kierkegaard's journals.)

Kierkegaard thought his age needed to be educated anew in the discourse and life of Christian faith.

The case of a contemporary pastor named Adler was the occasion for a sustained investigation by Kierkegaard of the Christian understanding of revelation.[2] Adler had been educated in the reigning Hegelian philosophy and had understood the Christian faith through Hegelian eyes. But in 1842, while serving a pastorate in a small Danish village, Adler experienced what he later described as a revelation from God in which a "new doctrine was communicated to him" (p. 19). He ostensibly gave up his Hegelian theories, even burned some previous work of his on Hegel. But he was judged by his bishop to be deranged and was suspended from the pastorate. Later, after replying in an evasive way to the bishop's official inquiries about his revelation, he was deposed from the church's ministry. In the course of about three years he published six books pertaining to his "revelation" experience.

For Kierkegaard, Adler was a protruding example of the fundamental confusions concerning the Christian faith that afflicted his time. While Adler started with a claim to a revelation and a new doctrine, his behavior and his talk gradually seemed to belie the claim. The vivid certainty of a revelation from God gradually gave way to doubt and was finally transformed into a profoundly moving religious experience. The authority of a revelation was slowly exchanged for the authority of a gifted and insightful religious genius. The new doctrine was strangely elusive with respect to its newness. According to Kierkegaard's diagnosis, Adler had such an "imperfect education in Christian concepts" (p. 167) that he could only confusedly use Christian terms to convey what had happened to him. Adler was too deeply mired in the volatilized religious talk of his day to be able to speak of revelation in a Christian context with clarity and circumspection.

---

[2] Except for a short piece on the distinction between a genius and an apostle, Kierkegaard did not publish his extensive reflections on Adler and revelation. He did, however, write three prefaces to his "Book on Adler" and those, along with the "Book," have been translated by Walter Lowrie under the title *On Authority and Revelation*. The bulk of my remarks have to do with this book, and further page references to it will be included in parentheses in the text.

II. Notice how Kierkegaard characterizes his perspective and purpose in writing about Adler. He suggests that the careful reader will perceive the respects in which Adler is "used to throw light upon the age and to defend dogmatic concepts" (p. xv). And a theologically inclined reader should be able to obtain "a clarity about certain dogmatic concepts and an ability to use them which otherwise is not easily to be had" (p. xv). Kierkegaard summarily asserts that "the whole book is essentially an ethical investigation of the concept of revelation; about what it means to be called by a revelation; about how he who has had a revelation suffers in our confused age. Or, what comes to the same thing, the whole book is an investigation of the concept of authority, about the confusion involved in the fact that the concept of authority has been entirely forgotten in our confused age" (p. xvi).

"An ethical investigation"? "Defend dogmatic concepts"? What is involved in Kierkegaard's speaking thus? I think he is initially reminding us that human speaking can also be ethically appraised. Lying is an obvious example of a morally reprehensible act of speech. But surely Kierkegaard does not intend to attribute lying, in any straightforward sense, to Adler. Perhaps Kierkegaard is pointing to some features of how we make sense in speaking, how we share a language, and how we are responsible in a variety of ways for what we say. While our speech may not be everywhere bound by rules, it is the case that rules are embedded in our speech. We cannot arbitrarily mean anything we want in what we say. To take a cue from Wittgenstein, say "the table is mahogany" and try to mean "the paper was destroyed."[3] But of course this example does not suggest any ethical considerations, and it should be obvious that not all rules of speech are moral rules or involve moral considerations. Correctness of speech is not always an instance of moral correctness.

But if we briefly consider a concept that has fascinated contemporary philosophy—namely, the concept of promise—we might better understand what Kierkegaard means by an "ethical investigation." When a person says "I promise," then in most cases, or as a rule, we do consider him bound, morally bound, by his promise. The utterance of these words, as a rule, brings the speaker under an obligation. Of course, people do also

---

[3] See Ludwig Wittgenstein, *Philosophical Investigations*, trans. G. E. M. Anscombe (Oxford: Blackwell, 1958), 139ff.

speak loosely and insincerely and will sometimes use these words even when they have no intention of trying to fulfill the promise. But in such cases we nevertheless hold them responsible for what they say; responsible for the deception involved in saying "I promise" without any intention of actually promising and being bound by the promise. Now in making comments of this sort about the use of "promise" I think we are noting ethical considerations embedded in the concept of promise; this would be an aspect of what Kierkegaard might call an ethical investigation of the concept of promise.

But now suppose that over a period of time many people came to use "I promise" as though they *meant* "I will if it is convenient." They no longer felt morally bound to keep promises beyond what convenience might allow. Would we not have in this case something like "having forgotten" what it is to promise, or having forgotten the concept of promise? While people still *said* "I promise" on innumerable occasions, they had forgotten how to promise without regard to convenience. Confronted with a situation such as this, I think we can appreciate the difficulty of undertaking to recover the concept of promise, of trying to reeducate people with regard to the practice of promising without regard to convenience. Likewise we should be able to appreciate Kierkegaard's concern for the forgetfulness and confusion that become evident when folk speak of themselves as Christians and use the terms of Christian discourse, yet now in diminished senses and without awareness of the incongruity between their speaking and living and the Christian faith.

But Kierkegaard's situation was even more complex than this. Not only was there a forgetfulness present in the careless and loose use of Christian terms, but there were also philosophers and theologians about who were offering new interpretations of Christian terms. The analogy to this would be philosophers coming on the scene to declare that the real and abiding essence of the concept of promise is the intention to do if convenient.

In the face of these complex confusions, I think we can understand the sort of considerations an ethical investigation of Christian concepts would involve. On the one hand, the recovery of the distinctive Christian concepts would involve showing their bearing on, their application to, how a person lives and showing the contrast with other ways of living. Ethical considerations would become evident in showing, for example, that a person had no right to speak of himself as a Christian, to continue the volatilized use of Christian terms, so long as he lived without regard to the concerns, dispositions, feelings, obligations, and convictions that are essential to Christian faith. Here Kierkegaard is trying to encourage honesty in folk about how they actually stand in relation to the task of becoming a Christian, and honesty of that sort will show itself in what a person says and how he says it.

On the other hand, in the face of the deliberate *reinterpretations* of Christian terms, Kierkegaard's ethical investigation seems aimed at sharpening the contrast in definition between the proposed reinterpretations and what he regards as the proper and distinctively Christian concepts. Here Kierkegaard is defending dogmatic concepts in the sense that he is attempting to preserve their distinctive meanings and applications. But even further, these two aspects of his investigation will often merge and coalesce around particular questions. For example, Kierkegaard wants to ask how one who has received a revelation ought to act; how does he comport himself in relation to others? Also, what is involved in acknowledging that another person has received a revelation from God? There is a deep confusion, a profound ethical issue, involved in speaking of another as a recipient of revelation and yet living, acting, in a way that seems unmindful of such an acknowledgment.

III. Of course, some difficult questions do arise at this point. It seems that a presupposition of Kierkegaard's exercise is that he does know which concepts are the correct dogmatic concepts so essential to authentic Christian discourse. Kierkegaard can identify confusions and mistakes only by reference to some sort of standard. And just here we might ask: How does one determine what the standard is? How can Kierkegaard justify his standard for discriminating between the correct and the confused or mistaken? Could not the so-called volatilization, at least that of some of the deliberate reinterpreters that Kierkegaard scourges, simply be a function of genuine and deep-going disagreements about the content of Christian faith? After all, the history of the church is full of serious doctrinal disagreements. Perhaps the polemical charge of "confusion" is unwarranted to the extent that it suggests thoughtlessness or ineptitude or intention to deceive, when in fact we may have a fundamental disagreement concerning the content of Christian faith. And with these considerations we are brought to the center of the issues concerning the status of doctrines and the nature of doctrinal disputes within the Christian tradition.

The question of the resolution of doctrinal disagreements is indeed complex and difficult, and I suspect doctrinal arguments have an inevitable circular character. But even so, it does seem that doctrinal proposals and arguments are attempts to identify, order, and elucidate the focal concepts and judgments of Christian discourse. And such proposals and arguments have a decidedly *ad hominem* character; they are attempts to confront those who intend to speak as Christians, to witness to Christian faith, with a variety of normative questions concerning the content and bearing of Christian faith. These normative questions direct our attention to the boundaries of Christian discourse, and it should be obvious for anyone acquainted with the history of the discourse of Christians that such boundary and normative disputes are not rare.

If we are to understand what Kierkegaard is doing in his critique of Adler, we must reckon with his assumption that his readers (and Adler) are familiar in some sense with the dogmatic tradition of the Lutheran church and with the Bible. His strategy is to use that tradition of teaching and the Bible as the sources for the dogmatic concepts he is defending. His comments will have force for particular persons to the extent that they acknowledge some allegiance to that dogmatic tradition and to the Bible. The analogy here with respect to our earlier example of promising would be that the folk have some memory of the practice of promising without regard to convenience; or if memory is insufficient, then they can imagine such a possibility. Obviously for someone who has no interest in becoming a Christian or using Christian discourse, Kierkegaard's comments will have no force beyond what curiosity might occasion.

In the light of these comments, it is well to consider a point made by Stanley Cavell in a remarkably supple essay on Kierkegaard's book on Adler.[4] Cavell argues that Kierkegaard's critique of Adler and the age is the type of work that Wittgenstein called "grammatical." And in a rough sense I can agree: Kierkegaard, like Wittgenstein, is attempting to dispel a confusion concerning the meaning and use of particular words and utterances by elucidating how they do make sense in an agreed context.

---

[4] Stanley Cavell, "Kierkegaard's *On Authority and Revelation*" in *Must We Mean What We Say?* (New York: Charles Scribner's Sons, 1969), 163–79.

For example, Wittgenstein attempts to meet some philosophical puzzles concerning the status of color-words like "red" by noting features of how we do, in ordinary non-technical talk, use color-words. Wittgenstein works by elucidating the grammar of our ordinary color-talk. His comments achieve, so to speak, a leverage on our understanding to the extent that they remind us of how we do, in fact, make sense with color-words. In our ordinary discourse there are deep agreements in what we say and how we talk, which are obscured by misleading *a priori* theories that declare how we *must* speak in order to make sense.

It is very tempting to say that Kierkegaard is, in an analogous way, making grammatical comments on the Christian concept of revelation. "In the face of the volatilized use of Christian terms and the confusion which has been created, Kierkegaard has attempted to recover the proper Christian concept of revelation and thus to sort out the legitimate from the illegitimate," we might say. But this does suggest that there is in Christian discourse something analogous to ordinary language: a field of talk and practice in which there are deep agreements in what we say and how we talk. Yet the question is whether there is such an analogous field of agreement in Christian discourse, and that is a difficult question to answer. It is difficult just because there is also significant disagreement and division evident in the discourse of those who claim to be Christians. This suggests that we might well have something like competing grammars among the different communities of Christians, even though there might be important overlappings and resemblances among what they say. But considerations of this sort do further suggest that a claim to have presented *the* definitive grammar of the Christian concept of revelation is not just a neutral, descriptive claim; it involves a normative doctrinal judgment as to what is indeed the correct Christian concept of revelation.

This much, however, is clear about what Kierkegaard is doing in his work on Adler. He is assuming that any Christian discourse worthy of that designation does involve some talk of revelation, some reference to the authority of the Bible, some recognition that Christian faith is not simply identical with paganism. In defending dogmatic concepts Kierkegaard is offering us a set of considerations that he thinks are unavoidable for anyone who thinks seriously about the distinctive character of Christian faith. By stating a few points clearly and crisply, he intends to obviate what he regards as some confusions concerning Christian faith.

And I think we must admit that his comments will have force—an *ad hominem* force—to the extent that he does elucidate concepts that appear in the speech of many Christians in their ordinary practice of the faith.

IV. In stating the purpose of his investigation of Adler, Kierkegaard indicates the central questions of what it means to be called by a revelation and how he who has had a revelation is related to the race, the universal, and how we others relate to him. He then asserts that these questions "come to the same thing" as "an investigation of the concept of authority"(p. xvi). For Kierkegaard, then, speaking of revelation is intimately connected with such acts as claiming and acknowledging authority. It is well to note that, even though Kierkegaard does question Adler's claim to have had a revelation, he does not ask whether it makes sense to speak of "being called by a revelation." Kierkegaard takes for granted that such talk is appropriate and intelligible within the Christian context. His task is to elucidate what is meant in the use of that locution; his task is to explore the *sense* such an expression does make.

Kierkegaard seems to be working with a basic picture of what divine revelation involves. I think it is obvious that the picture is suggested by innumerable biblical passages. This is the picture of God intentionally revealing something to a particular person (or persons); God is in some way communicating with the person. The individual to whom God has revealed something is placed in a privileged position; it is clearly not a position enjoyed by all persons. It is a special, extraordinary position. And by virtue of this special and privileged position, the recipient of a revelation is also placed in a position of authority with respect to other persons. The authority that the recipient has is conferred upon him by God's revelation; to that extent the authority of the recipient is founded in God's authority. God puts a person in a privileged and authoritative position by revealing something to him.

According to Kierkegaard, a recipient of God's revelation is thus placed in a "teleological" movement toward other persons (p. 105ff). He is called by a revelation not for his own benefit but for the benefit of others. The revelation that he has received is to be conveyed to others. "He is on a mission and has to proclaim the doctrine (which he has received) and exercise authority" (p. 118). In relation to others the recipient claims to speak in the name of God, to speak with divine authority. "He who is called by a revelation is called precisely to appeal to his revelation [and] he must precisely exert authority in the strength of the fact that he was called by a revelation" (p. 24).

That there might be something called "general revelation" Kierkegaard does not seem to have considered; in any case, it is obvious that he would draw a sharp distinction between such revelation and the special revelation in which God reveals something to a particular person. Such a distinction would be unavoidable because of Kierkegaard's emphasis on the authority of a recipient of revelation; there would be no positions of authority if revelation were a general or universal phenomenon.

Further, Kierkegaard does not use "revelation" in such a way that it also refers to the rise of faith in an individual. There are such experiences as "religious awakening" (pp. 163ff), but these are not strictly revelations of God. It appears that one symptom of Adler's confusion was that he wanted to use "revelation" to cover a variety of profoundly moving experiences or religious awakenings.

It is also worth noting that Kierkegaard shows no hesitation about thinking of revelation as a definite event in which some definite content is conveyed to the recipient. Being entrusted with a definite message or a definite doctrine is just the sort of consequence that revelation involves. Further, while Kierkegaard does not explicitly speak of the recipient as possessing knowledge by virtue of the revelation, he does repeatedly speak of the recipient's certainty both with regard to his having received a revelation and to the message that has been conveyed. In fact, Kierkegaard seems to regard uncertainty on these points as an indication that one has not received a revelation from God.

Christian faith is itself, according to Kierkegaard, "built on a revelation" and "limited by the definite revelation it has received" (p. 92). That revelation is, of course, the revelation of God in Jesus Christ; Jesus Christ is the God-man who speaks with divine authority (pp. 114–15). But in connection with the revelation in Jesus Christ, Kierkegaard also emphasizes the concept of apostle. While he does not put it exactly this way, we could say that for Kierkegaard the apostles of Jesus Christ are those who were specially called by the revelation in him to witness to him and to speak of him with divine authority.

In the Christian context, to acknowledge someone as an apostle is also to acknowledge that person as one who speaks with divine authority.

Kierkegaard is well aware of the obvious fact that terms like 'authority,' 'revelation,' and 'faith' can be used in ways quite different from the Christian use. For example, 'authority' is not limited in meaning and use to the Christian context; so too with 'revelation.' There is no conceptual mistake as such in speaking of a politician's revelation that he will not seek reelection, of a statue being revealed by being uncovered, of a novel as a revealing presentation of the corrupting power of envy. But one needs to beware lest the Christian concept of revelation be simply assimilated to such uses. In order to draw our attention to the peculiar meanings of Christian concepts, Kierkegaard speaks of their "qualitative" distinctiveness (p. 105). This is connected with his development of other concepts: "the new point of departure," "the eternal, essential qualitative difference between God and man," "paradox," and the distinction between "immanence" and "transcendence" (p. 105).

Christian concepts achieve their qualitative distinctiveness by virtue of their application to the paradoxical new point of departure that is the coming of God in Jesus Christ. In spite of the "eternal, essential qualitative difference between God and man"—a difference which stands as a limitation on all human speech about God—God has revealed himself in Jesus Christ. Such a revelation is a paradoxical *new point of departure* for human understanding of self and God; it is *paradoxical* in that there is no higher explanation of how such a revelation is possible. This new point of departure is not to be explained as the inevitable or necessary fruition of the historically previous or natural; it does not fit into the historical unfolding of human events in a calculable or predictable way. In relation to a human understanding that is tied to the previous, the predictable, or the necessary, the new point of departure will effect a collision. That new point of departure disturbs the understanding and resists attempts to assimilate and digest it in terms of what we already know, believe, and expect. The new point of departure, so to speak, posits itself as a heterogeneous authority; it is the revelation of divine authority. The new point of departure represents a transcendent authority, an authority not reducible to the variety of authorities that properly play a role in the "immanent" understanding of self and world.

V. Now Kierkegaard thinks the concept of an apostle, properly explicated, will show forth the special point of these distinctions.[5] Consider the various ways we have of speaking about Paul, especially how we might appraise Paul or commend him. We can appraise him as an agent in the history of the West, and such appraisals are often carried out by historians. Or we might appraise him in terms of intellectual brilliance, or practical and tactical shrewdness, or rhetorical style, or poetic sensitivity. Appraisals of these sorts, however, are within the range of appraisals we might apply to anyone, and there are criteria available to guide our judgments. But is the judgment that Paul is an apostle to be assimilated to the logic of judgments about historical agents, intellectual achievements, practical shrewdness, rhetorical style, or poetic sensitivity?

Perhaps such judgments do not properly convey the special and exceptional character of Paul so far as he is an apostle. But we do have a way of appraising people so as to set them apart from the common run of humanity. We will often call a person a "genius" when we wish to ascribe to him some distinctive talent or achievement. A genius is one who ranks highest in the grade of appraisals within some type; being a genius is a matter of having a superiority of some sort. With reference to intellectual capacities, a genius is one who has such capacities at the highest level. However, even though we use the term "genius" to register such an exceptional appraisal, we must admit that the judgment pertains to superiority within some type. That is, the judgment involves a quantitative appraisal. Hence, it also makes sense to speak of approximations to the superiority that the genius represents: "he was almost a genius."

Return now to Paul. What sort of appraisal is involved in acknowledging Paul as an apostle? Is this an acknowledgement that involves judging Paul in terms of historical agency, or in terms of being a genius of some sort? Would it be appropriate to say such things as: "With rare insight Paul discovered the fundamental difference between grace and law, faith and works," as though this were evidence for his being an apostle? According

---

[5] The following remarks are based largely on Kierkegaard's discussion of the distinction between a genius and an apostle on 103–18. This discussion was later published by Kierkegaard in 1849 along with another essay in *Two Minor Ethico-Religious Treatises*, which has been translated by Alexander Dru in S. Kierkegaard, *The Present Age* (London: Oxford University Press, 1940), 139–63. (This essay is newly translated and included in *Kierkegaard's Writings*, vol. 24, *The Book on Adler*, 173–88.)

to Kierkegaard, it is sheer confusion to assimilate Paul's status as an apostle to his status within the ranks of the historically important, the brilliant, the shrewd, the poetic, etc. The concept of apostle is qualitatively different from these other appraisals, and such matters as those appraisals indicate count neither for nor against Paul's being an apostle. The concept of apostle pertains to an individual's being called by God in a revelation, and herein "the divine authority is the qualitatively decisive factor" (p. 107).

For Kierkegaard, then, it is a mistake to defend or explain Paul's authority as an apostle in terms of these other appraisal concepts, for such appraisals have regard to Paul only in the field of immanent authorities, relative authorities, transitory authorities. Such appraisals, in spite of whatever truth they might indeed express, do not even approximate the acknowledgment that Paul is an apostle called by God and invested with God's authority.

Consider the logic of this. To acknowledge Paul as an apostle is to acknowledge him as one called by God's revelation. To be called by revelation means being placed in a privileged and authoritative position in relation to what we might call the "universally" human. The authority of the revelation—the authority that the revelation confers—is a heterogeneous factor in relation to the general situation of human beings. "Being called by a revelation" is a characteristic or a quality that is posited from outside the human situation: it is posited by God (p. 110). Hence this quality is not to be understood as a general possibility that might be realized in the natural development of a human being; it is not a quality that might be explained as a possible human achievement. It is a paradoxical quality, and that means that it does not fit into the scheme of possibilities that characterize what Kierkegaard calls the "sphere" of immanence (pp. 105, 112).

According to Kierkegaard, the concept of authority that is appropriate to the sphere of immanence is one that pertains to relative or transient conditions. By the sphere of immanence, Kierkegaard has in mind the "relationship between man and man qua man" including "political, social, civic, household, or disciplinary relationships" (p. 111). There are, of course, many authority relationships in human affairs. And while Kierkegaard wants to warn us against construing divine authority in terms of how we establish and recognize the legitimacy of authority in various human situations, he does intend for us to note well how the relationship of authority functions even there.

For example, we are to note that one who exercises authority should not confusingly defend his authority: a judge who wanted to defend his authority as a judge by citing his legal achievements as a lawyer would only appear foolish. He would be confusing his status as a juridical authority for the state with his status as a competent legal attorney. Also, the acknowledgment of the judge's authority by others, for example, in his courtroom, ought to be quite independent of their regard for his legal achievements or his personal features. Acknowledgment of his authority means obedience and submission, and within the courtroom contempt for his personality is not a legally legitimate excuse for disobedience. I take it that Kierkegaard wants to remind us that even in the sphere of immanence the acknowledgment of authority does in some instances involve obedience and submission to the exercise of that authority.

In speaking of authority relationships as transitory and conditional, I think Kierkegaard is drawing our attention to how authority is legitimized in human relationships. And herein the legitimacy seems to be a function of a complex set of arrangements in human society. These may change, and it would be foolish to suppose that they were unconditional in character. But divine authority seems to be just that authority that is unconditional and is not a function of human arrangements of legitimization. The concept of divine authority is confused if one supposes that it is an authority that can be legitimized by recognizing its role as one of the conditional authority relationships. If it is a mistake to think of the judge's authority as a function of his legal brilliance, it is, for Kierkegaard, an even worse mistake to think of an apostle's authority as a function of his genius. While the concept of divine authority does trade on the notions of obedience and submission, it is not a type of authority that can be legitimized by reference to the criteria of the sphere of immanence.

The authority of an apostle, therefore, is the special and paradoxical authority of one who has received a revelation of God. The apostle does not suppose that he can prove that he has had a revelation; he does not advance arguments with the intention of securing himself as an authority. That is, he does not seek to establish his authority by appealing to non-divine authorities. He can only repeat his claim to being called by a revelation.

According to Kierkegaard, it was one of Adler's mistakes that he wanted both to claim the authority of one who has received a revelation from God and to look for confirmation of his authority and his doctrine by appealing to authorities of the sphere of immanence. Under the initial impact of his experience Adler set out to break with immanence: he burned his Hegelian books and denounced his Hegelian ways. But under the questioning and skeptical eyes of church and world he began to look for legitimization in terms of what folk otherwise know and believe, in relation to immanent authorities. It is as though Adler wanted to make a case for himself; he looked for an inference license, an ergo, which would secure the conclusion: Adler had a revelation and speaks with divine authority. But for Kierkegaard such a conclusion could only be obtained at the expense of confusing the Christian concept of revelation.

VI. It is worth pausing now to see if we have adequately grasped Kierkegaard's points. The distinction between immanent and divine authority is crucial for him, and yet the distinction does raise some questions. Perhaps the following considerations will enable us to become clearer about what Kierkegaard calls "immanent authority." Let us say that A is a purported authority. Concerning A's purported authority we can always ask at least two questions: (i) with respect to what is A an authority? and (ii) by virtue of what is A an authority? In asking these questions we are inquiring about the conditions under which the authority exists.

Suppose that we are confronted with a claim by some A to authorize p, wherein p is either a belief or a course of action. It is with respect to p, or the sort of thing p is, that A claims to be an authority. When we ask, "By virtue of what is A an authority?" we are asking about the conditions that legitimize (or back and warrant) A's authority. For example, if A is a judge in a courtroom, he is an authority on the question of overruling or sustaining 'objections.' And the authority of the judge derives from his status as an official of the state.

Of course, questions and disagreements may easily arise concerning someone's claim to exercise authority. We may disagree as to whether the claim of A is the sort that can be a function of legitimizing conditions. And we might disagree as to whether A actually meets the conditions for being the sort of authority he claims to be. I think it is the case, however, that authority claims of various sorts are advanced and acknowledged—explicitly and implicitly—in an enormous range of human relationships. And in many cases there are relatively unproblematic ways of getting clear about both the grounds and the limits of the authority. In that respect we can say that all of these authorities have their relative conditions, and it seems to me that these authorities are what Kierkegaard calls "immanent authorities."

But Kierkegaard is emphatic in urging us to think of *divine authority* as quite different from all immanent authority. But in what respects different? I have already suggested that a start in the right direction is to say that, whereas all immanent authorities are conditioned, God's authority is unconditioned. God does not have his authority by virtue of anything else but himself. We might even say that it is a logical absurdity to question God's authority, just as it would be logically self-contradictory to assert that God lies. So it would seem that because God is God, he is the supreme authority and whatever he says is worthy of belief.

However, without disagreeing with these points, I think we can see that the dispute in discussions of authority and revelation in Christian discourse is not whether God has supreme authority but whether some particular claim to have the sanction of God's authority does in fact have that sanction. That is, for every claim to represent what God has authorized we still have the question of whether God did in fact authorize it. There is nothing logically absurd in asserting, for example, that God said "Jesus is my Son." The hard question here is not whether God is an authority to be acknowledged and believed. Rather, the hard question is whether God did in fact say what he is asserted to have said, and that leads to the further question of what criterion could be used to determine when some claim is indeed a proper claim of divine authority.

It should be obvious, then, that there is a difference between asserting that God said *p* and justifying that assertion. And without very careful qualification it does not seem appropriate to regard a challenge to the assertion that God said *p* as a challenge to God's authority. Put another way, there is a world of difference between the following utterances: (a) What reason is there for believing that God said *p*? (b) What reason is there for believing *p* even if God said it? Clearly (b), if it does make sense, might be considered a challenge to God's authority, for it suggests that God's saying *p* is not sufficient to authorize believing *p*. But (a) is not as such a challenge to God's authority. At most it could be regarded as a challenge to someone who claimed to speak for God. Hence, the question that disturbs Christian discourse is not whether God is the supreme authority but how to identify those claims that genuinely do have God's authorization.

The following dilemma thus gets posed even if we do think of God as unconditioned authority in distinction from all conditioned, relative authority. While God's authority may not be conditioned, it does seem that we cannot claim his authority without providing some criterion for justifying such a claim. But any criterion that we might provide would either be one that is reducible to some relative authority or it would appear to be itself a question-begging appeal to God's authority. Put another way, we need a usable criterion for identifying what does have God's authority, and we seem confronted with either deriving the criterion from relative authorities or justifying the criterion by appeal to God's authority. The latter alternative looks as though it is saying, 'This is what God has authorized, and we know it because He authorized it.'

In the light of these considerations it would seem that Kierkegaard's basic point is that the Christian concept of revelation is indeed question-begging in a crucial respect. There is no criterion contained in the abstract concept of divine authority that justifies of itself the designation of any particular claim as having the sanction of divine authority. But in the context of Christian faith the decisive point is that some particular persons are acknowledged as being bearers of divine authority. Hence, for Kierkegaard, Jesus and the apostles are the defining instances of divine revelation and divine authority. There is a necessary circularity here, and this circularity is the *logical knot* that the concept of revelation posits and conveys.

Kierkegaard is aware that his account of the Christian concept of revelation flies in the face of a conviction that is not only widespread among his contemporaries but is sometimes expressed in the Christian tradition. I have in mind the conviction that Christianity must somehow be defended as plausible, wherein 'plausible' is tied to noncircular argument. As some might put it, circular argument is no argument at all, or is question-begging. Being plausible about the Christian claims of divine authority would seem to require a noncircular way of defending that claim. In the face of just this sort of talk Kierkegaard says "Christianity is implausible" (p. 60). Cavell suggests that this remark is grammatical in character, and that would mean that Kierkegaard is pointing out a fundamental rule concerning the discourse of Christian faith; it is a rule that forbids all attempts to explain and justify the faith in terms other than the authority of the new point of departure which is Jesus Christ and the calling of the apostles.

It should be clear that Kierkegaard's "defense of dogmatic concepts" is not an attempt to defend Christian concepts against the skepticism of critics. His defense is not an argument for the truth of the judgments that dogmatic concepts can be used to make. Defending such concepts is not an attempt to make them plausible before the court of immanent human understanding. Rather, defense involves clarifying the concepts over against their illegitimate cousins, against the counterfeit substitutes, against the vain and trivializing uses that deflect and obscure the true character and point of Christian faith. We might say that the defense does in a sense represent the kind of understanding that thinks, lives, and speaks in the light of the new point of departure and within the limits of that point. In this connection dogmatic concepts do not render a higher understanding; instead, they are developed as the sentinels whose sole task is to demarcate the distinctive contents of Christian faith.

VII. The repeated use of "understanding" and "limits of understanding" may be creating some genuine problems for us that require some careful analysis. I can imagine the following comments: "Hasn't Kierkegaard tried to delineate the Christian concept of revelation, to make it clear and understandable in order that it might be distinguished from what you have referred to as counterfeit concepts? Hasn't Kierkegaard provided, therefore, an understanding; and if so, doesn't that mean he has brought the concept within the limits of understanding? Whatever else Kierkegaard might mean by this odd notion of the limits of understanding, surely you must admit that to the degree that Kierkegaard has been successful in his discussion, just so far also has he brought the concept of revelation within the "limits of understanding."

There is something in these comments, and among the difficulties in replying adequately is that which pertains to the varied meanings of the term 'understanding.' It is admittedly like Euthyphro's "piety," it gets up and walks around on us. And interestingly enough, even when we are not discussing "understanding," it—if I can here use 'it'—is what we are typically looking for and disputing about in philosophical discussions. Also, at various points in the history of philosophy, we have attempts to draw sharp boundaries around understanding in order to distinguish between the intelligible and the unintelligible. Not the least of those efforts was that of the Logical Positivists.

I do not want here to delve further into a criticism of those efforts, except to say that one of the more fruitful suggestions of Wittgenstein has been to warn us away from attempts to draw neat, across-the-board distinctions between the intelligible and the unintelligible. Instead we are to look more carefully at specific examples of how we do understand and what counts for understanding in this or that context. I do think Kierkegaard would have been appreciative of these cautionary remarks. On occasion, however, we can for a particular purpose cast our nets in a rather sweeping fashion, recognizing that not all of the fish we will catch can simply be put in one category.

There are, I think, at least two senses of the word 'understanding' involved in Kierkegaard's casting the net labeled "the limit of understanding" and that are meant in such expressions as "collides with the understanding." The first has to do with understanding so far as that covers the variety of human epistemic activities and theories. This is the understanding that some philosophers have been most interested in and inclined to regard as *the* understanding. In a book called *Human Understanding*, Stephen Toulmin identifies his inquiry in this way: "The general problem of human understanding is . . . to draw an epistemic self-portrait which is both well-founded and trustworthy."[6] "The final philosophical goal . . . is . . . to give an adequate account of the intellectual authority of our concepts, in terms of which we can understand the criteria by which they are to be appraised."[7] Toulmin goes on to say that such an account "must be relevant to the actual practice of rational criticism" and "must be given in terms which are operative in the light of our present knowledge."[8]

If I have properly grasped Kierkegaard's discussion of revelation, then it would have to be said that this concept of revelation does not fall within

---

[6] Stephen Toulmin, *Human Understanding* (Oxford: Clarendon Press, 1972), 3.
[7] Ibid., 11.
[8] Ibid.

the province of the well-founded intellectual authority of human understanding. To defend the Christian talk of revelation in terms of what we independently know and understand is to abolish the concept of divine authority. We should be rightly surprised to find Toulmin discussing the province of divine authority, unless he was surreptitiously reinterpreting that to mean some well-founded field of human authority. But further, it is not as though a Toulmin-like discussion could come up with a list of concepts that naturally fall beyond the limits of human understanding and that divine revelation and authority are on the list. Rather, Kierkegaard's point is that at the heart of Christian discourse is the paradoxical revelation in Jesus Christ, and to understand it as paradoxical is to understand that it does not seek certification at the hands of our understanding. There is, of course, a difference between (a) understanding that the concept of revelation involves the paradoxical identification of divine authority and particular persons and utterances and (b) striving to achieve an understanding that, without begging the question, could justify that identification. The latter, clearly, could be achieved only by eliminating the paradox.

The second sense of understanding that involves a collision with the claim of Christian revelation pertains to what we might call the informal, conventional, or ordinary understanding that human beings have concerning themselves and what is valuable in the world. We need not think of this in a theoretical way, though it may receive a theoretical form and argument in the hands of intellectuals. This is the understanding that manifests itself in actual life, in how persons live, in how they feel and are disposed toward other people and the world. Kierkegaard argues that Christian faith is bound to collide with this understanding. The claim to divine authority, to unconditional obedience, and the emphasis on a justification of life through grace and faith are bound to collide with the typical ways in which persons live and prefer to live.

Given this Kierkegaardian way of construing the dogmatic concept of revelation, does it follow that Christian faith is immune from philosophical criticism? Well, what does "immune" mean here? That such criticism is impossible? That would be a strange conclusion indeed. It certainly does seem possible that there will be severe criticism of Christian discourse, and the wisest course would be to look at such criticism piece by piece as it is presented. But it should be no surprise to the Christian that his discourse might be charged with being in some crucial respects question-begging or unverifiable. That is the sort of point Kierkegaard is trying to underscore in speaking of revelation and a new point of departure. To the extent that these concepts are both proper for Christian faith and understandable, they do make it evident that the Christian recognizes that a collision with the immanent criteria of understanding is unavoidable. The collision is not something that needs to be covered up or attenuated. This, of course, does not mean that any sort of philosophical criticism would have to be tolerated; much of it may be a function of misunderstanding and to that extent can be cleared up.

VIII. There is, however, something profoundly misleading about the discussion thus far. The tendency has been to characterize the concept of revelation in terms of logical considerations. That is, the emphasis has been on contrasting definitions, inspecting implications and inconsistencies; it is a picture of a logical structure of concepts and propositions. But when I suggest that this picture may be misleading I do not mean that I want now to correct the picture by modifying yet another feature of the logical relationships. Rather, I want to suggest that it is misleading because it is too abstract; it makes it look as though we were simply sorting out intellectual confusions. It has been as though there was an unstated qualifier in the background that can now be put like this: 'If you want to speak in terms of the Christian concepts, then there should be some gain in becoming more familiar with the logic of that discourse.' But perhaps the logic of the discourse has not yet conveyed a way beyond the 'if' of 'if you want to . . .' That is, the essay has not come to grips with the task of placing the discourse in a more concrete relation to human interests and dispositions.

Perhaps I can show why the discussion might be misleading by considering this. What has been presented can quite easily be construed as the exploration of a baffling puzzle, a knotty problem. It may look as though it all comes down to this: 'Do you or do you not believe the Christian revelation?' or, 'Do you or do you not intend to become obedient to God?' There we are, face to face with the central claim of Christian faith. Take your choice: this conceptual scheme or some other. But surely this is misleading, for it makes it look as though we have only our doubts and questions on the one hand and an authoritarian system of belief on the other.

It is one of the enduring merits of Kierkegaard that he was also acutely aware of just how this sort of situation can become profoundly misleading. How Kierkegaard also sorted out the possible misconceptions in this we do not have the space to pursue beyond some brief remarks. Kierkegaard's literature was designed to force our attention on the interests, concerns, and feelings of human subjects, of ourselves. How do these interests, concerns, and feelings hang together in actual life, in the concrete way a person lives? The Christian talk of revelation is not basically addressed to what we might call the interests of knowledge and curiosity. Rather, Christian concepts have their bearing in changing and forming the lives of folk; they have their bearing in relation to an acute awareness of one's own personal life, to how one is disposed to act, judge, and feel. Kierkegaard referred to these features of human life as *existential* matters.

Now consider how Kierkegaard construed the situation in the book by Johannes Climacus, *Concluding Unscientific Postscript*. The question being considered was how it is possible for a person to base his or her eternal happiness on an historical point of departure. While the question might receive an abstract or algebraic discussion as in *Philosophical Fragments*, the task in the *Postscript* is to concentrate on the individual who might genuinely ask such a question. 'Genuinely ask such a question?' Yes. It is possible not to ask it genuinely. But to understand how such a question could be a genuine question for an individual subject, we need to become clear about what sort of an *interest* this eternal happiness represents. How must the individual subject be qualified in order for this question about eternal happiness to become a serious question? The assumption, of course, is that not all of us will have sufficient seriousness of interest to grasp the point and weight of the question. Not that we need more intellectual training. Rather, Kierkegaard is saying that there must be a requisite development in the individual before this question can be seriously asked. So, too, with the concept of revelation in Christian discourse: the vitality of its use is quite obscured apart from the appropriate interests and passions.[9]

---

[9] See the new translations of these great works of Kierkegaard: *Kierkegaard's Writings*, vol. VII: *Philosophical Fragments; Johannes Climacus*; vol. XI, 1 and 2: *Concluding Unscientific Postscript to Philosophical Fragments*; edited and translated by Howard V. Hong and Edna H. Hong (Princeton: Princeton University Press, 1985, 1992).

The other side to this is that for Kierkegaard faith involves being *schooled* in the distinctive Christian concepts, for these concepts themselves should give shape and continuity to the life of an individual. The concept of revelation does confront the individual with an authoritative demand for obedience. And one should not pretend to acknowledge the Christian revelation if one is subjectively indifferent or indecisive at the point of obedience. There really is no acknowledgment of divine revelation if there is not also the deep realization that this revelation is decisive for one's life.

These considerations must be linked with Kierkegaard's judgment that another of the ills of his age is that everything has become an object of reflection. And he thinks such a tendency creates confusion in the sphere of faith. "It is . . . in relation to the spiritual life the most injurious thing when reflection . . . goes amiss and instead of being used to advantage brings the concealed labor of the hidden life out into the open and attacks the fundamental principles themselves" (p. 30). Assuming that Kierkegaard is thinking of revelation and authority as "fundamental principles," we can see that for him reflection brings confusion in its train when it openly seeks a non-question-begging justification of those principles. Instead of using reflection to intensify and clarify the shape and course of one's spiritual labor, one is caught up in the endless dialectic of whether it really is divine revelation one is confronting. "The appearance of being in suspense always results when one does not rest upon the foundation but the foundation is made dialectical" (p. 30). For folk who are incessantly preoccupied with the attempt to resecure those foundations, Kierkegaard's words may be like salt on a wound.

IX. It should be apparent to any student of contemporary theology that the volatilization of Christian concepts remains an ominous problem today. Considering that the concept of revelation is certainly one of the most volatilized concepts, I hope these remarks on Kierkegaard provide some insight into a few of the issues posed in Christian talk of divine revelation. It is a profoundly serious matter to speak of and make claims about divine revelation. And surely Kierkegaard is challenging in his contention that human reflection encounters a logical knot in the Christian concept of divine revelation and that such reflection cannot discursively establish that God is revealed in Jesus Christ and the witness of apostles.

Admittedly, many issues remain. We are *inter alia* still confronted with questions concerning the content of revelation, including the question of what in the New Testament is to be explicitly identified as bearing divine authority. Further, considering that our own culture is even more secular than Kierkegaard's Christendom, there is the persisting question of how Christian faith can be articulated so as to lead to a decisive engagement with the actual lives of folk. Kierkegaard's work is important in this regard also, for he held together the concern for the logical integrity of dogmatic concepts and the concern for showing how those concepts relate to and shape the subjective interests and passions of persons. Kierkegaard does not seem to have succumbed either to the temptation to attenuate the dogmatic concepts for the sake of touching the lives of contemporaries or to the temptation of ignoring the concrete lives and sensibilities of folk for the sake of declaring a dogmatically *correct* gospel. Precisely because his work unfolds in the tension between these two temptations, Kierkegaard remains provocative and challenging to Christian theologizing.

6

On Understanding God and Faith

This essay is an address given at the time of my installation as Dean and Professor of Theology at Christian Theological Seminary in the fall of 1988.

I propose to share some of the influences and conversation partners I have had and continue to have. This may give, for whatever it's worth, some insight into what animates some of my instructional concerns as a seminary professor and dean. A person may be widely read, and those of us in theological education certainly should. But, for me, there are some writings I read, re-read, ponder, and re-read; and I find new challenges with each reading. These conversation partners are important. One may disagree with such partners, but the mere fact that the partner wrote it or said it is sufficient to make the matter worthy of my consideration. I will not bore you with a complete list of these partners, but I will mention a few.

Let me first identify the *Holy Scriptures* as a partner. From one point of view there are many voices in Scripture, but the many voices develop a powerful focus and intensity when I read them as one being addressed by the Word of God. These words I need to read and to hear. Some parts I will read quickly and not tarry over too long. Other parts resonate, challenge, judge, and lift up. More than this I will not say on this occasion.

Next I would mention the writings of *Søren Kierkegaard*. Here I find such a rich display of distinctions and insights, such an amazing range of different types of literature, that I return again and again. From several angles of diagnosis, Kierkegaard thought his contemporaries existed under the monstrous illusion that they were Christian and had forgotten what the distinctive concepts of the faith are and what it means to become a Christian. He designed his literature to gain the attention of his time and to move his readers against the inclinations of the age. Kierkegaard thought he was a corrective, and a sobering reminder to me is that he is a corrective even today.

Then there is the massive theological production of *Karl Barth*. When I first read Barth I felt that every basic premise and principle I held as obvious and intelligent was under sharp rebuke. The sustained emphasis on the sovereignty of God's grace as revealed in Jesus Christ, the subtle critique of tradition, and the unsurpassed freshness of scriptural exposition mark Barth as the magisterial theologian of the twentieth century. As with Kant in philosophy in the nineteenth century, one hasn't started theologizing until one has come to grips with Barth. I don't think of myself as a 'Barthian,' wedded to every move and utterance of his theology. I haven't even read all of what he wrote! But he is a partner, and I could not think about Christian faith without being interrogated and guided by his theologizing.

The philosophical writings of *Ludwig Wittgenstein* have had a liberating and chastening effect on me. His is not a philosophy of 'conclusions' that can be neatly summarized in textbooks. The way he philosophizes, the suggestions and distinctions he makes, and the fruitful, surprising examples he chooses convey a radical impression. His assembled reminders about how we use language, how we make sense, how certain pictures can exercise a bewitching grip on our thinking, and how easy it is for contrived 'intellectual' languages to go on a holiday and lose sense have proven helpful in thinking about Christian faith and its many-sided discourses. Under the tutelage of Paul Holmer and O. K. Bouwsma, I have come to see the remarkable continuities between Kierkegaard and Wittgenstein. But I should also say that I am not much impressed by some of the quick and easy adaptations of Wittgenstein to Christian theology. Wittgenstein gives you the courage to acknowledge that many intellectual issues are not so clear and that getting clear about a few elemental points is astonishingly laborious but praiseworthy.

Finally, I should mention a school of philosophers and theologians that nudge, stimulate, and provoke me. I refer to *Alfred North Whitehead* and *Charles Hartshorne* and their followers, generally called 'process theologians.' For many years I pored over the writings of Whitehead and Hartshorne and was attracted by the prospect of a metaphysical scheme that could effectively and rationally ground Christian theology. I almost went all the way. But for a variety of reasons, I drew back, concluding that Christian theology did not need that metaphysical backing and that its concept of God was not compatible with orthodox christology and trinitarian belief. Yet this alternative approach continues to be a partner with whom I converse. And I look forward to a continuation of that argument with those colleagues of mine here at Christian Theological Seminary who profess a more positive leaning toward process concepts and themes.

There are many more in tradition and contemporary life who do get my attention. Liberation theologians certainly raise questions that are far-reaching and compelling, and perhaps some will emerge to be as seminally powerful as the ones I have mentioned. But I *think* under the impetus and dialogue that my partners elicit. In the remaining moments of this address let me suggest a few considerations that grow out of these conversations.

I have long been convinced that there is no simple definition of 'theology' and that theologizing covers a complex range of activities. There is no hidden essence of theology that our intellectual deliberations must finally lay bare. When we do try to draw lines of distinction and continuity, we need to be quite clear about our purpose. I do not want to draw a tight picture of what theology is, but I do want to probe several activities that appear under that rubric and are worthy of our reflection.

Let me begin my brief investigation by way of an example drawn from a course I am currently co-teaching. This course, required of all senior ministerial students, aims toward a paper that will convey their understanding of the basic concepts of Christian faith, how this understanding might be justified, and how this understanding relates to the mission of the church and their understanding of their own ministerial calling. This is a large agenda. The students approach it with varying emphases and convictions. But notice the big words in this assignment: "understanding the basic concepts of the Christian faith," "how this understanding might be justified," and "their understanding of their own ministerial calling." What am I asking for when I ask for *understanding*? How will I, the teacher and reader, know when they have succeeded in this understanding?

At one level, when I ask them to understand basic concepts, I think I am expecting a demonstration of familiarity with a host of utterances of Scripture and the traditions of the church. With that familiarity I expect them to have the ability to identify and sort concepts and to explain them by executing several operations. I want them to explain what the concepts mean—often by using other concepts—and to make concepts into sentences and propositions, to connect these sentences together and overall to show what could be called the *logic* of the concepts. It is a sophisticated skill and requires sustained attention and learning to do it well.

Demonstrating that they understand the concepts, however, goes with the second part of showing how these concepts and propositions might be defended or justified. I mean nothing highfalutin or absolute by this 'justification.' I don't suppose there is a perfect argument or a complex set of arguments that will lay to rest all objections to Christian faith. But I do want them to *reason* with the concepts. I want them to begin asking *why* they say this rather than that and how they would *explain* what they say. I assume that if they are going to teach the faith, they need to be clear about why they believe their basic concepts are appropriate to the Christian faith and why they think the propositions are true. *What do they mean when they speak as they do and by what authority do they speak?* Here I want them to reflect on how they use Scripture, how they sift tradition, and how they relate the teachings to contemporary learning and cultures.

In conjunction with this sort of talk I often mention the need for a *theological method.* Sometimes I create in myself and in others the impression that such a method must be something strict, perfectly lucid, and easily applicable to data in order to derive certifiable results. But this must be wrong-headed in theology. In actual practice we just do not have those kinds of tight procedures. In fact, striving for this understanding of Christian faith is complex and complicated, and no one has it all perfectly in place. So maybe I should be more circumspect when I speak of method. Maybe method is just a way we have of organizing our material and showing what we mean and why we think it is true.

This quest for understanding, which I urge the students toward, is part and parcel of our human quest for knowledge, and is an unavoidable engagement for persons of learning and sophistication and an undeniable task for persons of leadership in the Church. But my depiction of what is involved in understanding would be incomplete if I did not point to a set of issues—issues of a peculiar sort—that confront persons in relation to understanding God, faith, and oneself. We could say these issues are there for anyone who is deeply serious about the life she lives. There is an understanding appropriate to faithful living that uses the concepts and sentences of the language of faith to deepen, discipline, and shape the labors of the spiritual life.

Kierkegaard's literature is unmatched in developing a range of distinctions to keep us from forgetting that there is an understanding he called *existential* and there is an *edifying* language appropriate to it. There is much talk today about 'spirituality,' 'character,' 'faith development,' and the proper purpose of theological education. In this connection I want to suggest some diagnostic points that grow out of my conversations with those partners mentioned previously and that often perplex me in my teaching.

The *first diagnostic point*: prolonged preoccupation with those concerns of understanding that I first described can conjure some misleading pictures for the second understanding, namely the understanding Kierkegaard calls *existential*. This preoccupation can suggest that we are concerned for the truth, and the truth is what is the case about reality. Christian teachings declare the truth or purport to—and must therefore meet the contemporary tests for what counts as truth-claiming and fact-stating. If we can just marshal our arguments in cogent and clear language, then we can defend the truth-claims of the Christian faith. This makes it look like the really difficult task is justifying the truth-claims—or at least reinterpreting the truth-claims in such a way that the re-interpretation is justified. Hark to those who defend the truth-claims! It almost seems that the life of faith follows naturally if one can just be *sure* the teachings are true. But diagnostically I want to suggest that there is little to support this notion that if the claims are defensible, then faith will follow as a matter of course.

This presents a host of puzzles. What are we to do? We want the truth-claims defended by the best of intelligence. But even if—and this is a big 'if'—we have the claims defended, then what is implied about faith, the faith of a person? Yet surely faith, as the labor of spirituality, is not just a formless mass of subjectivity and emotion. Following Kierkegaard, faith has to do with *how* a person lives, with the shape of the passions and the overriding intentionality of her actual living. Kierkegaard goes on to say that the distinctiveness of the *Christian "how" is shaped by a relationship to Jesus Christ.* But Kierkegaard is clear that there is no logical transition from believing any purported fact about Jesus Christ to the concrete living in which Jesus is Lord and Savior. Objective, detached understanding never makes that transition. Kierkegaard is so daring at this point that he declares that objectively there is an unavoidable and irreducible uncertainty—no compelling, non-question-begging, irrefutable arguments are available to assure us that Jesus is the Son of God.

As you may have surmised by now, I am perplexed. I spend an adult lifetime explicating and defending the teachings of the faith, trying to show a passion for the truth about God, world, humanity, contending that God is for humanity in grace—and that that is the truth! Even though I know, in spite of my appeals to revelation and to sound reasoning, that I cannot lay to rest all the questions that can be put to my defense of the faith, I still play the game of probing those teachings. And yet it appears that there is no necessary correlation between understanding my defense of the faith and a faithful life's understanding. Kierkegaard suggests that people often build intellectual castles in which they don't live in the humdrum of decisions and everydayness. But surely I have gone too far and put matters too severely. How do I work my way out of this? Do I need more understanding?

Diagnostic point two: the labor of faith cannot be cut off from the teachings of the faith. Faith needs the shaping of the teachings, and faith cannot avoid reasoning and thinking. In fact, faith is unintelligible to us apart from the teachings. Yet, in a certain respect, it never follows necessarily that if you have skill in the understanding—the identification and explication—of the teachings, then you have faith's living understanding. There is no simple recipe of how these interrelate. Maybe the explanation of the teachings must show that their proper home is not in the interest of objective, detached knowledge. One learns how to assert—to say and mean—the concepts of the teachings when one engages the teachings at the deepest levels of one's life—in how one lives. *There is truth about God and the world, but it is only fully understood in the practical labor of how one lives.*

Diagnostic point three: the intellect can be used to pursue endlessly the interpretation and justification of the teachings, but that pursuit is infinitely *dialectical*. Even Barth's appeal to revelation cannot, in the court of detached intelligence, refute Feuerbach. Only the fundamentalists and the Roman Catholic Church and some liberals believe there are incorrigible and infallible utterances that can objectively assure faith and produce God. As long as one stands transfixed by this epistemic situation of uncertainty or kicks repeatedly against it, the soul's wound is great and the spiritual life hemorrhages. But the intellect can—without a false construal of the epistemic situation—be used to strengthen the character of faith, to illuminate and discipline the infinite and daily details in how a person lives her life.

Diagnostic point four: it is possible to say, 'God loves me and the whole creation,' and yet speak emptily and fail to make sense. It is even possible to have the intellectual skill to *explain* what one *means* by this utterance by having a *theory* about God, love, and the world. So, in a way it is possible to understand and yet fail to understand in a way appropriate to the context of faith. *To understand this utterance—to be able to say and mean it—goes with a pattern of practices that show how one regards God.* The meaning of this utterance is not a private mental event independent of those practices.

Diagnostic point five: I have tried to make some distinctions and draw a modest map. We can argue about these distinctions and this map and we should. It is always possible, however, that a paradox may arise: that one 'understands' the teachings and yet 'understands' nothing important and decisive in one's life. Let no one—student, professor, minister, or lay person—forget himself and the task of living before the living God who loves us with an unremitting love. It is the truth that God loves every human being; but this truth has no currency, no cash value, in the encyclopedia of knowledge apart from the consuming passion of a concrete, laboring soul. When one is engaged in this latter way, it shows. *Not everything can be said.*

7

Schematic Reflections on Salvation in Jesus Christ

The first version of this essay was presented to the Faculty Colloquium at Christian Theological Seminary in the spring of 1989. The themes of the essay achieve further expression in GCF, 503–9, 709–48.

1. It is obvious that the term 'salvation' is subject to various and different and even conflicting uses and interpretations in the contemporary life and discourses of the church. In this brief essay I will attempt to identify a general schema or model of how soteriological themes hang together in Christian discourse. And then I will sort out two different, even competing, ways of interpreting the model. I will argue that one of these interpretations is more adequate to the distinctive themes of the Christian Gospel centered on Jesus Christ. Throughout, my aim is to be diagnostic, acute, and illuminating, if not exhaustive and complete. The issues being identified and argued require much more elaboration and dialectic than can be mustered in this limited and concentrated presentation. I hope what is presented will not be without usefulness and merit to concerned thinkers and to the church.

Before elaborating the model, it is important to note my belief that biblical language does not contain one uniformly consistent theory of

104

salvation. There are several terms, emphases, and images for salvation, including deliverance, freedom, redemption, reconciliation, justification, liberation, resurrection, and eternal life. There is no simple congruence in how these terms are used in Scripture; and when we get into the larger church traditions of interpretation, we find multiple accents and theories. There are indeed thematic continuities, but there is hardly universal agreement about the details and explanations. In this sense, then, every generation of the church has had to wrestle with how the Gospel is to be understood for its time; this is *faith seeking understanding* and is a necessary feature of the life of faith. In our time it is internally important to wrestle with the Gospel and the full meaning of salvation, given the multifarious ways of speaking of salvation in the church's contemporary life and discourse.

2. A general schematic model of salvation issues and accents can be garnered by considering the following questions and their possible answers:

1. What is the condition from which persons need saving?
2. Who is the agent who does the saving?
3. How does the saving agent accomplish the saving?
4. What is the condition to which persons are saved?
5. Who is saved?

Let us now look at the various answers to the first question: *What is the condition from which persons need saving?* There is general agreement that in some sense the condition from which persons are to be saved is *sin and the effects and consequences of sin.* But what is sin? However analyzed, sin is at least rebellion against the rule of God, who is the Creator of all things. It is understood that the persons who rebel are responsible for their rebellion. And what are the consequences of sin? Variously stated, the consequences are alienation from God, other humans, and one's proper good and fulfillment as human. These consequences of sin are destructive of human life and well-being, of which death looms as the most threatening destruction and annihilation.

Shifting the emphasis somewhat, we can ask as well about being saved from the effects upon us of the sins of others, such as Israel being saved from the evil Pharaoh who had oppressed them. This is a saving or liberating from the conditions of injustice and oppression created by the sins of others. This sort of saving from oppression and enemies is the primary focus of the so-called liberation theologies that are prominent today. Where one places the emphasis between *my sins* and *their sins* will make a big difference in how one talks about salvation. Yet it can be argued that a complete understanding of sin and its consequences will grasp both the individual embrace of sin and the systemic sin of social structures, relationships, traditions, and powers that oppress people and seek to destroy human well-being.

The second question—*Who is the agent who does the saving?*—has been persistently answered by pointing to God. *God is first and last the One who saves*, and here the accent is typically on the mercy, grace, and love of God. God's saving can be contrasted with all those other attempts by humans to save themselves by their own efforts. Only God can save and such saving is the free grace of God. Yet even though this answer is virtually unanimous in mainstream Christian traditions, how the third question is answered opens up considerable room for disagreement.

We turn now to the third question: *How does the saving agent accomplish the saving?* But this cannot be answered without specifying *what* the saving agent does that is efficacious in accomplishing the saving. It is here that the church typically centers on Jesus Christ, and, because only God can save, the church had its basic reason for saying that Jesus Christ is divine. Yet answers and their nuances offer significant variety. Notice at least the following differing accents as to what the saving agent does:

a. God, out of love, forgives the sins of those who repent.
b. God becomes incarnate in Jesus Christ to overcome the sins of the world and defeat the powers of evil.
c. God acts in Jesus Christ to reconcile the world to Godself.
d. Jesus Christ atones for the sins of the world.
e. Jesus Christ exemplified and enacted the new path to follow in order to be saved and fulfilled.
f. Jesus taught a new set of commandments, a higher righteousness, the following of which leads to salvation.
g. Jesus proclaimed and exemplified the grace of God that is always available to all humans.

h. God acts ever and always in and through the powers of righteousness
   to overcome the injustice that oppresses people.

I am not saying that it is impossible to accommodate all these in a
single complex interpretation. But notice that *a* and *h* do not require any
reference to Jesus Christ. Also, *e*, *f*, and *g* do not require that Jesus be
divine. While *h* does not require Jesus, it may at least include Jesus among
the powers of righteousness. That Jesus be divine, as well as human, is in
some sense required in *b*, *c*, and *d*.

Yet another question is implied in this third question, namely, 'Does
the saving agent save completely or partially?' That is, in the requisite
sense of saving, does God alone achieve the saving or does it require human
response and cooperation? Of course, every interpretation says that humans
should respond positively to God's gracious acts, but the nuances of
meaning come in their analyses of how the response is related to the saving.
The tradition that comes from Augustine through Luther and Calvin tends
to say that God's grace is the necessary and sufficient condition for salvation.
Other traditions indicate that God initiates the offer of grace but humans
have to accept the offer before the saving is complete. In this sense, then,
God's grace is a necessary but not sufficient condition of salvation. Hence,
it can sometimes be said that one must repent and be baptized in Jesus'
name in order to be saved. When this latter emphasis is decisive, we have
positions similar to *e* and *f*. The logic of this strand of tradition is this:
God through Jesus offers grace; humans must accept the offer in order to
be saved, whether that means following his example or his teachings or
some other specification of what is involved in an authentic accepting
and following. God goes so far, then humans must go the rest of the way.

We turn now to the fourth question: *What is the condition to which
one is saved?* Again nuances to answers vary, saying one is saved to the
condition of:

a. freedom from the effects and consequences of sin;
b. experiencing the love and forgiveness of God;
c. faith as living trust in God;
d. being justified before God;
e. being obedient to God's rule;
f. flourishing and well-being;

g. social peace, justice, and love;

h. being freed from social oppression;

i. a future historical fulfillment;

j. a future transhistorical fulfillment.

By *historical* I mean what can be described in some spatial and temporal frame, while *transhistorical* refers to that which transcends space and time. We can quickly see that the condition of being-saved can be described in various ways, from an emphasis on i) a present quality of a person's life, irrespective of social conditions, to ii) a present historical social condition, to iii) a future historical social condition, to iv) a transhistorical future condition. These need not be mutually exclusive, and different combinations are possible. For example, the saved condition of faith may be thought of as itself a necessary condition of being saved in some transhistorical future. Or, one can reject a transhistorical future and emphasize only being saved in present and/or future historical conditions.

The very mention of future in this connection shows that we are inextricably dealing with *eschatology*, the doctrine pertaining to the ultimate and final aspects of human and world destiny. Here I use *destiny* to refer to both the *process* and the *end* toward which the world and humanity are moving. Here *end* includes both *telos* (goal or fulfillment) and *finis* (what is final or conclusive). Sometimes this is thought of as a *dual destiny*, namely, the destiny of the saved and the destiny of the damned.

But this moves us to face the fifth question: *Who is saved?* This question is first a conceptual question, not a simple factual question. That is, we are asking for the identifying traits of the logical class of the saved, even though we may not be able in concrete fact to determine which persons have the traits. As we consider the question of who is saved, we see that the answers to the first four questions will already determine the answer to this question. If, for example, we say that God saves by revealing in Jesus a path of higher righteousness, then those who follow that path are the saved, whether now or in the future. If we say that God's saving act is freeing people from oppression, then those who are so freed are also the saved.

In order to see the interrelated logic of various answers to the question of who is saved, however, we need to make some further diagnostic distinctions. Under the rubric of 'salvation' we are dealing with several distinct but related issues. Hence, we need to distinguish three senses or foci of salvation. First, we will say *Salvation I* refers to what the saving agent does. So, It might be said that Jesus Christ, the God-man, atoned for the sins of the world. Or, one might say that God gave a path of higher righteousness in Jesus. On their face, these seem to be different *whats*. Second, let us call *Salvation II* the receipt and appropriation of *Salvation I* in the life of some person's or persons' historical experience. Third, *Salvation III* refers to the ultimate future or ultimate destiny, however that may be characterized. Hence, the question of who is saved may be answered differently according to which salvation one is talking about.

Before leaving this general schema on salvation, it can be pointed out that it is conceivable to have a contrast at all three foci of salvation between the saved and the unsaved (damned or rejected). What this contrast comes to in the three foci is a crucial question.

3. I next want to look at a set of concepts that frames many ways of answering the five schematic questions. Even when the set does not explicitly frame the answers, it continues to exercise strong sway over other possible answers. I call this set of concepts the *Reward/Punishment—Just Deserts* frame. It will become obvious that this frame is represented in much biblical language, and this has been used in the church to justify the frame.

The fundamental concepts are that human beings are responsible for what they do and what they do has deserved consequences. If what they do is good or right, then they deserve reward or blessing. If what they do is bad or wrong, then they deserve punishment. Aside from the general notion that doing good or right is to be obedient to the rule of God, I am not here interested in the further possible specifications of that good or right or obedient activity. The basic point is that persons are accountable agents who deserve certain consequences according to the moral or religious character of their activities.

God is understood as that agent who not only creates humans but lays down the standard for their lives and conduct. Further, God is the One who is the primary executor of the deserts of humans. God creates, commands, rewards, and punishes. In this sense God is *just* as the one who sets the standard and who metes out rewards and punishments. In other words, it is a matter of God's justice that persons are held accountable for their lives and conduct and that such accountability necessarily involves rewards and punishments. It is part of the just moral/religious order of God's world that the morally good be rewarded and the morally bad be punished. This moral/religious order gives clout to the following summary of the human situation:

All humans have sinned in being disobedient to God's rule.
All humans deserve punishment by God's justice.

Up to this point most of the traditions of the church agree with this analysis of the human situation. But how can humans be saved from this sin and consequent punishment? Within this frame, answers have varied. But typically they appeal to God's mercy and grace to provide another opportunity for humans to escape sin and their deserved destiny. However differently they may be analyzed, I am grouping all these theories together and calling them *Second Chance* theories. In the language of my previously developed schema, the Second Chance is anything that God has done (*Salvation I*) that requires an appropriate response from persons (*Salvation II*) as a precondition for a positive ultimate destiny (*Salvation III*). God graciously provides the Second Chance—that is, a second chance for sinners—but it is up to the individual to accept or reject this new chance. But here the frame is adamant and remains intact: if the individual accepts the second chance, then the individual deserves blessing and reward; if the individual rejects or ignores the second chance, then the individual deserves appropriate punishment. God's justice may be tempered by God's grace and mercy, but finally it is God's justice—as *retributive justice*—that frames and controls the destiny of humans insofar as they get what they deserve. (Note: nothing logically changes in this interpretation if there are more chances than a second one.)

We could fill in the details of some differing interpretations that employ this basic Just Deserts framework. But no matter how the details may vary and differ, this frame requires that persons finally receive what they deserve, and in this sense their destiny is decided by their own lives and conduct, decided by themselves. God may supply a *Second Chance* and be the executing power of justice, but it is the life and conduct of persons that crucially determine whether they are rewarded and saved or punished and damned. Hence, it is the person's doing or working in appropriating the Second Chance that is the *destiny-determiner* under God's justice. However nuanced we may strive to make this position, in the final analysis it is a matter of *works righteousness*, scorned by Paul, in which our acts achieve for us the worthiness to be loved and saved by God. Even though this Second Chance position, framed as it is by Just Deserts, wants to speak of God's grace, I will contend that it finally dissolves into lip-service grace inasmuch as the real destiny-determiner is the character of the life of the individual.

Most theories of dual destiny are rooted in this framework: according to God's justice, some are saved and some are damned. And it is clear that obedient response to the Second Chance is a necessary precondition for a positive, saved ultimate destiny. But we could also point out that this justice scheme could be skewed by saying that it is God's sovereign free grace that of itself decides who shall be saved and who not, which is the position of some Calvinist predestinarians. For them, all humans deserve punishment because of sin, but God graciously decides to save some, through no merit of their own, and to allow the rest to perish. The saved are saved by grace alone, and the damned are damned by Just Deserts.

4. I will now briefly sketch an *alternative frame that is centered in Jesus Christ and the Pauline-Reformation principle of salvation by grace alone.* In answering the five diagnostic questions and showing an interpretation of the three foci of salvation, I hope it becomes clear how much this position varies from the Just Deserts frame previously discussed.

First, the starting point for this frame, which we know only from the biblical testimony, is that the Creator God has acted in the history of Israel and decisively in Jesus Christ in a self-disclosing, self-revealing, and self-communicating way. Humankind is basically rebellious about its creatureliness and is confused about deity, apart from this definitive self-revelation of God in the life, death, and resurrection of Jesus of Nazareth, a Jew of Israel. Jesus is the life of God incarnate in the midst of finitude and sin in humanity's historical existence. *In Jesus we come to see truly who God is and who humans are.*

Second, in Jesus Christ, God is revealed as free, self-determining love who acts to save the world from its sin and the effects and consequences of sin.

What is done in Jesus Christ is the free grace of God acting on humanity's behalf. God is not required by necessity or human merit to save the world; to say 'grace' is to say that it is free, uncompelled, and unmerited.

Third, *in Jesus Christ God acts to take the sins of the world upon Godself for the benefit of the world.* How does this happen? God's life is actively identified with the life, death, and resurrection of Jesus of Nazareth, a specific, concrete, historical human person. This is what is meant in saying that God is incarnate in Jesus in a unique and singular way. Hence, Jesus' life and death are also God's, and in the terrible death on the cross, Jesus the Son of God experiences the full alienating and annihilating power of a sinner's death. This is death under the sway of sin, and God's judgment on sin is to allow it to traverse its course toward nothingness and alienation in death. Sin pretends to be the determiner of human destiny, to control what life comes to and means. *In Jesus' death on the cross God allows God's judgment on sin to fall on Jesus, one without sin and God's own Son, and therefore to fall on God's own self.* And this judgment and death are met and overcome in God's life as manifested in Jesus' resurrection from the dead.

These are the bare elements of a *doctrine of atonement or reconciliation* in the event of Jesus Christ. God reconciles the world unto Godself and does not count its sin against it. Humans no longer stand before God as sinners punishable in alienation from God and in death. Instead, because of what is done in Jesus Christ, humans are forgiven and justified sinners: sinners who do not have to face the consequences ultimately of their sin before God. We are obviously dealing here with *Salvation I:* God has acted in Jesus Christ to change the real situation of sinful humanity as requiring annihilation or ultimate punishment. This salvation is the event of Jesus Christ as incarnation, atonement, reconciliation, and justification, which is the self-revealing work of God.

Fourth, God in Jesus Christ through the Holy Spirit calls humanity—all humanity, for all humans have a new situation before God's grace—to receive and acknowledge this new standing and justification. It is God's Spirit that moves persons to participate in, to appropriate, to say 'yes' to this prior work of God's grace. Here we begin to deal with *Salvation II*. It is the doctrine of the *Trinity* that is unfolded in trying to express adequately the fullness of the divine Life that creates, reconciles, and redeems as Father, Son, and Holy Spirit. God is self-revealed as One sovereign subject who lives in three modes of being and acts as Father, Son, and Holy Spirit. This triune God is infinite, free, self-determining love who has freely chosen in love to create the world, to become incarnate in it, and to call all humanity to the acknowledgment that God is for and with humanity and the world.

Note carefully that the *Gospel* is essentially this Good News of what God has done in Jesus Christ to save humanity. The Gospel declares the priority of this objective happening as the self-revelation and self-enactment of God's being and life. In the life of Jesus, God has reconciled the world to Godself, and the world is no longer under the condemnation of its sin and God's justice. And this is done on behalf of all humans and the whole world. *Salvation I* is the foundation of *Salvation II*.

To elaborate now on *Salvation II*, it is simply persons coming through the Spirit to say 'yes' to God's prior acts of grace to justify humanity. It is not that they will be justified and forgiven *if* they say 'yes' to Jesus Christ. They are *already* justified and forgiven in Jesus Christ and now are called to live the whole of their lives in the manifest gratitude for this wondrous grace. One repents of one's sin because one has already been forgiven, not in order to be forgiven. This is the life of faith, love, and hope in which persons are baptized, accept the gift of reconciliation, receive the forgiveness of sin, receive the freedom of the Spirit to not be determined by sin, and strive to live the *ethics of grace*. This ethics is in contrast to an ethics of Just Deserts in which one strives to be good and therewith also to be worthy of being-saved. Ethics of grace starts with God's gracious justification in Jesus Christ and then asks: "If God has done this, then how am I called to live?" It is the believer who lives daily by grace and confesses gratefully that Jesus is the very being of God and thereby Lord and Savior. The believer is called to live in community with the neighbor, even if the neighbor is also the stranger or enemy.

This *life-in-the-Spirit* of authentic Christian existence is a new creation and is a being saved in the here and now of one's historical life. It makes a difference in *how* the believer lives and is in contrast to the life of the world. Yet, there is still an incompleteness in the believer's situation. Though God has acted in Jesus Christ to defeat the powers of sin and evil and has in ultimate fact defeated these powers, the believer's life does not seem so complete and sin-free. The world is still in its historical existence bedeviled by destructive principalities and powers and human rebellion against God's rule. Even though in Jesus Christ the believer knows that these powers cannot finally determine one's being before God and one's final destiny, she still lives concretely in the midst of ambiguity and conflict. The Kingdom of God as the presence of peace, justice, and love among humans before God does not seem to be fully embodied in history. The believer says 'yes' to God's grace, but the 'yes' is not perfect or complete. Hence, the believer *hopes* in God's further work in the future in which the Kingdom might fully come.

Indeed, in her own life the believer knows the inviting lure of God's future work and the foreshadowing of a completion yet to come. God has been at work, is now at work, and will be at work in the future. God is faithful to God's promises, and God has promised in the Spirit that nothing can separate persons from the love of God, come what may. Christians hope in God in at least two basic senses: hope for the historical future of the world and hope for an ultimate transhistorical future. For the historical future Christians trust in God's continuing salvific activity, however ambiguously evident or even unevident such activity may be, and they work with God to proclaim the Gospel, to free the sinful and oppressed, and to pursue concretely a Kingdom of peace, justice, and mutual love.

But this historical horizon of hope does not exhaust Christian hope. Christian hope also resonates to God's promise that death is not the last destructive word about life and that resurrection from the dead is resurrection to God's life. Further, Christians look to a *transhistorical future* in which all things, the whole of creation, will be taken up into God's eternal life and fulfilled. There are many images for talking about this ultimate situation, but human language has definite limits in trying to speak lucidly and truthfully about this ultimate future and destiny. The Christian's hope is that God's grace will meet us in death and will meet the whole world in its final end. This is destiny both as goal (telos) and as conclusion (finis) and is thereby the supreme fulfillment of human life in a transhistorical future. Our destiny—the destiny of all humanity and the world—is to be ultimately saved by God whereby none shall perish unto nothingness. *Ultimately before God, hell is empty.* These are the lineaments of *Salvation III*.

5. However briefly and inadequately, I have now sketched an alternative to the Just Deserts reading of salvation. Next I want to deal with some predictable questions and to elaborate some of my reasoning. Let me start

by addressing the fifth question of the schema: "Who is saved?" In the focus of *Salvation I*, all humans are saved in the sense that their situation before God has been changed from one of condemnation to one of reconciliation and justification. This is not a changed situation only for those who repent of sin and accept Christ. That is, this changed situation is real before God and is not conditioned in its reality by any human response.

In the focus of *Salvation II*, it is obvious that not everyone says "yes" to God's reconciliation, and there are many who either reject God's offer of grace in Jesus Christ or live in actual ignorance of it. So, not everyone is saved in *Salvation II* because not everyone says "yes" to God in Jesus Christ by the Spirit.

We might inquire, however, in the sphere of historical existence, which is the sphere of *Salvation II*, whether some non-Christians nevertheless know God and live faithfully before God and others. This is a keen question in our age of pluralism, and it is not easy to answer wisely in this short space. But a few remarks will show the direction of my thinking on a cluster of complex issues.

First, the very character of Christian existence is its acknowledgment of God in Jesus Christ; this is a specific cognitive intentionality and apart from this intentionality one's existence would seem to be something quite different. There is no 'real' God who transcends Jesus Christ and who is readily identifiable and intendable in some universal way.

Second, I see no compelling reason to believe that human 'religions' have something in common that could be considered salvific in any recognizable Christian sense of salvation.

Third, for the Christian, the devout Jew does stand in a unique situation. This Jew does know the grace of God in the election of Israel and the establishing of covenant and Torah. Yet this Jew does not acknowledge that the God of Israel was uniquely and singularly present in the Jew, Jesus of Nazareth. While God has not broken God's covenant with Israel, Israel is not prepared to see God for Israel and the world in Jesus Christ as atonement and justification.

Fourth, is it possible to live justly, generously, and well, whether in a religion or not, without acknowledging God's grace in Jesus Christ? It seems to me that in some relative sense, persons can live more or less justly, generously, and well in the world and therefore live a real presentiment of the life in the Spirit of Jesus Christ. However, I do not want to identify this situation with the situation of the true, self-conscious yes-sayer to God in Jesus Christ, with its clear recognition of sin, grace, forgiveness, and hope before God.

Fifth, in all these reflections we must be absolutely clear that it is not a question of whether God loves the non-Christian or whether God is punishing the non-Christian. From my discussion of incarnation and atonement it should be clear that God loves all persons regardless of their own disposition toward God.

Sixth, I find undaunting the accusation of some ardent pluralists who contend that any exclusive focusing of God's grace in Jesus Christ means necessarily that non-Christians are ungraced and unsaved. My reasoning on these matters of salvation is intended at least to deprive this contention of its force and misleading analysis. Beyond these remarks I am not prepared now to go.

6. We now further consider *Salvation III*, and we are faced with some compelling questions. Is the life of saying 'yes' to God's work in Jesus Christ a *precondition* to any positive ultimate salvation? That is, are only those who live obediently in faith in Jesus Christ going to be ultimately saved in death and in world consummation? I am denying that *Salvation II* is a necessary condition for receiving *Salvation III*. Much harm has come to Christian witness and humility by refusing to sever the logical and ontological connection between the life of faith and ultimate redemption. Because of the magnificence of God's atonement in Jesus Christ, we should resolve to see God's faithfulness in grace carried to its ultimate conclusion.

More precisely, what are my reasons for denying the linkage between faith and ultimate salvation and for affirming a *single, universal ultimate destiny*? First, we do not know how to answer the question of when a concrete life is 'faithful enough' to be a precondition for ultimate salvation. If this cannot be done, then in point of actual fact the Christian is trusting not in her own faithfulness but in the continued graciousness of God. If this is the case, then it should be realized that God's grace, as grace, is without conditions and is freely given. To be sure, grace cannot be acknowledged without recognizing that it gives directives for one's life. But the directives and the obedience to the directives are not the conditions

116

for being graced by God, even though they may well be conditions for the personal acknowledgement and appropriation of God's grace.

Second, to posit a dual destiny means either falling back into a destiny determined by Just Deserts or a destiny determined by the arbitrary decision of God. The Just Deserts frame, no matter how subtly or nuanced it is stated, fails to carry through completely both the sufficiency and the ultimacy of God's grace as the real, final judgment on humanity. The arbitrary decision of God to save some and not others is not the God we know in Jesus Christ and does not appear to be even a just and loving God. Christians have idolatrously worshipped this *potentia absoluta* long enough, and it is time to give it up for the sake of the real triune God.

Third, one might advance a pious agnosticism that says, 'Only God can ultimately decide who is saved, and we don't know what that decision is.' But this position fails to confront its own logic seriously. God will appear to have three types of options: (1) to decide according to the Just Deserts frame, using some definite criterion for discriminating deserts; (2) to decide arbitrarily to save some and not others; or (3) to decide in love to save all. And if in the light of the Gospel there is good reason for rejecting the first two options as inappropriate to the God we know in Jesus Christ, then we are left with the third choice of universally saving all. Pious agnosticism may be no more than a refusal to take with ultimate seriousness God's self-declaration in Jesus Christ.

We might next inquire whether this universal salvation renders our historical lives pointless. If, in spite of what we have done with our lives, God will nevertheless save us, then why worry about any moral seriousness, repentance, striving, and faith? But when it is put this way it makes it sound as though the only compelling and legitimate motive for moral effort is the desire to be rewarded for goodness. I have already suggested the inadequacy of this motive for Christian ethics and existence. Christians strive morally because of what they know about their own and others' forgiveness in Jesus Christ. They are moved by gratitude and love, not by the selfish hope that it pays in the end to be good. For the Christian, there is great point to her historical life precisely as the experience of sanctifying growth in *Salvation II*.

Further, I would argue that anyone who says, 'Why be faithful if God will save all in the end?' does not in fact properly understand what the Christian means when she says 'God,' 'faithful,' and 'saved by grace.' What appears to be meaningful talk is in fact *empty* of Christian intention, point, and content.

But won't persons use this view as an excuse for ignoring the Gospel and the call of the Spirit, because it doesn't pay to believe the Gospel? Why be Christian if there is no dual destiny between Christian and non-Christian? But surely Christians are not believers in order to have some advantage over a non-Christian, and Christians should have no interest in a salvation that logically requires that some others be damned. Such motives and reasoning are the opposites of Christian humility, gratitude for grace, and love.

Even more one might sharply ask whether my position is the epitome of so-called *cheap grace*. But the point of cheap grace talk is not that grace is really conditional. Rather, the target is that some folk speak of being saved by grace, but saying this makes no concrete difference for how they should live before God. Anyone who confessed salvation by grace alone but who did not actually live a transformed life would be cheapening the grace confession and would be misunderstanding the language of grace. Certainly we are not to think that the opposite of 'cheap grace' is 'earn your own salvation.'

7. Further, it might be asked, 'What about all of those biblical images that at least seem to posit a dual destiny and a real hell for the damned?' I must admit that these images are there in some biblical texts, even as I contend that there are other images that lead in a different direction. And I will admit that mainstream Christian traditions have assumed, if not always emphasized, a dual destiny. Yet, in fear and trembling and joy, I think there is a central theme issuing from God's incarnation in Jesus Christ as the free gift of Godself to sinful humanity that has not received the riveting and consistent attention it should. At its best, *Christian hope has always been hope in God's grace* and not a hope founded on confidence in one's own virtue or righteousness or religious correctness. What is the logic of this hope? I have tried to make it explicit.

The biblical images of dual judgment and destiny can, however, be given an alternative interpretation. These images convey bluntly and graphically that sinful humanity, *left to its own devices*, cannot find fulfillment and is instead destructive of life and comes to an alienated end. These images can vividly drive home that human sin in itself is alienation and hell and has only the dismal prospect of more hell, of leading only to nothingness. But in the Christian Gospel sinful humanity is not left to the wages of sin. God takes up the human plight and in Jesus Christ acts to overcome sin as the determiner of destiny, of ultimate destiny. God graciously in love gives humanity a new future. Without the confidence and joy in what God has done, sinners are driven to despair and are without legitimate hope. Living in the Spirit of Jesus Christ is a concrete and definite saving and makes a difference in one's life. The images of hell and damnation remind us of the threatening potential of sin, while the teachings of hope in God's grace persuade us that the *domain of hell— however persistently it stalks and demeans our historical existence—is finally and ultimately empty*!

It should be pellucid by now that the ultimate universal salvation that I am espousing is to be sharply distinguished from any so-called universal salvation that liberally and optimistically considers humans 'good enough' to achieve their own salvation or to deserve it. The universal salvation I posit is founded on the atoning work of Jesus Christ as the authentic self-revelation and self-communication of God's reality. This gracious God has done this and is this and will be faithfully gracious in the future.

8. One problem with the particular trajectory of tradition that emphasizes the sovereign efficacy of divine grace is that it is repeatedly co-opted by a picture of dual destiny. With dual destiny as an indisputable requirement, this trajectory is often driven to conclude that only some will be ultimately saved by grace and that some will be untouched by grace and thereby damned. And the dual destiny language seems to fit quite well the experiential judgment that some persons live profoundly and egregiously evil and unjust lives.

It should be clear that I am proposing that dual destiny language can be misleading and confusing to an adequate characterization of the foci of salvation. I am arguing that the logic of a radical incarnation/atonement view centered in Jesus Christ moves resolutely to the final conclusion that all will be ultimately saved by God's sovereign grace. With the universal efficacy of grace firmly secured in *Salvation I* and *III*, we can then understand some of the 'semi-Pelagian' talk about *Salvation II*: the 'yes' of the believer to God's grace in Jesus Christ is a genuine human decision and a necessary constituent in the salvific movement of this focus of salvation. To be sure, the human decision is a grateful response to Jesus Christ and is empowered by the Holy Spirit and is therefore not quite so autonomous as the semi-Pelagian suggests. But here in *Salvation II* we can acknowledge a duality of historical destiny: some persons say 'yes' to the Gospel and some persons say 'no' or are ignorant of it. We can thus be clearer and firmer about the real but penultimate importance of faith if we are clear about the universality of atonement and ultimate salvation by God's grace alone. Yet this grace talk finally dissolves if we make the life of faith a necessary precondition for a positive ultimate destiny. And the talk of God's love dissolves if we make a dual destiny ultimately dependent on an arbitrary decision of God.

We can also parenthetically note now how vulnerable the phrase 'justification by faith' is to ambiguity and misuse. It may be, and has been, interpreted as though it is the believer's *faith* that justifies her before God. So, then, without faith a person is not justified. But I am arguing that this interpretation easily deteriorates into works righteousness whereby having faith is something the person achieves and is therefore deserving of being justified. To preclude this unhappy development, I am arguing that justification is rooted in the event of Jesus Christ in such a way that all persons, sinners that they are, are justified by Jesus Christ's atoning work, whether or not they have faith. Hence, I prefer *justification by grace alone* to *justification by faith*. The justifying is in the atoning grace not the faith. And this is not to deny the real importance of a person having faith, which is crucial for *Salvation II*. But a person has faith that she is justified by grace alone.

9. Have I dealt yet with the concerns of some *liberation theologies* with their focus on historical liberation from injustice and oppression? It seems to me that the Christian knows at least two senses of historical liberation or freedom. First, there is the freedom that comes, even in the midst of injustice, when a person acknowledges that she is loved by God and not determined in her standing before God by either her own sin or the sins of her oppressors. From Paul through the centuries, oppressed Christians have experienced this freedom and liberation: they are not defined and destined by the powers of the oppressors. Second, there is the freedom from actually being oppressed and unjustly treated in one's social setting. The Christian hopes, prays, and works for this liberation for herself and for others and looks to God for continual historical, social liberation. The ethics of the Christian life aims directly at working for justice and peace in the common public world.

But we should not allow the concept of this social liberation to be the sole meaning of salvation nor the condition of ultimate destiny. If salvation were to be reduced to only historical, social liberation, then we would have the unhappy logical consequence that most of the human population through the ages have been unsaved or damned insofar as they were oppressed and never socially liberated. This would have the further consequence of giving to the oppressors the power to be determiners of others' ultimate destiny, a power that is God's alone. Many liberation theologians avoid this reduction, but it is a profound temptation in the midst of rhetorical 'prophetic' exhortation in which the Gospel and the ethics of grace can be forgotten.

10. *Is Jesus Christ the only Savior of the world?* From my perspective how could it be otherwise? Jesus Christ is not a quasi-divine mediator that helps people and of which type there may be many other mediators in other religions. Jesus Christ is God incarnate graciously acting to reconcile and redeem the world. God is the Father, Son, and Holy Spirit, and there is no other God. Hence, Jesus Christ is the only Savior of the world precisely because only God saves and Jesus Christ is of the very being of God as the One who graciously and universally loves all humanity. But this is a comment about Jesus Christ as Savior; it is not a comment about Christians alone being ultimately saved.

The Gospel of John has Jesus saying: "I am the way, and the truth, and the life. No one comes to the Father except through me" (John 14:6). Traditional interpretations tend to emphasize that Jesus is the only way to come to the Father and to infer that only those who have faith in Jesus will be saved. But this interpretation, powerful as it may be about *Salvation II*, tends, when isolated from other themes, to subvert John's prior declaration that Jesus is the Word made flesh and comes from the Father's love to a lost world as grace upon grace. The way of salvation is first the way of the Son *from* the Father *to* a lost humanity, and then secondarily and derivatively the way of humanity *to* the Father. *There is no human approach to God that in itself is effective and saving apart from the encompassing actuality of God's gracious approach to humanity in Jesus Christ.*

But the ultimate effect of what God has done in Jesus Christ through the Spirit is not limited to only those who have faith in Jesus.

So, are only Christians saved? All human persons are saved in God's atoning and reconciling work in Jesus Christ (*Salvation I*). Christians are those who gratefully acknowledge this and strive to live by the Spirit (*Salvation II*). This living by the Spirit makes a real difference in a person's life and is reason enough to witness before all humans to the wondrous things God has done on behalf of all. Christians also hope that all humans will ultimately be saved by God's sovereign resolve to be gracious and to gather all into God's own eternal life (*Salvation III*). Narrow may be the way of salvation in the life in the Spirit, because few will know the freedom, suffering, and joy that come with following Jesus. But wide and universal is the way of God's grace in incarnation, atonement, and ultimate redemption.

11. In conclusion, I hope my diagnostic schema helps us to understand salvation more clearly and complexly. The distinctions I suggest should enable us to ask sharper questions and to discern subtle but important differences, as well as similarities. To talk adequately of salvation in Jesus Christ requires that we see the range of meanings in which the word 'salvation' works. I have argued for one way of connecting the foci of salvation-talk and centering them on God's salvific work in Jesus Christ, which can only be explicated as the full work of the triune God, Father, Son, and Holy Spirit.

8

God: Triune in Essence
and Actuality

This essay was written for a Festschrift *edition of* Encounter *honoring Professor Richard D. N. Dickinson upon the occasion of his retirement as President of Christian Theological Seminary. See GCF chapter four for the fuller statement of the positions developed in this essay.*

It is a remarkable consensus in late twentieth century theology that the doctrine of the Trinity is regarded as important for a correct understanding of the Christian doctrine of God. Not since the fourth century have we seen such a prolonged and vigorous discussion of trinitarian doctrine.[1]

---

[1] Much of the twentieth century discussion has been stimulated by Karl Barth and Karl Rahner. See Karl Barth, *Church Dogmatics*, I/l, trans. G. W. Bromiley (Edinburgh: T. & T. Clark, 1975) 295–489 and *CD* II/1; IV/I; IV/2; Karl Rahner, *The Trinity*, trans. Joseph Donceel (New York: Seabury, 1974). Other heavy hitters are Jürgen Moltmann, *The Trinity and the Kingdom*, trans. Margaret Kohl (San Francisco: Harper & Row, 1981); Robert W. Jenson, *The Triune Identity* (Philadelphia: Fortress Press, 1982); Eberhard Jüngel, *God as the Mystery of the World*, trans. Darrell L. Gruder (Grand Rapids: Eerdmans, 1983); Wolfhart Pannenberg, *Systematic Theology*. vol. 1, trans. Geoffrey W. Bromiley (Grand Rapids: Eerdmans, 1991); Catherine Mowry LaCugna, *God For Us: The Trinity and the Christian Life* (San Francisco: HarperSanFrancisco, 1991); Thomas F. Torrance. *The Christian Doctrine of God: One Being Three Persons* (Edinburgh: T. & T. Clark, 1996). Good introductions to

Yet in the midst of this remarkable consensus there is still ample room for significant disagreements over several issues of trinitarian formulation. It is the fundamental thesis of this essay that the failure of contemporary trinitarian discussion to attend to a clear distinction between God's triune essence and God's triune actuality seriously hampers the development of the full conceptual potentialities of trinitarian doctrine. I will argue in this essay that this distinction facilitates a trinitarian doctrine that is radically incarnational and relational and that steers through the perilous waters of classical theism on the one hand and process theism on the other.

To make the argument concerning the importance and usefulness of the distinction between God's triune essence and God's triune actuality, I will first discuss the importance of the concept of the *Economic Trinity*, and then I will turn to a discussion of God's freedom and love. It is this later discussion that will be a launching pad for the development of the distinction between God's essence and God's actuality. Every theological effort intends to develop an answer to the questions: 'who is God?' or 'how is God to be identified?' or 'how is the term "God" to be used in Christian discourse?' At stake here is what I call the 'identifying references' or 'semantic rules' for saying who God is.[2] Every use of the term 'God' is employing some such identifying references or semantic rules.

In so-called *classical theism* the basic rules are that God is one, simple, infinite, eternal, immutable, and impassible and the first cause of all things. These identifying references sometimes seem even more basic than the biblical testimony and come to provide the foundational rules for the development of the doctrine of the Trinity. These rules presuppose that God's essence and existence are identical. The consequences for trinitarian doctrine are devastating: how can we talk of a triune God who becomes

---

contemporary discussions are: Ted Peters, *God as Trinity: Relationality and Temporality in Divine Life* (Louisville: Westminster John Knox, 1993); and John Thompson, *Modern Trinitarian Perspectives* (Oxford: Oxford University Press, 1994).

[2] For a discussion of 'identifying references' in ordinary language, see Peter F. Strawson, *Logico-Linguistic Papers* (London: Metheun, 1971). Robert W. Jenson also uses the terms 'identifying references' in developing his doctrine of the Trinity. I have been helped by his discussion, but I phrase the identifying references for God rather differently than his. See Robert W. Jenson, *The Triune Identity*, 1982; and "The Triune God" in *Christian Dogmatics*, vol. 1, ed. by Carl E. Braaten and Robert W. Jenson (Philadelphia: Fortress Press, 1984); and *Systematic Theology*, vol. 1: *The Triune God* (Oxford: Oxford University Press, 1997.)

incarnate in a particular human being while at that same time maintaining that God is simple, immutable, and impassible in both essence and existence?

If trinitarian considerations are to be central in identifying who God is, then we cannot begin with these rules of the natural theology of classical theism nor, I will argue, with the rules of the natural theology of process theism. Rather, we will begin with those considerations included in the concept of the economic Trinity. Relying on the authoritative priority of the biblical testimony, the term 'economic Trinity' refers to God's acts of self-communicating disclosure in the history of Israel and of Jesus Christ and the calling of the church. It is the *oikonomia* of God's disclosive management of salvation history in creation history. Hence, when we talk of the epistemic priority of the economic Trinity, we are referring to these self-disclosures of God in which God *identifies* Godself for Israel and the church and thereby for the world. We learn, therefore, who God is by looking at what God does in these self-communicating, self-identifying actions.

I propose that we can formulate *three foundational self-identifying references by God in God's economic life with the world*:

1. God is the One who elected, liberated, and covenanted with Israel and thereby is the One who is the sovereign Creator of all things.
2. God is the One who is singularly incarnate in and thereby definitively self-revealed in the life, death, and resurrection of Jesus of Nazareth.
3. God is the One who empowers the church into being and moves within creaturely life to give life, new life, and to draw all creatures into a redemptive future.

These fundamental self-identifications of God are the trinitarian trajectories requiring some explanation of the *differences* and *otherness* in God as well as the *oneness* of God. The doctrine of the Trinity is the attempt to provide coherent rules for talking about the God who self-identifies, who self-communicates, who self-reveals in these three differentiated ways of being God.

It should be relatively clear that it is the doctrine of the incarnation, as the assertion of the divinity of Jesus Christ, which propels the doctrine of Trinity into sharper formulation. While the God of Israel—as represented in the Old Testament—can be interpreted in ways that suggest some differentiation within God's life, it is the *identification of God with Jesus of Nazareth that posits a hitherto troublesome sense of otherness and differentiation within the divine life*. Drop the singular identity of Jesus with the God of Israel and there is no need for the doctrine of the Trinity. But with that identification, it becomes impossible to identify adequately who God is apart from some triune way of understanding that includes Jesus and the Spirit and grasps the otherness within God's actuality.

The more radical the insistence on the singular identification of God with the human Jesus, as the becoming human of God, the more radical is the doctrine of the Trinity and the less it can be co-opted by some metaphysical theory of the dialectical unity of the world spirit or some theory of the ultimate reality of community or togetherness or abstract relationality. Trinity is fundamentally about saying that the God of Israel has become incarnate in the creaturely otherness of a Jew—named 'Jesus' and located in first century Palestine—for the salvation of the world through the Spirit. When we say 'economic Trinity' we are reminding ourselves of *this specific narrative history of God's self-identifications*.

In all three of these self-identifications, the themes of *God's freedom and love* are central. The One who elects and liberates Israel is the One who self-names as YHWH: "I will be who I will be" (Ex 3:13-15). YHWH is the One who is free and self-determining. And the election of Israel is altogether a free and loving act. Likewise in Jesus Christ, God comes freely and lovingly to the rescue of a humanity that has repeatedly broken covenant with God, and in the Spirit God freely and lovingly moves persons to newness of life in response to the cross and resurrection of Jesus Christ. Throughout these disclosive acts, *God is the One who loves in freedom*.

The characteristic New Testament name of this loving freedom is '*grace*' (see Acts 15:11; Rom 3:21; 5:15-21; 6:15; 11:6; 2 Cor 8:1,9; Eph 3:7). Grace is a free gift of God that is undeserved and has beneficial, salvific effects for persons. It would not be a free gift if it were a necessity of God's nature. It would not be undeserved if it were given as a reward for merit or justified cause. Hence, we misconstrue God's grace if we think of it only in terms of undeserved beneficial effects. They must be freely given.

In our trinitarian discourse about God we cannot prioritize or separate God's love and God's freedom. Keeping these two essential attributes of God together is decisive for the explication of the biblical witness to God as a triune personal agent who is freely and lovingly gracious to the creature. But it has been a profound temptation of the church to separate and explicate God's freedom and love independent of each other. When this separation occurs in the church's discourse, we have, on the one hand, a freedom that makes it appear that God is free not to love. This is the tendency of emphasizing that God is primarily *potentia absoluta*, absolute and unconditioned power. On the other hand, we have a love that makes it appear compelled or necessitated by God's essence or nature, as though God's loving is not a personal, free decision, relationship, and gift of God. Therefore, in the church's discourse we must keep the concepts of God's freedom and love dialectically distinct and interrelated in such a way that they are never interpreted in independence of each other or that one is prioritized over the other. Freedom and love are the two attributes that will shape our understanding of the other traits of God's life and actuality.

There are two significant meanings in the understanding of *God's freedom*: 1) God can will and decide among alternatives and 2) God is self-determining will and power. But God is neither, except as the One who loves. Here love dialectically qualifies the first meaning of freedom: God is not free not to love. But God is free in what and how God loves relative to the creature and creation. As self-determining, God is free to self-determine Godself to-be-determined-by-another. God can determine Godself to be affected by and limited by another, and such self-determination to be so affected is a self-determination of God's love. But such determination by another is never the determination of some metaphysical necessity. Rather, God's being determined or conditioned by another and thus being affected by another is always God's free decision to be so determined, conditioned, and affected. Thus we do not characterize God's freedom as an impassible self-sufficiency or aseity that exists without being affected by any other actuality.

The New Testament is replete with references to *God's love* (see John 3:16, 16:27; Rom 5:5,8; 8:35,39; 2 Cor 13:11,13; Gal 2:20; Eph 1:5; 2:4; 5:2; 2 Tim 2:16; 1 John 3:16; 4:7-16; Rev 1:5). In trinitarian terms we can distinguish between two different types of objects God can love: 1) God's own internal loving among the persons of the Trinity, and 2) the creature. It is God's triune nature to be loving among the Father, the Son, and the Holy Spirit. But God's loving the creature is a free, self-determined act of openness to the being of the creature, to bringing the creature to be and to letting the creature be. God freely and lovingly comes to the rescue of the creature that is otherwise mired in sin and its destructive consequences.[3]

Nothing that we have said thus far would lead us to say that God is simple, immutable, and impassible.[4] In fact, by taking our lead from the biblical narrative we would never arrive at such conclusions; rather we are led in another direction in which we want to be able to say intelligibly and consistently that:

1. God freely and lovingly creates the world and is affected by the world;
2. God freely and lovingly elects, liberates, and covenants with Israel;
3. God freely and lovingly becomes incarnate in Jesus of Nazareth at a particular point in time for the salvation of the creature;
4. God freely and lovingly moves within creaturely life to renew and restore the creature's life and well-being;
5. God has an interactive history with the creation, Israel, and the church.

Given these trinitarian themes and activities, it seems appropriately implied that God *becomes* in God's life with the world, that God is *affected* by the world and its becoming, that God has an *interactive life* in and with the world. It is impossible for classical theism, given its basic semantic rules, to say these utterances intelligibly. As the Creator who is in actuality impassible and immutable, the God of classical theism metaphysically *cannot* be affected by the world and *cannot* become in any manner and

---

[3] The most discerning discussion of God's freedom and love is provided by Karl Barth, *Church Dogmatics*, II/I, 257–321. While my discussion has been influenced by Barth, I suspect that some of my points would not sit well with him. Jüngel helpfully reinforced some convictions I had about God's self-determination. See *God as the Mystery of the World*, 35–38.

[4] This is not the occasion for discussing the problems with the traditional interpretations of God's simplicity. If it meant no more than that God is not composed of quantitative parts, then it would not be objectionable. But the concept of simplicity is also used to deny real distinctions within God, and especially the denial of the distinction between potentiality and actuality in God, thus requiring that God is pure actuality. But precisely here there is the negation of that movement—albeit self-movement—in God that seems essential for trinitarian thinking. Further, simplicity seems to deny that otherness in God that incarnational thinking seems to demand. On another occasion I will make a case for revising the tradition on God's simplicity such that for God there is a special kind of simplicity that does not negate a special kind of complexity and otherness in God.

cannot have an interactive history with the world. And it would seem utterly unintelligible what it might mean to say God becomes incarnate in a finite, changeable, human life.

Process theism seems quite able—on the surface—to affirm that God has an interactive history with the world and lovingly becomes in relation to the world. But it has difficulty saying that God is triune, that God freely creates the world, that God becomes singularly incarnate in a human being. Rather, it seems by metaphysical necessity of God's love—as the capacity to be universally affected by all other actual entities—that God must have some world to love. Hence, some creature is necessary for God to be God. God could not be God without some world.[5]

Accordingly, we need a grammar of the Trinity that will steer us between the two alternatives of classical theism and process theism and will give us intelligible ways of talking about God as the triune One who loves in freedom. I am proposing that we revise the traditional grammar of God's essence and existence or actuality (I am using the terms 'existence' and 'actuality' interchangeably herein). This revision is adumbrated in the Cappadocians and Barth and is suggested in nontrinitarian ways in the process theology of Charles Hartshorne.[6] I am proposing *a new way of understanding God's trinitarian essence and God's trinitarian actuality.*

---

[5] It is generally acknowledged by process theologians that *this* world is not a metaphysical necessity for God, but that *some* world is. This is because it is a metaphysical necessity for God to be in relation to some other actuality. Without this relation, it is impossible for God to exist. Hence, process theologians generally speak of the co-eternality or co-everlastingness of both God and the world. I am arguing that this system of metaphysical principles is not adequate to understand the freedom and love of God in their triune manifestations. See Alfred North Whitehead, *Process and Reality* (New York: The Humanities Press, 1957), esp. 519–33.

[6] The Cappadocians at least recognized that the essence (*ousia*) of God is not another acting subject beyond the three persons. Barth's language about 'essence' and 'actuality' and 'being' is notoriously unstable, but I do believe he saw that the Godhead, as the essence of God, does not do anything; only God the triune subject acts. See Karl Barth, *CD*, IV/2, 65. In utterly nontrinitarian ways, Hartshorne is quite clear about the distinctions between God's essence, existence, and actuality. For our purposes here I am not concerned about his distinction between existence and actuality. While these distinctions are evident in much of Hartshorne's writings, they do not receive systematic clarification until he strives to state the ontological argument with logical rigor. See *The Logic of Perfection and Other Essays in Neoclassical Metaphysics*, (LaSalle: Open Court, 1962), 61ff. and *Anselm's Discovery* (LaSalle: Open Court Publishing Co., 1965), x.

What sort of talk is this talk about 'essence'? Philosophically it goes back to Socrates, Plato, and Aristotle, but it is deeply rooted in ordinary discourse about many things. Typically, we are stating the *essence* of something when we answer the following questions: '*What* sort of thing is this?' and 'What is it that makes it to be the sort of thing it is?' So we might ask 'What sort of things are Priscilla, Fred, and George?' and the answer might be: 'They are human beings.' *Being human* is the sort of thing they are; it is the *essence* or *nature* they have in common.[7]

But Priscilla, Fred, and George are more than just this human essence; they are concrete particular human beings. Being the *particular* human beings they are, they are also different from one another. Further, as a particular human being, each is subject to conditions of change and finitude. But to remind us of what each has in common, we can say that each is an *instance* of the human essence.

While it is clear that each human being is subject to change and becoming, the human essence itself does not change. The essence is just what it is and does not change from person to person, even though Fred and Priscilla do change. This unchanging essence we can also call the human 'nature' or 'form' or 'structure.'

Following this line of thought we can understand what is meant when we say that the essence of humanity is a *logical subject* but not an ontological subject. That is, as a logical subject, the essential traits of humanity (whatever they are!) can be spelled out and predicated of the essence. For example, we might say that being a personal and spiritual creature is an essential trait of human being. We can now predicate the human essence, as a logical subject, of Priscilla, Fred, and George. But George, Fred, and Priscilla as particular human beings cannot be predicated of anything else; they are *ontological subjects*. So, in this limited context it makes sense to say that Priscilla can do something, can act and become in time, but it makes no sense to say the human essence acts and becomes in time.

But we have a problem stemming from Plato: he thought the essence of something was what was most real about that something. And since the essence of something is an unchanging form or structure, he believed that it was more real to be unchanging than to be a changing, transient,

---

[7] That historically humans have often misconstrued the essence of something does not of itself cancel the usefulness of language about essence.

finite particular something. Hence, the semantic/ontic principle: *the unchangeable is more real than the changeable*; and thus when we ask about the essence of something, we are asking about what is most real about that something.

Sadly for Christian intelligibility and self-understanding, the principle that the unchangeable is more real than the changeable gets adopted in the post-apostolic church as a fundamental theological rule. In the developed tradition the further rule is advanced that God's essence and existence are identical. Hence, we see how easy it was to say that immutability and impassibility are traits of the essence of God. This is saying more than that God's essence is unchanging; it is saying that it is one of the unchanging, essential traits of God that God is immutable and impassible. And whatever is an essential trait of God's essence is identically a trait of God's existence or actuality.

We can subvert and dismantle this grammar of essence and actuality, if we *make a distinction between God's essence and God's actuality* and if we posit that *God's actuality is the more fundamental reality*. It is the actuality of God that is the fundamental ontological subject, and the essence of God is simply the necessary structure that is always present in God's actuality. God's essence is itself a logical subject, but it is not an ontological subject. Only the actuality of God is the ontological subject.

It is this subject that we have trinitarianly identified in the economic self-communications of God. In the actuality of these self-communications we have a basis for identifying God and talking about God's actuality. In actuality God is Father, Son, and Holy Spirit in dynamic, free, and loving interaction with the world. While the essence of God is itself unchanging, *the actuality of God can change, become, be affected by the world, become incarnate in the world, die a human death in the world, and actually consummate all things in redemptive fullness*. The essence of God is thus a predicate of God's actuality and is not more real than God's actuality. In short, the essence of God does not do anything; it cannot act; only God the actual triune subject acts.

We can now clearly affirm that God's essence, as structure, is unchanging or immutable, without also saying that immutability is one of the traits included in God's essence. An *essential attribute* or trait of God is a trait without which God could not be God. So, God's essence is that structure of attributes without which God could not be God. It is

God's actuality that has the essence, but God has other attributes as actual that are not included in God's essence. We are now in a position to see the intelligibility of saying that God has some traits or attributes essentially or necessarily and some contingently. We thereby avoid saying that every attribute of God's actuality is an essential attribute, without which God could not be God. Rather, God can actually have some attributes in self-determined contingency, which does not mean that they are any less real than the essential attributes. The *attributes of self-determined contingency* are those attributes of God that presuppose the world and God's relationship with the world. Here we would at least be talking about God as 1) perfect, 2) omnipresent, 3) holy and righteous, 4) patient, merciful, and gracious, and 5) constant or faithful. All of these are relational attributes of God. And, of course, all the essential attributes would apply as well to God's relationships with the world, but, as such, an essential attribute does not presuppose the world.

How then do we arrive at the essential attributes of God that comprise God's essence? We *infer* them from the triune actions of God's economic interaction with the world.[8] As we have seen, the attributes of freedom and love are central to God's economic actions, without which they would not be the distinctive actions of God. Further, precisely as economic actions, the triune self-identifications of God presuppose the givenness of the world as the world created by God. In order to preserve the graciousness of God's triune actions, we need to see God's interactions with the world as the contingent actions of God's freely self-determined love for the world. Hence, it is not of the essence of God that God be Creator of the world, the incarnate Reconciler of the world, and the Redeemer of the world. But, of course, these actions and their traits are constitutive of God's self-determining actuality.

What, then, might we say are the essential attributes of God? I would suggest the following: God as 1) loving, 2) free, 3) almighty, 4) wise, 5) eternal, 6) living, 7) triune, and 8) necessarily actual.[9] These are the traits

---

[8] The reasoning here is a form of that reasoning called by some 'transcendental reasoning.' As such, it means that we start from a given actuality and ask the question how this actuality is possible: what must be actual if this actuality is the case? Hence, what must be the case about God if the economic actualities are real and possible?

[9] Of course, justifying just these attributes and interpreting them are matters not pursued in this essay. They are noted here to give some content to the concept of essential attribute.

without which God could not be God; God does not *decide* to have these attributes. These attributes are the necessary structure of God's living actuality. While these attributes are necessary to God, *how* God has the attributes *in actuality* is subject to God's own disposing and enactment. For example, God is necessarily and immutably loving, but how and what God loves is subject to God's self-determined disposing and enactment.

This essay is not the place to elaborate and explain these attributes, but let us consider the attribute of *triunity*. I am arguing that God is in essence triune; that is, God has the attribute of being triune as essential to God's actuality and without which God would not have any actuality. This excludes saying that God first *becomes* triune in creating, reconciling, and redeeming the world. It also excludes saying what the Cappadocians said: that God's essence has three instances or persons.[10] Rather, precisely in God's triune actuality, there are not three instances of triunity but only one. Since we know no God except the One who is triune, we cannot speculate about an essence that is other than triune itself. Being triune, being Father, Son, and Holy Spirit, is not something God *decides*. But *how* God is these three modes of actuality is subject to God's loving self-determination and self-differentiation. Hence, we can say intelligibly that God, as triune actuality, creates the world, reconciles the world, and will redeem the world.

We are now in a position to affirm that *God could be God even without the world*, which puts us in direct conflict with process theologians. God actually is the One who freely and lovingly creates and governs the world, but these are contingent actions of God's actuality. While admitting the paradox in saying that God is actual even before creating the world, we are entitled to assert that God is *Primordially Triune* even before the world.[11] God is in loving actuality the One who loves within Godself as Father, Son, and Holy Spirit. And there is nothing about this loving triune actuality that requires or necessitates the creation of the world. That God does

---

[10] When the Cappadocians argue this way, they seem to me headed towards the heresy of tri-theism. While the definition of tri-theism is controversial, it seems that a divine essence that has three instances is about as clear as one might want concerning what it means to say there are three gods. On another occasion I will develop the argument that God is best thought of as a single triune subject who lives in three modes of being-in-act.

[11] See Jürgen Moltmann, *The Spirit of Life*, trans. Margaret Kohl (Minneapolis: Fortress Press, 1992), 292.

actually create the world can only be characterized as a free and loving action in which God self-determines Godself to become the Creator of the world.

But given that God has created the world, God's actuality is affected by this creating and by the creation itself; God's actuality is self-determinately limited by the creation in the primary sense that God does not choose to have God's life without the creation. Thus we can see the intelligibility of being able to say the triune God in living actuality is affected by the world, suffers with the world, and is powerful enough in actuality to suffer a human death on the cross of Jesus without ceasing to be God. Central to this intelligibility is the concept that God's actuality is inclusive of God's essence and is the fuller and richer reality of God. The triune God who is actual can become, have movement and life, and interact with the world. To put it vividly, God, in God's primordial triune actuality before the world, has the power to become the economic triune actuality in relation to the world. This, of course, means that we will have to talk about a *sequentiality* in God's life, and therefore God's eternality cannot mean simple timelessness as the negation of time. Without the distinction between God's essence and God's actuality we could not render intelligibly how God was actual and could have been actual without the creation but is now actual with the creation,

The concept of the *Immanent Trinity* has had a tortuous history of interpretation. We can now see how our distinction between God's essence and God's actuality enhances our ability to talk aptly of the immanent Trinity. The concept of the immanent Trinity has been variously used to mean:

1. God *in se*, or God-in-Godself or God as internally related as Father, Son, and Holy Spirit;
2. God *in se* as distinct from God-in-relation-to-the-world;
3. God's essence;
4. The deepest reality of God.

We must first affirm that the economic Trinity has epistemic priority here, and everything we say about the immanent Trinity is derived from what we know of the economic Trinity. That is, we have no independent access to a triune being apart from the economic self-revelations of God.[12]

The concept of the immanent Trinity affirms that God is not just triune in salvific self-communications in creation history, but is triune in Godself. Here the concept is used to defeat *modalism*, which can be interpreted as saying the economic Trinity is but the transient appearances of a primordial One who is not triune in itself. Modalism believes that God is primarily a simple monad who is unrelated to the world and for whom the distinctions of Father, Son, and Holy Spirit are unreal or merely temporal distinctions. Hence, in saying that God is immanently triune, we are negating modalism and affirming that the distinctions among the Father, the Son, and the Holy Spirit are real distinctions and involve real otherness within God's actual life. Modalism also challenges an abiding belief of trinitarian theology: that the revelations of God in creation history are *self-revelations* and that therefore we can trust the revelations as truthful disclosures of the very actuality of God. Sound trinitarian theology forbids us to believe that there is some more real God *hidden* behind the revelations who might be quite different than the revelations have led us to believe.[13]

The concept of the immanent Trinity has also been used to preserve the freedom of God in creating the world and becoming incarnate in the world. It is used to affirm that God *in se*—God in God's immanent and eternal self-relations—is self-sufficient in love among the persons of the Trinity and that God does not need the world in order to be loving. Therefore, it is not a necessity of God's loving nature that God have a

---

[12] Contra LaCugna, we do have reason for saying something about God apart from God's relation to the world, precisely for the sake of speaking aptly about God's gracious relationships with the world. Her demur about saying anything about God before the creation inadvertently renders her unable to speak acutely of the freedom and love of God in God's triune interactions with the creation. See *God with Us: The Trinity and the Christian Life*, 175–76, footnote 93.

[13] Whenever someone posits a hidden God who might be different than God has shown Godself to be, we can always inquire concerning what semantic rule is being thereby invoked. Do we have some more fundamental rule that can relativize God's self-revelations? If we do, then that is the real foundation (or anti-foundation) for Christian theology. But trinitarian theology must aver never to fall back on some more primitive semantic rule or identifying reference—such as the rule that God is ineffably infinite—for understanding who God is. If God is ineffably infinite, then it is false that God has given us authentic self-revelations of God's reality.

world of otherness to love. If something other than God comes to be, it comes to be only because God has freely and lovingly willed it to be.

Thus far we agree with this important point, for without the concept of the immanent Trinity we might be led to see the economic acts of God as the necessary unfolding of God's essence, perhaps in the fashion of Hegel. But the peril to the doctrine of the Trinity comes when tradition combined the concept of the immanent Trinity with the concepts of immutability and impassibility and therewith concluded that the immanent Trinity—God in Godself—is unmoved and unaffected by the economic activity of God. Our understanding of God's essence and actuality subverts and prevents any such misconstrual of God's immanent life. Further, our distinction helps us clearly affirm that in God's actual life with the world there are continuing internal relations—God *in se*— among the Father, Son, and Holy Spirit. And we can say that these internal relations are affected by the interaction of the persons of the Trinity with the world: for example, the Son's going to the cross of death affects the internal life of the Father and the Spirit and is the atoning movement of God's own life.

Given our distinction, we can see how unintelligible it would be to identify God *in se* with the essence of God. God *in se* is simply that dynamic internal relatedness among Father, Son, and Holy Spirit that is primordially actual and is economically actual as the coming-to-be of God's actual life with the world. The essence of God is merely the structure of God's actuality and is not itself and as such related to anything. The essence of God is not itself an actual relationship among the divine persons. I am arguing, therefore, that the concept of God's immanent Trinity becomes less confusing and still useful if we affirm the following:

1. God's essence is triune;
2. God *in se* is triune;
3. God's living actuality includes God's essence and God *in se*;
4. God in primordial actuality is triune;
5. God in economic actuality with the world is triune.

To recapitulate the argument for the usefulness of the distinction between God's essence and God's actuality, I have argued that the distinction will make it more intelligible how God can have a triune interactive life with the world, without thereby asserting that the world is necessary to God and without falling into the trap of classical theism with its emphasis on the immutability and impassibility of God. Without my distinction, we will have the continuing confusion about how to speak of God's having a real relationship with the world, of God's suffering with the world, of God's becoming incarnate in the world. With my distinction, we are empowered to talk about God's free and loving actuality that is free to become the Creator, Reconciler, and Redeemer of the world. Indeed, my distinction allows new intelligibility to shine through some of the prime utterances of the faith that have hitherto been difficult to interpret.

9

Christology and Jewish-Christian Dialogue

It is a pleasure to write an article in this *Festschrift* issue honoring my friend and colleague of many years, Clark Williamson. We taught systematic theology together for several years at Christian Theological Seminary, and I confess that his passionate concentration on Jewish-Christian dialogue deeply aroused and influenced my awareness of the issues and necessities of engaging in the dialogue in our post-Holocaust situation. Without his insistent arguments, I might well have neglected issues that have profound implications for how we construe Christian faith. While it has been clear to many over the years that Clark and I disagree over important matters in Christian theology, it may have been overlooked that we also agree on a wide range of Christian concerns. This essay on christology is written in gratitude for the conversations and writings of Clark and for the persistent passion of his theologizing in a way that does not forget the Holocaust. I choose to write on christology because that is an area in which our strongest theological convictions sometimes collide.

I am under the impression that we are now entering a phase in Jewish-Christian dialogue in which Christian guilt is no longer the shared premise of the dialogue. When this premise is given full reign, we often have

Christian theologians eager to diminish distinctive Christian claims and to find ways in which the common ground between Jew and Christian can be emphasized. In this situation, the more liberal voices in both traditions can play out the agreements and neglect the differences. In the course of this phase of the dialogue, Christian christology often became the scapegoat for the sins and guilt of the Christian tradition. It was not seldom in this dialogue that it seemed that Christianity had become a slimmed down Judaism for Gentiles with a prophetic Jesus and a Christ idea without the particularities of incarnation.

We are now in a new phase of the discussion, beyond Christian guilt, in which a resolute honesty on both sides is emerging with a new acceptance of both the profound continuities and significant differences that obtain between Jewish traditions and Christian traditions. The recent publication by Jewish scholars, *Christianity in Jewish Terms*,[1] is a bold attempt from various Jewish perspectives to characterize Christian faith and to identify those areas of significant agreement and difference. At many points in their essays, the issues of christology and incarnation come repeatedly to the fore as a set of beliefs that dramatically differentiate Judaism and Christianity.

I think they are on target in identifying these issues as the deep markers distinguishing Christianity and Judaism, and it is important that the disagreements in christology be discerningly articulated. It is my project in this brief essay to explore a schematic understanding of christology and the doctrine of God that acknowledges the differences without: a) advocating a supersession of Judaism by the church; or b) diminishing an incarnational christology; or c) lapsing into the glib locution that 'Judaism is for Jews and Christianity is for Gentiles.'

From the Christian side there is general agreement that all forms of supersessionism are to be repudiated, but the term 'supersessionism' often gets up and walks around on us. I find there are at least two different meanings attached to the term 'supersessionism':[2]

---

[1] Edited by Tikva Frymer-Kensky, David Novak, Peter Ochs, David Fox Sandmel, and Michael A. Singer (Boulder: Westview, 2000).

[2] Most of the following and much else in this essay is developed further in my two-volume text: *A Grammar of Christian Faith: Systematic Explorations in Christian Life and Doctrine* (Rowman & Littlefield, 2002).

S1: the belief that since most Jews during the time of Jesus (and most since) rejected him as Israel's Messiah, God has rejected Israel as God's people, canceled God's covenant with Israel, and replaced or superseded Israel with the church; and therefore only those Jews who accept Jesus as Messiah and Savior will be saved.

S2: the belief that Jesus Christ is the fulfillment of God's work in Israel and that Jesus Christ therefore has salvific import for the life and destiny of Israel.

I reject S1 as an illegitimate and unfortunate belief of the Christian church through many centuries. But I am concerned about those Christian theologians who would also call S2 a supersessionism to be rejected. With the apostle Paul in Romans 9–11, I affirm:

a. that what God has done in Jesus Christ has been done in the history of Israel, in a Jew, and in fulfillment of God's intent with Israel as covenant people and therefore for Israel;

b. that God is faithful in God's promises, and God has not rejected Jewish people who have not accepted Jesus as Messiah;

c. that what God has done in Jesus Christ has been done for all God's children, Jew and Gentile alike;

d. that a Jewish person is not making a conceptual mistake in believing that Jesus Christ has salvific meaning for Jews; certainly Paul the Pharisee, and all the other NT authors who were Jews, thought Jesus was their Savior and Lord;[3]

e. that it is, therefore, not the case that Jesus Christ is for Gentiles only and Judaism remains theologically untouched by the life and destiny of Jesus.

Of course, a Christian theologian who denies that Jesus is salvifically for Jews and important for Judaism has subverted most of the New Testament and has reduced Jesus to the proportions of an interesting and provocative social prophet carrying the 'universals' of Judaism to the Gentiles. When I say 'universals,' I mean those aspects of Judaism that

---

[3] See Gal 2:19-20.

can be universally held by 'reasonable people,' such as some form of monotheism and a set of social justice principles.

However, when well-intentioned Christians try to diminish Jesus in the interests of defanging a presumably supersessionist Christianity, they also collide directly with the profound Jewish and Christian belief that Israel is a people specially elected by God. To affirm the special election of Israel by God, however, is also what opens the door to affirming that the God of Israel has become a Jew on behalf of the salvation of the whole world, including Jews. Only a God who does special and particular acts in the world, such as specially electing and covenanting with Israel, is a God who can become a human being. Other gods, of which there are many in our day, including a vague deistic god, do nothing in particular in the world. Hence, the special election of Israel is a common belief that Jews and Christians should share.

In order to appreciate the realism of this shared belief, it must not be seen as emerging from the modern historical study of religion and democratic theories of pluralism, in which a mutual tolerance among religions is appropriately encouraged. But that sort of discourse and perspective could never of itself assert the theological belief that the Creator of the world specially elected and covenanted with Israel. Notice the extraordinary grammatical difference between saying 'Israel believed it was elected by the Creator of the world' and saying 'Israel was elected by the Creator of the world.' The first utterance can be spoken with complete personal detachment and neutrality, pretending to be no more than a verifiable historical belief about Israel's religion. The latter utterance can only be authentically spoken with passion and commitment such as one might find in synagogue or church.

This shared belief in a God who has specially elected and covenanted with Israel is compelling, and no credible theologian, Jew or Christian, should allow it to be neglected or omitted from his discourse. And from a Christian point of view, the particularity of Israel's election and the particularity of Jesus Christ are indissolubly bound together. What distinguishes Christian and Jew theologically is the further Christian belief that the God of Israel acted uniquely and incarnately in Jesus of Nazareth for the salvation of the world, including the ultimate salvation of Israel.

It is, however, one of the appalling tragedies of church history that a crucified Messiah, who was believed to be of the very essence of God and who preached peace, love of enemies, and nonretaliation, was converted into a triumphalist Emperor in whose name it became appropriate to kill and persecute Jews and heretics and all other enemies of the imperial god. The way of the cross, instead of being the way of the Christian disciple and the church, became the despised way of weakness in the face of enemies who are bent on doing harm to one's family, clan, nation, or religion. When attacked and in self-defense, it becomes mandated that the followers of the Emperor Jesus are justified in killing either in return or in anticipation.

The agenda for a full-bodied Christian post-Holocaust christology is to recover the crucified Messiah and Son of God as the one who was the definitive self-revelation of God and of the way in which God's people are called to live in the world. There is no reason emerging from the Holocaust to retreat from the belief that the God of Israel became incarnate in a Jew for the salvation of the world. But this incarnate God is not one who is immutably above the fray of life and enmity and is not one who is impassible in the face of human suffering. Instead, such an incarnate God, one who is the very essence and actuality of God, is the one who comes to live in the midst of enmity and suffering, in the midst of oppression and misery, in the midst of the least of those in human social arrangements, and he is brutally slain by the powers that think they are ultimately in control of human life and destiny. The moral/theological character of Jesus' resurrection from the dead is the validation that his life, teaching, ministry, and death are revelatory of the ways of almighty God, who created heaven and earth and elected Israel. The divine reality that is claimed for Jesus is a reality that can die a human death and take the sins and evil alienation of the world upon Godself. The sins of the world include the sins of Jews and Gentiles alike. And, we must admit, if the God of Israel has done this incarnate act in Jesus Christ, then that very belief itself begins to transform how we Christians understand the reality of the God who elected Israel. Herein lie the roots of trinitarian belief among Christians: a complex and multi-relational divine Life has crossed the boundaries between Creator and creature to become a creature and take up the cause of the creature and shape the creature's destiny.

For Christians to say, then, 'Jesus is Lord' is not merely to say that he is ruler in their hearts, however much that may also be true. It is boldly to say that Jesus is truly the Lord who reigns over all human life, history, and destiny. And his Lordship is that of peace, self-denial, cross-bearing, agapic love, and resurrection from the dead. Affirming these beliefs is what was at issue at Nicaea and Chalcedon: Jesus' life and destiny, his suffering and cross, is the life and destiny of God and the people of God. And it is appalling how quickly these huge theological claims got sidetracked, even derailed.

Hence, the need today in the church is not a diminished christology but a robust christology that is faithful and truthful about the reality of Jesus and the God of Israel. Such a christology will give no justification for the coercion of anyone in Jesus' name, for it cannot endorse coercion or violence. Such a christology could never be used to warrant persecution, harm, and violent treatment of any human being, for it stands for the dignity of all human life before God and God's suffering solidarity with human life.

If this Jesus is Lord of life and human history and destiny, then a Christian would be irresponsible if she did not affirm that this Jesus is also salvifically for Jews. From this christological perspective, whether any contemporary Jews accept Jesus or not, Jesus is for Jews of all times and places. To say this Jewish Jesus is only for Gentiles is to deny that Jesus is Lord of history. It is to deny that Jesus is of the very essence and actuality of God and is the incarnate work of God on behalf of a rebellious and sinful humanity.

There are, then, some significant differences between Jewish theology and Christian theology. It cannot be true that the God of Israel both did act incarnately in Jesus of Nazareth and did not so act. It cannot be true that the God of Israel both acted for the salvation of the world in Jesus Christ and did not so act.

But Christians need to remember as well that it cannot be true that God in Christ both prohibits violence, retaliation, and killing among humans and sanctions violence and killing on select occasions when some of God's sinful children deserve to die. It cannot be true that Christ is both Emperor like Caesar, ruling by fear behind armies and fortresses, and the slain Lamb of God, the crucified Messiah dying at the hands of the sinners of the world. It cannot be true that killing and violence are ever justified by appeal to the name of Jesus.

Do Jews have a right to exist as Jews now that the Messiah has come? Of course. Is a Jew making a conceptual mistake to believe that Jesus is the Messiah? In the times of the apostolic church, when the New Testament was being written by Jews who thought Jesus was Lord and Savior, they could never have thought they were making a conceptual mistake. So we have in New Testament times many Jews believing salvific things about Jesus. Yet it may well be that today a Jew by birth would cease being Jew, in the eyes of some, were he to become a Christian. But these are matters so complex for Jews themselves that I will say no more. My point is simply that the earliest followers of Jesus were Jews who did not think they were betraying Israel in believing Jesus to be Israel's Messiah.[4]

While Christians must continue to be vigilant in their discourses and practices about Israel and Jews, they are not expected to be endlessly guilty for the Holocaust. The Holocaust is a horrible marker in human history as to the extent and ferocity of human sin, of the human inclination for scapegoating, for retaliating, for revenge, for hatred, and for a demonic will to power over others. The history of the church contributed to these inclinations as they came to expression toward Jews over centuries of contempt and persecution. The most enduring way in which the church can prevent such inclinations from finding habitation in the church's discourses and practices is for the church to be truly and profoundly christological. If Jesus is God incarnate and lived, taught, and died without violent resistance at the hands of the powerful in the world, then his Lordship commands that Christians live in the same way: the way of agapic love and peace. It is a narrow way not often taken. Jews have no reason to fear these Christians, though they might be annoyed at the Christian's insistent confession that Jesus the Jew is the incarnate Lord of history.

I hope, therefore, that I have shown a way in which a genuinely New Testament, Nicene, and Chalcedonian christology might be reclaimed by Christians without fearing they are giving comfort to those who would condemn or eradicate Jews and Judaism. I would also hope that I have shown how those sincere and honest Christians who are valiantly trying

---

[4] Of course, there are significant differences in what later Jews and later Christians mean by 'Messiah.' These differences are explored further in my *A Grammar of Christian Faith* and in my earlier article, "Jewish and Christian Theology on Election, Covenant, Messiah, and the Future," in *The Church and the Jewish People*, ed. Clark M. Williamson (St. Louis: Christian Board of Publication, 1994), 51–58.

to construct a post-Holocaust theology by evacuating Nicene christology and theology can now desist from those enervating efforts.

Finally, while I have not been able to develop it in the limits of this essay, I think the sort of christology I have outlined is so deeply grounded in the free grace and love of God that it leads directly to the eschatological hope that the triune God, who lived amongst humans, was crucified, and rose from the dead, will ultimately gather all—Jew and Gentile alike—into God's own eternal Life. It is inconceivable that the God who became incarnate in a Jew would have any other future with Jews than that of Ultimate Companionship and Redemption.

10
Jesus, the Incarnate Word
Grace upon Grace
John 1:1-18

A sermon preached in St. Paul United Methodist Church, Muskogee, Oklahoma, on January 2, 2005.

The passage I have just read from the Gospel of John is typically referred to as the "Prologue" to the whole gospel. In it we have one of the most profound and influential statements of the significance of Jesus of Nazareth that exists anywhere in the literature of the early church. It is fair to say that what came to be known as the 'orthodox' tradition of the church was deeply dependent on the language and theology of the Gospel of John. It is, I hope, a special blessing for us to have this text as the lectionary reading for this Second Sunday of Christmas, at the beginning of this new year of 2005. I propose to give the text a close reading and interpretation in the hope we all might find ourselves better grounded in the understanding of Jesus as the Incarnate Word of God and enlivened in our faithful living by that understanding.

Let us start by looking closely at the first five verses:

In the beginning was the Word,
and the Word was with God,
and the Word was God.
He was in the beginning with God.
All things came into being through him,
and without him not one thing came into being.
What has come into being in him was Life,
and the Life was the Light of all people.
The Light shines in the darkness,
and the darkness did not overcome it.

In its originating context—a largely Hellenistic world in Palestine under Roman rule and domination—anyone who might be entrusted to read the scroll upon which this whole gospel was written would know that the gospel is about Jesus the Jewish prophet from Nazareth. And in knowing that, they would also know that he preached the coming Kingdom of God, was crucified on a cross of shame by the principalities and powers of his first century world in Palestine, and that his followers had claimed that—though he died a terrible and brutal death—he was raised from the dead by the One he called Father, the God of Israel.

We can now understand that anyone reading this gospel in that early context would be astonished at the claims now being made about the significance and reality of Jesus' life, death, and resurrection. If anything is clear in this gospel, Jesus of Nazareth is being placed in a cosmic drama with significance for every being that has existed, does now exist, and might exist in that cosmos. But we will not get very far in our understanding if we do not appreciate some dimensions of the Palestinian world in Jesus' time.

Remembering now that the New Testament was written in Greek by Jewish followers of Jesus, let us look at two Greek words that are crucial to this text: *theos* and *logos*. Our translators have rendered them "God" and "Word." We should not suppose, however, that, in their Palestinian setting in a Roman subjugated world with many religions, these terms had agreed on—or common—meanings and references. Quite simply, *theos* refers to whatever is regarded as in some sense divine. As such the word *theos* does not tell us anything further about who or what is divine. Hence, the divine could be the many gods of the Roman mythological pantheon, and a succession of Roman Caesars claimed to be divine, while the various Hellenic philosophers had teachings as to what should be regarded as divine. Hence, there was a continuing linguistic battle going on as to what or who is divine.

The sole exception is that among Jews—and Jesus and this gospel writer were Jews—*theos* referred first and only to the God of Israel, who created all things, elected and covenanted with Israel, spoke to Israel in giving her commandments and in giving her guidance through prophets who declared God's Word to the people of Israel.

That other word, *logos*, had a rich linguistic context as well. We certainly must believe that the writer of this gospel was reaching into the deep resonances of other uses of this word in the Hellenistic world. *Logos* is translated "Word" here largely because of its Jewish background: the God of Israel is a God who speaks words, who creates a world by speaking and who sends prophets to speak God's truth and commandments.

But even a Jew in this Hellenistic world would know that the word *logos* was related to logic, to right order and meaning among words and to right order within the world, to the basic rationality that it is at the heart of how things go in the world. To have fathomed the *logos*—the intelligent and understandable order—of the world was to have grasped what it means to live as a human being in this world. To grasp the word or *logos* is to have grasped something meaningful and intelligible.

A skilled carpenter—who knows how to identify types of wood, who knows how to read the grains of the wood and knows how to use tools to fashion wood into attractive and useful forms—is a person who has understood the *logos* of wood and carpentry.

In our time we do not seem to value words very highly, being aware that people often use them superficially and chaotically. But I have argued elsewhere that the length and breadth of the language we have available to us and in which we are skilled in speaking, in hearing, and in writing is precisely the most basic way in which we have a world and live in it. The language a person possesses is the foundation of how she has a world, and the limits of her language is the limit of her understanding.

Put another way, I think one of the most basic challenges to any one of us is how to make sense out of our lives and the world in which we live. *Sense-making* is a fundamental human activity and it is profoundly dependent on the words—on the language—we know how to use and understand.

If we call ourselves 'people of the book,' then surely we all know that words do matter and that the words of this gospel matter; these are the words that we need to be able to speak and to understand and by which our lives should be formed.

Further, the very words "In the beginning . . . ," which come first in this Prologue, remind us of the words in Gen 1: "In the beginning God created the heavens and the earth." *God speaks the cosmos into being.* And this God who creates by speaking is the God whose Word forms and orders and enlightens all things and is the Word that comes into the world in Jesus Christ.

So, let us note firmly that this profound language is referring to the reality that is Jesus of Nazareth and is saying something like this: if you want to understand how things are and who is finally in charge of all life and light and truth, then come to grips with the reality witnessed in the narrative of the life, death, and resurrection of Jesus of Nazareth.

As the prologue narrative goes on, the One who is the Word and Light of the world came to "his own people" who by and large "did not accept him"(v. 11). We know, of course, that all of Jesus' earliest followers were themselves Jews, and they did "receive him," and "believed in his name," and to them he "gave power to become children of God"(v. 12).

These followers, however, became children of God born "not of blood, or of the will of the flesh or of the will of man," but born of the grace of God (v. 13). This means that they are so decisively born of the Word of God that it is sheer grace that they come to believe and to become children of God. They are not children of God by their own arduous exercise of their presumably free wills: they are children by the *grace of God.*

Then, the narrative goes on: whether the Word was well received by all, whether the Word that enlightens every person that comes into the world is acknowledged or not, and whether the persons of the world cry 'hallelujah' or not, "the Word became flesh and lived among us"(v. 14). Here the narrative joyfully exclaims: "we have seen his glory, the glory of the Father's only Son, full of grace and truth"(v. 14).

The stark boldness of this claim should not escape us—I mean escape us present-day Christians. Some of us say loosely that Jesus is God but we say it without passion and life-shaping power. Some of us prefer to say

Jesus is merely a man, perhaps a good and interesting man, but nevertheless finally only a man. It should not escape us that this gospel writer is claiming *that the very Word that is God and is the Word of truth and light that is at the heart of the universe, has become a human being—a Jewish human being,* born of a Jewish mother in the turbulent times of first-century Palestine, and named Jesus, which any good Jew would know means "God saves."

The gospel writer is careful not to say that the Word that is with God and is God became flesh in such a way that the Word ceased to be God and became instead a human being. Rather, let us read this carefully: it means that the Divine Word itself became a human being without ceasing to be the sovereign reality of the Divine Word itself. It also means that in Jesus, the Incarnate Word, the reality of God becomes *vulnerable* to the human world. Yet it is a vulnerability—even on the cross—for the sake of the redemption of the world.

This is not entirely easy of understanding, and the church has grappled through the centuries in trying to unfold the thick richness and boldness and beauty of this claim about the Word becoming the human being Jesus of Nazareth.

The gospel writer says: "No one has ever seen God. It is God the only Son, who is close to the Father's heart, who has made him known"(v. 18). A *palpable bodiliness of God* was not what a learned person would expect of God. Yet to see this bodily Jesus with the eyes of faith is to see the love, grace, forgiveness, reconciliation, and peace that are the heart of God, even at the heart of the universe.

However much people repeatedly choose to live in the darkness of hate and lies, the darkness of violence cloaked as justice—choose to live, in other words, as though the darkness is itself the power and truth that engulfs and rules over every human that comes into the world—*Jesus nevertheless reveals the true heart of God and the universe.*

Let us pause now and think about what is being said in this Prologue. We have seen that it starts out using words many of us would regard as somewhat abstract and even obscure: words like 'Word' or '*logos*,' and "that all things came into being through" this Word or *logos*. I have already called our attention to the fact that the God of Genesis is a God who speaks the world into existence, is a God who speaks through the covenantal law and speaks through the prophets. Surely our awareness of these uses of the phrase 'God speaks and it is so' gets us more anchored.

This gospel writer is telling us here in the Prologue—will tell us throughout the following gospel text—that it is only in Jesus that we are to understand how we ourselves are to grasp and speak such words as "God," "*logos*," "truth," "light," and "life." It should now be apparent to us that this Jesus of Nazareth—the one who proclaimed a Kingdom of peace and reconciliation, who was crucified by the powers in charge of the political order of the day, and who was raised from the dead in vindication of his life—this Jesus speaks and enacts that power and truth that is at the heart of the universe and that is the gracious truth about every human being that has come into being or will come into being.

Jesus as the Word made flesh has enacted how things really are about a world that has repeatedly refused to dwell in the light of truth and peace. Jesus enacts that "grace upon grace" that is the rational, intelligent, and sense-making Light at the heart of all things.

Notice further that—because Jesus was himself crucified by those who thought themselves in control of the known world—it is also the case that *Jesus is the suffering of God on the cross of human arrogance, pride, and violence.* Jesus—the *logos* of all things—has suffered death on a cross that symbolizes the human claim that we humans are in charge of the world.

In all of the world's dark messiness, in all of its violence, we humans—just like the Romans—repeatedly claim that we are just doing what is realistically necessary to protect ourselves from the rage of others who envy our power. We live as though the real *logos* of the world is the power to do as we please and to impose our will on others as we please. In fear we rush to embrace this darkness of power and conflict.

God suffers this arrogance of ours and yet offers us grace and reconciliation—offers the most basic truth of the universe—and those who receive this Jesus gladly will know the very heart of God.

Here we must emphatically say that, for the church and Christians, the word "God" can never be used to refer to a reality that vaguely transcends the world and is hidden behind the scenes. The word "God" for Christians can never again be used to refer to One who is above the fray of human life and aloof from human affairs. No, *now our use of the word "God" is tethered to and ruled by Jesus Christ, the Word made flesh.* The words Jesus spoke and preached and enacted, the pattern of life he lived and died, the suffering he endured on behalf of the world, the grace he expressed—these are the clues to who God is and what is the final *logos* of the whole creation.

We live in a turbulent time as well. We live in a time when some church leaders teach that the *logos* of the world is quite different from what John has declared to us. As these teachers forecast the imminent end of the world, they see a different Jesus coming back to do something vengeful and destructive to those who will be "left behind" by Jesus. They see a Jesus who is not the grace upon grace, the truth and light, that is at the heart of the world God has created. They see a dark angel of violence bent on revenge.

But I ask you, could anyone who has seen Jesus with the eyes of faith ever construe Jesus as the One who is out to destroy and incinerate this world God has created? Could anyone construe this Jesus as the great provocateur of hate for enemies near and far? Could anyone construe God, therefore, as the One who will finally punish and banish to hell all those who might still live in darkness unaware of God's love and grace in Jesus Christ? Is it not then the case that folk who continue to construe God in ways that repudiate Jesus as the very gracious truth about human life and God—these folk speak lies and covet the darkness, even if they know it not.

Yet is it not also true that those who live in the darkness of untruth have not overcome or extinguished the truth and light of Jesus? He still shines brightly and is that ultimate Word of Grace that is already in charge of the destiny of the world and of all of us humans who live in the world. God's truth, God's true word from the beginning of all things is *undefeatable and irresistible grace*. We come to be through acts of grace, and even when we and the world fall into darkness, God's grace is the true and final Word that will be spoken even unto the end of the ages.

There is much herein for us to ponder. May it be that as we enter this new year, we Christians might become knowledgeable—even intelligent— about that Word that is at the heart of the world God has created and is intent on redeeming. Grace upon grace! Can we hear it, can we feel it, can we live it?

All this, dear friends in Christ, I have dared to preach in the name of the Father, the Son, and the Holy Spirit, one God, Mother of us all. Amen.

11
Kierkegaard: Spy, Judge, and Friend

This is a community-wide lecture given to students, staff, and faculty at Christian Theological Seminary in the spring of 1999.

I first became acquainted with the Danish philosopher and theologian Søren Kierkegaard as an erstwhile pre-ministerial undergraduate majoring in philosophy at the University of Oklahoma. For my generation of religious types, Kierkegaard was required reading. He was fascinating and exciting, very much at the center of the existential philosophy that seemed to be dominating theological circles. Upon arriving at Yale Divinity School in 1958, I discovered that most of my entering divinity student colleagues had read and reveled in Kierkegaard. One colleague in particular enjoyed late hours of intense wrestling with me over Kierkegaard and Dostoyevsky. His name was Gary Hartpence, a sober Nazarene who later became politically famous as Gary Hart, an ill-fated presidential candidate. Later in my studies, a new professor named Paul Holmer came to Yale with the reputation of being the freshest and most philosophically acute interpreter of Kierkegaard. After a year of pitched battle with Holmer, I had to admit that he was very much changing and deepening my understanding of

Kierkegaard. To this day I remain in Holmer's debt for opening up Kierkegaard in ways new and compelling.

So why am I speaking on Kierkegaard today? Primarily because I find him endlessly challenging and a wonderful conversation partner, and I want to introduce him to you. But why do I need to introduce him to you? After all, wasn't he the major inspiration behind the so-called existentialist movement in philosophy and theology? Wasn't he that astute critic pronouncing with relish the death and end of that infamous arrangement between culture and church called "Christendom"? Wasn't he the first intellectual to diagnose and identify the demonic seductions of modern mass culture and the all-powerful *crowd*? Didn't he decisively influence twentieth century theologians such as Karl Barth, Paul Tillich, Rudolf Bultmann, Reinhold and H. Richard Niebuhr? Haven't hundreds of books and thousands of articles searched, scoured, and critiqued his literature and life? Haven't a host of contemporary analytic philosophers, including Ludwig Wittgenstein, found him intricately fascinating? Haven't some therapeutic types invoked his name repeatedly as truly the first great psychologist of modern humanity? Yes, all that; he was one of the most influential intellectuals for the twentieth century.

But today I find few entering divinity students that can spell his name, fewer still who have read anything of his, fewer yet that have benefited from his friendship. So I want you to begin to get acquainted with Søren Kierkegaard: a *Spy* who will push you into inward places of hiddenness you are reluctant to explore, a *Judge* who will indict your vagaries of life with inescapable and relentless precision and vivacity, but finally a *Friend* who might spiritually edify you on the multifaceted journey of *becoming a Christian.*

Kierkegaard was born in Copenhagen, Denmark, in 1813 and died in Copenhagen in 1855 at the age of forty-two. From 1843 till his death, he published thirty books and scores of articles in Danish. At his death, about eight more book manuscripts were discovered, including one on logic, one on a theory of communication, and one on revelation and authority, and over twenty big volumes of journals, diaries, and notes. George Brandes, a well known European cultural critic, has made the judgment that Kierkegaard did for the Danish language what Shakespeare did for the English language, and that had he been writing in English, German, or French, he would have been instantaneously famous in Europe as an author. As it was, outside Denmark, Kierkegaard would have to wait until the early twentieth century to be 'discovered.'

With uncanny prescience, Kierkegaard knew he would someday be famous but feared and loathed the prospect that he would fall into the hands of the professors, who would analyze and reduce his life and writings to a thumbnail sketch or footnote, or even to a voluminous narrative, but would never realize that the whole of his literature was directed even to the professor as an existing person who still had to exist somehow. He criticized professors, philosophers, and theologians unmercifully for building grand mansions of theory and thought only to live their actual, existing lives in the barnyard, feeding daily out of the pig trough. The point here is this: intellectuals are given to the pursuit and development of thought, concepts, and ideas, and they can easily fool themselves into supposing that if they have thought the thought they have also lived the thought. No, says Kierkegaard; to live the thought means to have one's living passions and decisions shaped by the thought. Intellectuals are inclined to forget the actual passions and concrete decisions that shape their daily living, and therefore are forgetful of their actual existing. Their theories cannot—of themselves—encompass and shape the theorist's existential reality without decision and persistence in passions.

It should take only a modest gift for irony to understand that it is not easy to be a professorial admirer and lover of Kierkegaard. But he never lets me forget that I am also "that individual"— that "reader"—for whom he writes in the interest of edifying me in how to live and how not to forget that the raw material of my life is there to receive some decisive form, that I can never forget that I must exist somehow in some way. He lovingly but insistently asks: "Are you a self, Joe, or are you a mere loose collection of grunts, hunches, aches and pains, rampant and tepid desires, desperate needs, fears and anxieties, a mere cloudy mirror-image of your time and culture, a perhaps clever and well educated individual in theory and argument who feasts on keeping the personal questions of existence up in the air for endless discussion, speculation, and postponement? Are you yet a self, Joe, who is ready to decide your existence and take on responsibility for how you live?" He asks with insistence: "You do understand, Joe, don't you, that thinking the thought that you are called to love the neighbor is not itself loving the neighbor?"

Kierkegaard can be an exacting and unyielding judge of those of us inclined to take some more time to consider the question of how we might exist, while all the time postponing becoming a self who is decisively bringing his or her existence under the governance of an overarching moral *telos*. That is the demanding part, and most of us—especially intellectually educated and gifted folk—flee from its urgent, practical implications.

Allow me now to sketch the briefest of historical notes about Kierkegaard. He was the youngest of seven surviving children born to Michael Pederson Kierkegaard and Ann Sørensdatter Lund. His father was fifty-six when Søren was born, and it was obvious to all in the family that little Søren was his father's favorite. A markedly melancholic person, Michael Kierkegaard was born in abject poverty on the Jutland in Denmark and spent his early childhood tending sheep. At age twelve he became an apprentice to his uncle in the hosiery business, and it was as a hosiery businessman that he made a fortune so substantial that he was able to retire at the age of forty. A close friend of the Bishop of Denmark, the father was well-read in philosophy and theology, though largely self-taught.

Kierkegaard recalled for us how his father used to hold his hand in the family living room, strolling around the room narrating for little Søren fascinating adventures of the imagination. But the father brooded over life and guilt, and especially over the crucifixion of Jesus, and was intent on impressing on little Søren the tragic grandeur of Christ's sacrificial death for humanity's sin. Kierkegaard later tells us that he never had a real childhood, that he went straight from the cradle to adulthood. It was this strangely tender but brooding old father who was to be a provocative foil for much of Kierkegaard's introspective life and literary productions.

In bodily form, Kierkegaard was small and a bit humped in the spine, and no doubt this created health difficulties that would result later in his early death. His voice was raspy and could crackle with wit and laughter and sarcasm. He went to college to study for the ministry, at his father's insistence. During his 'college' days he fell into a period of riotous living and dissipation and rebellion against his father's authority. He loved to drink and party, exercising all the time the rapier-like and lacerating tongue for which he was already then famous. Hans Christian Anderson, later to become heralded as a children's storywriter, was one of the crowd that caroused with Kierkegaard. Kierkegaard's father had to pay off a debt incurred by lavish spending in the amount of today's value about three thousand dollars. Kierkegaard apparently had cultivated a taste for fine wines, rare brandies, and foppish, *avant garde* clothes. He thought he had perhaps outgrown Christian faith.

A touching story survives of these times. Paul Møller, a professor of philosophy important to Kierkegaard, is reported to have said to him after a ribald party in which Kierkegaard had dominated at his wittiest best: "You are so polemical through and through that it is utterly terrible." That remark got Kierkegaard's attention, provoked a period of profound self-examination, and enabled him to muster sufficient seriousness to proceed on to the completion of his doctoral dissertation on *The Concept of Irony in Socrates*. Møller was later to say on his deathbed: "Tell little Kierkegaard not to try to accomplish everything."

After the death of his father in 1838, Kierkegaard became engaged in 1840 to Regine Olsen, a seventeen-year-old beauty. She was to remain a muse to his imagination and thought for the rest of his life. He fell hopelessly in love with her. But after the engagement was announced, he began to query himself thus: "I have no doubt that I love Regine, but what is marriage morally understood, and am I fit for it?" After agonizing self-analysis and a deep probing of the meaning of marriage, including his own reckoning with the possibility of a vocation for himself as a religious author, Kierkegaard concluded that he could not marry Regine. I think he understood that marriage required an openness and forthcomingness between the spouses, presupposing that each could handle the other's openness; it haunted him whether he could be so open to Regine and whether, if he could, she had the seriousness necessary even to understand him and his religious calling as an author. Yet he never forgot that he did love Regine. Need I indicate here that much ink has been spilled by the professorial class explaining the 'real meaning' of Kierkegaard's decision not to marry Regine?

Having decided against marrying Regine, Kierkegaard moved to launch a career as an author who was no more than a mere *poet without authority*. As a poet, he saw himself attacking the grand illusion of his church and culture: namely, that we all are already Christians. The grand truth for Kierkegaard was that his culture had in fact forgotten what was truly involved in becoming and being a Christian and having one's life shaped by the decisive Christian existential categories of living.

This illusion expressed itself in Christian discourse being emptied of its decisive meanings by two astonishing historical developments. On the one hand, there were the people of town and market who were no longer shaped in their actual lives by having a crucified and gracious savior. On the other hand, there were the intellectuals among them who were rapidly reinterpreting Christian faith into concepts that omitted having a crucified savior and that were depleting Christian faith of its radical existential character. These intellectual reinterpreters of Christianity were busy translating the faith into concepts a bit more acceptable to the modern, enlightened age. They were "going further" than the original terms of simple faith, which, after all, is content with merely "edifying." The paradoxical and offensive character of *needing a savior* was being quietly edited out of Christian theology.

How then to dismantle and subvert the grand illusion by the folk and the intellectuals that they are already Christians—perhaps even scholarly theologians—when their lives are deeply antithetical to Christian faithfulness? He was convinced that people do not respond well when their illusions are attacked directly or head on, for that makes them defensive and stubborn, only further entrenching the illusion. No, the attack must be "indirect," to *wound from behind*, to create a literature in which persons might come to see themselves truly and honestly for the first time. As Holmer puts it, Kierkegaard was aiming to provide a map of human subjectivity, showing the characters of the various forms of passions and decisions in which persons exist.

Hence, as a *corrective* to his church and culture, Kierkegaard developed a two-pronged literature. On the one hand, he composed a series of works by pseudonymous authors in which he simply and artfully depicted persons in their different ways of existing. On the other hand, he was writing in his own name for the "individual who was his reader," offering edifying discourses of spiritual discernment and encouragement, designed to lead the reader into a deeper relationship with God. His enormous literary production was moving down these two tracks simultaneously.

Incidentally, I should note that Kierkegaard regarded his literature as his own education in the faith. As his journals reveal, Kierkegaard subjected himself to continuous and excruciating introspection, examining and re-examining his own motives in every major decision. Obviously, it was in these depths of his own soul that Kierkegaard found the raw material for his profound analyses of the many shapes of the human soul—its attractions to pleasure, its proneness to dread and despair, its deep reluctance to be an accountable self, and its ambivalence toward a gracious savior who refuses to become subservient to culture's principles of explanation and value.

In February 1843, Kierkegaard published *Either/Or*, a large two-volume work, and thus began his authorship with the *aim of reintroducing to Christendom what it means to become a Christian*, but now by indirection and edifying discourses. From this date until February 1846, Kierkegaard published fourteen works that must comprise one of the most prodigious and profound literary explosions in the western world. Let us briefly review this literature.

Either/Or was pseudonymously published under the name of Victor Eremita in two large volumes: one narrating the personality of an aesthetic young man given to grand designs of sexual seduction and sophisticated cultivations of pleasure, and one narrating the personality of an older man, a civil judge given to expressive praise of and wise counsel about the moral life. The either/or is between the *aesthetic life*—preoccupied as it is with pleasure and the avoidance of pain—and the *moral life*—preoccupied as it is with bringing the whole of one's life under a moral ideality. Victor Eremita does not recommend one or the other, but lets his personae stand entertainingly before the reader, indirectly posing the question: "How then do you live, dear reader?"

Then in October came two extraordinary pieces: *Repetition* under the pseudonym Constantine Constantius, and *Fear and Trembling* under the striking pseudonym Johannes de Silentio. Consider *Fear and Trembling*: in an intellectual culture given to supposing that real thinking requires one to go further than mere faith and to grasp philosophically what is only pictorially represented in simple faith, Kierkegaard examines the situation of Abraham, referred to in the New Testament as the father of faith. Is this Abraham, proceeding up the mount to sacrifice his beloved son Isaac, the one who fears the Lord above all things? In trying to fathom what faith is, Kierkegaard imaginatively examines Abraham's fear and trembling in all its terrible complexity. What does it mean to have an absolute obligation to God? Is this faith of Abraham something that philosophers in their superior knowledge can go beyond; or is it something unfathomable and about which the philosophers hardly have any existential inkling of what it means to be gripped by that fear before the Lord and the Lord's commands? These are questions we are indirectly invited to ask.

In June of the next year, he published two pieces of singular conceptual exactitude: *Philosophical Fragments* by Johannes Climacus and *The Concept of Anxiety* (or, Dread) by Vigilius Haufniensis. *Fragments* examines in unremitting precision the question of whether it is possible to base one's eternal happiness on a relationship to a savior who existed at a point in time. Is it too slight a thing to say that Kierkegaard posed the question that stalks the halls of contemporary discussion even today? Is it too much to conclude that Kierkegaard forever discriminates between those christologies for whom Jesus is a mere Socratic occasion for the movement of faith and those christologies for whom Jesus is himself the very condition of faith and salvation? *The Concept of Anxiety* has this subtitle: *A Simple Psychologically Orienting Deliberation on the Dogmatic Issue of Hereditary (Original) Sin.* Here the concept of anxiety was introduced into the theological discourse of the church.

In April 1845, a huge volume entitled *Stages on Life's Way* by Hilarius Bogbinder was published, developing further the depiction of stages in *Either/ Or* between the aesthetic and moral stages, now going on to the religious stage. In early 1846, the monumental *Concluding Unscientific Postscript to Philosophical Fragments*, again by Johannes Climacus, asked the penetrating question: how must the self be constituted so that the question of basing one's eternal happiness on a relationship to a historical savior can be seriously considered? Apparently, not everyone is sufficiently a self that they can ask the central question of faith in Jesus Christ with real seriousness.

While publishing these pseudonymous works, Kierkegaard was also regularly publishing eighteen edifying discourses for his reader who is serious about how it is to be related to God.

Our time is short. Let me be brief. Personally exhausted by this prolific undertaking, Kierkegaard took some time off from writing and considered entering the ministry. But he decided against that for complex reasons, and found his own voice in further publications. Forthcoming in the next few years were distinctly Christian books: *The Works of Love, Christian Discourses, Two Minor Ethical Religious Treatises, The Sickness unto Death, Practice in Christianity, For Self-Examination*, and *Judge for Yourselves*.

Already critical of the established Lutheran church of Denmark in the 1850s, after the death of his father's friend, Bishop Mynster,

Kierkegaard began his open and direct pamphleteering critique of the institutional church. This is a bitter attack on the public, state-sponsored, established church—the *attack on Christendom*. Kierkegaard declared that the established church was in fact not the church of Jesus Christ as we see it in the New Testament. He refused to participate in Holy Communion and urged others to abstain as well, contending that this established institution had no real theological authority. The idea that such an institution could be so thoroughly corrupt and still be the Body of Christ was an anathema to Kierkegaard. Simply put, whatever else the established church might be, it was not the church of Jesus Christ.

In October 1855, in the midst of this vicious controversy in which he was being stringently criticized by all the established personages and religious authorities, little Kierkegaard—always sickly—collapsed on the street. He was taken to the hospital, where he died a few days later at the age of forty-two. Ridiculed and humiliated in his own time by his own contemporaries, who despised his literary corrective to the illusions of their age, Kierkegaard has found friends in the twentieth century. He may not have gotten everything right in his literature, but he is sufficiently imposing as an intellect that if he thought something, it must be worth our serious consideration. I invite you to become more familiar with this brilliant author, who will spy out our deepest illusions, who will judge us harshly into decision, and who will befriend us on the arduous journey of becoming a human being and maybe even becoming a Christian.

(Bibliographic notes: All the works mentioned in this chapter have been translated by Howard V. Hong and Edna H. Hong in the twenty-six volume edition, *Kierkegaard's Writings*, published by Princeton University Press. Indiana University Press, under the editorship and translation of Howard V. Hong and Edna M. Hong, has published six volumes of *Søren Kierkegaard's Journals and Papers*. Paul L. Holmer never did write that definitive book on Kierkegaard that so many of us had anticipated, but his *The Grammar of Faith* (New York: Harper & Row, 1978) reveals the influence of Kierkegaard on Holmer's own theologizing. Yet, Holmer's influence can be seen in *Essays on Kierkegaard and Wittgenstein: On Understanding the Self*, eds. Richard H. Bell and Ronald E. Hustwit, (Wooster, Ohio: The College of Wooster Press, 1978) and *The Grammar of the Heart: Thinking with Kierkegaard and Wittgenstein*, ed. Richard H. Bell (San Francisco: Harper & Row, 1988). There are too many 'lives' of Kierkegaard to mention. *The Cambridge Companion to Kierkegaard*, eds. Alastair Hannay and Gordon D. Marino (Cambridge: Cambridge University Press, 1998) is a nice recent collection of essays on Kierkegaard.)

Part Three

Church Discourses and Practices in Tumultuous Times

12

Is Jesus Lord in Time of War?

or

What Does it Mean to Say 'Jesus is Lord' in Time of War?

This essay was prepared for a workshop of this title given at The Leadership Training School of the Oklahoma Region of the Christian Church (Disciples of Christ) in Oklahoma on January 31, 2004.

Fellow members of the Christian Church (Disciples of Christ) in Oklahoma, at the beginning of our discussion of this topic, I want to make a couple of points about our shared tradition.

First, I would have you recall the question that was put to you at the time of your baptism. With a few variations, I suspect what you were asked is similar to this question put to me: "Do you believe that Jesus is the Christ, the Son of the living God, and do you accept him as your personal Savior and Lord?"

Second, I would remind you of the oft-repeated phrase in our tradition of "No creed but Christ."

In the autumn of a lifetime of living in Disciples churches and teaching in two Disciples seminaries and a Disciples university, I have come to the reluctant and painful conclusion that these phrases are by and large empty of *communal content*. Both the baptismal question and "no creed but Christ" have been shibboleths—passwords—for being a member of the Disciples tradition, but we dared not venture to give either shibboleth the content that would make it binding and meaningful. Both locutions are seemingly Christ-centered, but it appears that our tradition has been persistently adamant in refusing to give any further communal definition to what it means to say 'Jesus is Lord' and 'Jesus is the center of our faith.' *We are christocentric—Christ-centered—in appearance but not in substance or in actual practice.*

Let me make some expansions on these two locutions about Jesus being Lord. Taking first the baptismal question, it is meet and right to ask the baptizee whether she will accept Jesus as her personal Savior and Lord. But this is almost meaningless without some grounding in Jesus being in actuality Savior and Lord, whether or not the baptizee really does accept Jesus as *her* Savior and Lord. Surely we must also be claiming that Jesus is Savior and Lord not just insofar as the baptizee accepts him as her Savior and Lord but in such a way that he is of the reality of God. Calling Jesus Lord was a great transformation of concepts for Jews for whom 'Lord' named only Yahweh, the God of Israel. But *if Jesus is Lord, then, he is of the very reality of the God of Israel.* Further, if he is Lord indeed, then he is Lord over all the creation and of all human history. Simply put, if Jesus is Lord, then his followers are to discern in him the character of that power that reigns over all things as the Alpha and the Omega of the whole creation. Hence, how he lived his life, how he taught about God and human life, how he was crucified by the powers of the world, and how he was raised from the dead all become pertinent to how we Christians understand God and ourselves and how we are to live, even in times of war.

Because we Disciples have refused to affirm together in a public confession of faith the things I have just said, it is questionable whether we have ever had a *common understanding* of who Jesus is and why we might call him Lord and Savior.

Likewise, take the statement "No creed but Christ." It seems to be telling us that creeds—as those confessions of faith that intend to state what is central to Christian faith—are all negligible compared to Christ.

But who is this Christ anyhow? Are there some *teachings* about this Christ that are central to Christian faith and the church? Or, is it all up for grabs, left to each person and each pastor to interpret who Christ is according to his own predilections? I think, in fact, our tradition has been ruled by no common confession as to who Christ is and why he is significant. But we have been ruled by a veritable chaos of individual creeds that each local pastor might lay on the congregation. Put simply, if there are no firm and truthful teachings about who Jesus is as Lord and Savior and it is all left up to the individual believer to determine for herself what any of this might mean, then it is utterly opaque who Jesus is, and the center of our faith is not Jesus but whatever we *prefer* to say about him. This leaves us basically deciding theology and ethics by our own individual lights. The real *dogma* at the center of our church's discourses and actual practices is that it is left to each individual to decide what is credible. *Beyond that dogma we have no common mind, no common Gospel, no common understanding of who God is.*

Let me clarify my concern about a common faith with some definiteness of meaning as central to the discourses and practices of the church. Let us admit that in the actual life of any particular person it is always the case that she has to construe for herself what it means to be a disciple of Jesus. But that is not to say that there should be no common teachings or doctrines about Jesus as Lord and Savior that comprise the *core of the faith of the church* and in relation to which any particular member of the church must make up her own mind and live her life. Hence, the very integrity of the church, as called into being by the Gospel of Jesus Christ, depends on having a *common articulable and public faith* that shapes the beliefs and actions of the living faith of the individuals who participate in the church's life.

In my judgment, our steadfast refusal to put any common and shared conceptual meat on the mantra of "Jesus is the Christ, the Son of God and Savior and Lord," is at the heart of the widespread disarray and even discouragement in our tradition today. Our discourses and therefore also our practices in regard to Jesus are in chaotic discord. This leaves us vulnerable to having the center of our faith occupied by *idols* of the moment, whether those idols are the politics of the state or the fear of enemies far and wide. When the discourses and practices of the church are in disarray, then we can also conclude that the way its members construe themselves, construe Jesus, and construe the world may be in stark contrast to how the NT and earlier traditions have construed Jesus and the reality of God and the destiny of the world.

If it were the case that our tradition understood in common language that Jesus is Savior of the world and the Lord who truly reigns over all creation and the destiny of the world, then you would think that *the character of Jesus' life, his pattern of acting and teaching concerning the Kingdom of God, his crucifixion, and his resurrection would affect how Christians would construe discipleship to Jesus, construe war and violence, and how they would act in time of war.*

Yet here we confront one of the strangest reversals of meaning taking place among Christians in the United States and among Christians in many of the nation-states that have sprung into existence in the last two centuries. All of these nation-states are founded in and sustained by violence. Their borders drip with wars of conquest and wars of self-defense. The reversal is that the Christians in these states regularly go to war as though they are in utter denial or ignorance of how Jesus is relevant to their war-making. Jesus may be a comfort to the soldier and those left at home, but that Jesus' life, death, and resurrection have some bearing on how Christians should construe the justification of going to war seems utterly denied. When we want to justify our wars, Christians here and abroad repeatedly appeal to some other lord or principle or necessity that justifies fighting war.

So, if we ask now whether Jesus being Lord has anything to do with the war against terrorism, and, as our president would have us believe as well, has something to do with going to war in Iraq, we seem tongue-tied. Why is this? I suggest to you it is because our Jesus—the one we have left up to each individual to construe for herself—is so thin and threadbare in ethics and theology that we can easily put him on the shelf and do our warring on the grounds of other lords and principalities and powers.

So let us look again at *what it might mean to say Jesus is Lord in time of war.* Surely even a cursory look at the New Testament would reveal that Jesus consistently taught that we were to love others and seek their good, even to the point of self-denial. His followers referred to themselves as slaves and servants, and they did not mean that they supported the social practice of chattel slavery but that they were to serve others as Jesus did precisely because he is the Lord who truly reigns over life and death. Jesus spoke of loving strangers and enemies, and we are not to suppose he had in mind a mere strong inward affection about enemies. His disciples were to turn the other cheek, go the second mile, refuse to return evil for evil, give up the inclination toward revenge, and seek peace nonviolently in the whole of their lives. Are these not *cross-bearing acts* fitting for those who follow the cross-bearing Jesus?

But the practical political codes of the nations of the world in Jesus' time and in ours are that any nation has the moral right to defend itself against enemies and go to war when its leaders judge it necessary. That has usually been interpreted as going to war as a *last resort*, but we now have the aura of moral legitimacy being cast over the belief and practice that a nation can go to war to *preempt* what it judges an enemy might do. Further, according to these codes some lives are justifiably expendable, both ours and the enemy's. Whence cometh this logic, this discourse, and this practice into the discourses and practices of the church? It seems to me particularly to be the case in the time of this war against terrorism that Christians should wonder whether we have suddenly permitted another lord—the nation-state and its leaders—to determine how we are to live, how we are to construe enemies, how we are justified morally in doing what we do.

So, let us admit, all Christians in the United States are also citizens of the U.S. And let us admit that most of us have deep regard for our nation, however critical of it we may be from time to time. Hence, we seem to be citizens both of the nation-state and of the church. *The nation-state is called into being and maintained by acts of violence; the church is called into existence by Jesus Christ to live in conformity to Jesus and his coming Kingdom.* Why is it that our citizenship in the church and the Kingdom are not the decisive determinants of how we live our lives? Is it not true, then, that when we make the state the formative power in how we understand ourselves and our enemies, we also thereby make the state into an idol—a surrogate god that we revere, adore, and obey and in which we trust to protect us and give us meaning?

Let me admit that I have many reservations about going to war against Iraq that I might offer simply as a citizen concerned about the governance of this country. But what truly overwhelms me is how this going to war corrupts the understanding and the practices of the Christians who support going to war. How does this happen?

I am really interested in, not so much what it means to be a citizen of the U.S. in time of war, but *what it means to be Disciples of Christ in time of war*. My suspicion is that we Disciples—having spent generations fleeing from the central questions of who Jesus is and what it means to call him Savior and Lord—simply have no means to fend off the overwhelming power of the state when it identifies enemies, arms itself for war, and then goes to war. *Our language in the church is already so wishy-washy about Jesus Christ that we do not know how in crisis times to actually be the church of Jesus Christ.* And when we are unclear and confused, then what the New Testament refers to as the principalities and powers of the world in our land will tell us who really is lord over history, and his name is Legion, and his armies are dominating and to be feared by all the peoples of the world.

The practical reality seems to be that the real lord for Christians, time and time again, is the politics of the nation-state and the maintenance of its dominating power and supremacy in relation to other states and over the lives of its own citizens. At the core of its power is the coercive use of violence and the credible willingness to use superior violence to preserve the state's power and supremacy. It is upon the state that we rely for security and the preservation of our preferred styles of life. The discourses and practices of patriotism, with its overweening passion, shape us in times of crisis much more radically than the discourses and practices of a church called into existence by Jesus Christ.

Surely these words should sound a theological alarm for the church as it struggles to be the church of Jesus Christ in times of war and terror.

13

What Sort of People Dare to Ordain for Ministry in These Tumultuous Times?

2 Corinthians 5:14-21

This ordination sermon was preached on July 20, 2003, in Tuxedo Park Baptist Church in Indianapolis, Indiana.

It is an enormous pleasure and honor to be here today to participate in the ordination of Janet to the ministry of the church of Jesus Christ. Janet has extraordinary gifts to bring to her ministry, and this should be an occasion full of celebration and much promise. It is not only the promise she herself has for ministry, but the promises we will ourselves make today to support and nurture her in her ministry.

Ordaining someone for the ministry of the church is an earnest exercise in *church politics*, and it should be done with great seriousness and with resounding joy. But our joy might be too hollow if we neglect to consider the truly astounding act we are performing in daring to ordain someone in these perilous and challenging times for the church. Properly performed, this ordination—done in and by the church before the world—should be a defiant and defining act that we intend to be the church of Jesus Christ

171

and that we refuse to merely be a miscellaneous collection of Americans who also, sometimes, gather together for sentimental gestures of hymn singing, Bible reading, and self-help homilies.

I want to invite us to remember anew what it is to be the church of Jesus Christ, with helpful reminders from the Apostle Paul writing to the church at Corinth.

Having written that "we are convinced that one has died for all; therefore all have died. And he died for all, so that those who live might live no longer for themselves, but for him who died and was raised for them . . . ," Paul goes on to say that "from now on, therefore, we regard no one from a *human point of view.*"

Christians and the church are the sort of folk who know themselves as the beneficiaries of Christ's living and dying and being raised and who, therefore, know themselves as *in Christ*. And they are the sort of folk who now regard other folk from the point of view of Christ, which means they regard others as *in Christ* as well. Or to put it succinctly: the church is the sort of community that regards all other people from the point of view of their being in Christ. Because of Jesus, Christians construe the world differently from the many human points of view that shape human identity and living.

We can make no progress toward the renewing of the church or revitalizing the church if we do not digest what Paul is saying to us. Without Paul's guidance about what point of view the church has, we the church, in our desperation to fill our pews and pay our bills, might succumb to points of view that are quite antithetical to that view rooted in Jesus Christ.

What are these all too human points of views that, according to Paul, misconstrue the truth about human life and God? Of course, these views are many and are as old as human kind. We can minimally say that for Paul the *human points of view* are simply those communal points of view by virtue of which persons have an identity and a way of living and of construing a world. These points of view enthrall folk and help them to construe who they are and who the others are who are not like them and are not part of their community.

This ordination service is taking place in an American Baptist Church in Indianapolis, Indiana, in that nation that calls itself the United States of America. We cannot escape doing what we are doing in just this social environment. But what points of view are deep within us precisely because we are Americans living in Indiana and variously related to the Baptist traditions?

Well let us look at the points of view that stalk our hearts and experiences these days. We have the *point of view of a people who are at war*, in which the war itself has been promoted as a just war of self-defense and liberation. We have been attacked by folk who identify themselves as our enemies, and we so identify them as well, which means that our fear of these enemies drives us to defend ourselves with great ferocity of force. Whatever may be the truth about the motivations that have led our leaders to push into the further Iraqi war, we seem to be the sort of people for whom going to war is viewed as a justifiable and necessary action, however reluctantly we might perform the action from time to time.

From this point of view, our soldiers—the ones who are killing and being killed and who have come from all walks of American life—are declared to be 'fighting for our freedom' and to be 'sacrificing themselves for us.' This is how we construe going to war in general and going to this particular war—it's a point of view, an all too human point of view.

Looking further we see that it is a point of view that teaches us that there are some human beings we can identify as *enemies* and they are appropriate targets of killing. Their lives are forfeitable and expendable. And, it seems, our soldiers' lives are forfeitable and expendable in 'defending our freedom.' O yes, from this point of view, it is also the case that killing some noncombatants, however regrettable, is unavoidable.

Now here is a point of view about ourselves, about other human beings, and about our wars that is deep and identifiable; and it is present among us as we meet today. If it is any comfort to us, it is also a point of view similarly present in Russia, in Israel, in Iran, in Germany, in France, in Egypt, and in almost all other nations of the world. It is deeply human, and it shapes how we construe the world and others and, therefore, how we live. It is like an *iron mask* we think is necessary for us to wear and to bear.

This point of view is in the church right now, right here in Indianapolis, even among Baptists and other Christians; and we might even say it is so powerful and dominating that it makes it difficult to have and live a different point of view.

I propose to you that we have no theologically justifiable business engaging in this ordination to the ministry of the church if we are no more than a people shaped and formed by this human point of view. If we are merely a people shaped basically by an American point of view, we simply are not the sort of people Paul is talking about when he talks about seeing all others from that point of view that is rooted in Christ. *People rooted in Christ construe the apparent enemies as those for whom Christ lived and died and for whom he was raised.*

Is it really possible to be the sort of people who see things through the lens of Christ? Is it really possible to be that sort of people who dare, in the face of war and declared enemies, to ordain folk to give leadership in proclaiming and living that radically new point of view of being in Christ?

We must seriously ask these questions of ourselves or we will be forever a church dominated by its surrounding culture in ways similar to the way the church has allowed itself to be dominated by other national cultures. Instead of proclaiming Christ as the Lord of history, we will pray that our nation might be the lord who will protect us from harm and who will lord it over others, of course, in the good cause of something called 'peace.' We will, then, accept that war is a moral necessity in a world full of sin, and we will be ready to go to war when our leaders tell us it is time to go, as in Vietnam, as in Panama, as in the Gulf War, as in the Iraqi War, and as in this haunting, elusive, but all-encompassing War on Terror. *We will, then, be a people who go to war when the leaders of our nation state say we should.*

But we do think we are a people created by Jesus Christ, and that very self-designated fact about our language and Scriptures is an awesome challenge to our inclinations to adopt and hold other human points of views.

So, given Jesus Christ, eternal Son of God, Lord of all time and history, the one who was reconciling the world to God, yet the one crucified as a criminal and enemy of the state, and the one raised from the dead, the one who is the grace of forgiven life for us—*given this Jesus*, how are we called to live and to view other persons?

Paul is ahead of us. He says we are to live as *ambassadors of reconciliation*, no longer regarding anyone from an all too human point of view and certainly not counting their sins against them. Rather than being warriors of an angry god out to slay the evildoers, we are to be the reconcilers of a world loved by God in Jesus Christ. For the sake of that reconciliation, we Christians ought to be ready to die, to be ridiculed as weak and passive and as those unwilling to kill others. The church itself ought to be a witness to an *alternative way of living and construing others.*

Dear friends in Christ, I am not inventing just another political ideology either from the left or the right on the national political spectrum. I am just reading and reflecting on what the Apostle Paul said in writings the church regards as Holy Scripture. Paul seems to be telling us that we the church—all of us together, not just some who are specially designated or called—have the ministry of reconciliation as our defining mission. Being reconcilers of humans—who are full of fear, conflict, and enmity— is an alternative way of living in the world.

In performing this ministry we might also call special others to give leadership in guiding us in being a reconciling and peaceable people who vividly know and live as though nothing can separate us from the love of God in Christ Jesus.

In this ministry of reconciliation, we the church will be the sort of people who construe the world differently from many others. We will construe the least of these in the world as the ones who need our extended and nonviolent help. We will see the enemies that seem bent on doing us harm as the ones to be reconciled by new and resourceful means of witness. We will refuse to construe some of the others in the world, however horrific might be their sins and evil deeds, as the ones who must be slaughtered, whether in jails or on fields of battle.

This is an awesome task, and without continuous prayer, earnest conversation, strenuous love among us, and the guidance of the Spirit, it is impossible. But it is possible given who God in Christ is. *It is not true that the Christ way of life is an impossible ideal,* which the real world and the church must reject because of the evil and sin in the world.

We are simply being asked to be witnesses in this troubled era that there is an alternative way of living. We are being called to be the Body of Christ in the world and for the world and to be that with faithfulness. In living and witnessing in these ways, we are empowered to have a joy and hope in our work that is not rooted in that human point of view of enemies and wars, of conquest, victory, and defeat.

From the point of view of our being in Christ, we, the church of Jesus Christ, now *dare to ordain* one of our own to lead us, to inspire us, to love us into constancy of faith, and to pray steadfastly for us as we intend to be the Body of Christ in the world.

I want to confess to you this afternoon that it is a special blessing from the Spirit of God that Janet has been raised up among us as one strongly called to leadership. She has been a special blessing to me as one graced to have her as student colleague, as loyal friend, and as fellow disciple of Jesus.

We must not, however, ask of her that she be less than a reconciler in and for the Body of Christ. We must not cajole her into adopting those human points of views that bring enmity and strife and partisan degradation of others. We must not pin her into leading what is no more than a gathering of Americans, wanting to do a little good here and there, keep our bills paid, and endure a few years by not being too visible and too vulnerable for the Gospel.

We may, however, pray for her and for the church. We may love her with a passion commensurate with her passion for the Gospel and the church's mission. We may cajole her a bit when she loses perspective and becomes discouraged. We may open our arms to supporting her family that will surely experience her absence more than they would prefer. We may pray for her family that her ministry may be a blessing to them as well.

If we do truly intend these beliefs and practices, then let us be the church of Jesus Christ and ordain this beloved woman to the ministry of reconciliation, in which—for her and for us—whether we live or whether we die, we are the Lord's.

All this, dear friends in Christ, I have dared to preach in the name of the Father, the Son, and the Holy Spirit, one God, Mother of us all. Amen.

14

Teaching Sound Doctrine and Itching Ears

2 Timothy 4:1-5

An ordination sermon preached in Allisonville Christian Church in Indianapolis, Indiana, on January 14, 2001.

Dear friends and family of Susan, it is a pleasure to be here for her ordination into the ministerial leadership of the church. It has been my delight to have had Susan as a student in several theology and ethics classes at Christian Theological Seminary and even as my teaching assistant in two other courses. I can testify before you that she is an exceptional student and an earnest person of faith. She is well prepared to receive the awesome ordination we the church are intent on conferring today and to assume the responsibilities of leadership that such ordination implies. You folk here at the Allisonville Christian Church have been especially privileged to benefit from her student ministry and to observe with tender and sweet joy the many gifts she has displayed among you. I am sure all of us here today are confident of her promise for ministry, and this is properly a grand occasion not only for her but also for us the church.

But even in our joy and delight, it is well that we understand that this *act of ordination is a grave and serious act of the church*: an act that reminds

177

us of our fundamental calling as the church of Jesus Christ and an act that is profoundly defiant of the inclinations and ruling powers of our contemporary social world in North America. We are not ordaining her to run for the school board, to serve on the Mayor's commission, to be pleasing to the ruling powers in this city or in another town or in this nation. We are not asking her to be all things to all people, though she will be tempted by our desires to be what we variously want her to be.

Rather, we are ordaining her to give leadership to the church in a time in which the many churches around us and in our Disciples tradition seem not only to be in numerical decline, but to be dramatically uncertain about their own basic calling in Christian life and witness. We are ordaining her for leadership to help us understand more clearly and profoundly— day in and day out—just who we are before God and just who that God is and what we are to become. Were she to fudge or burke or shirk in that task of leading us, she will have forfeited the good faith authority of this very ordination.

What then are we to make of her ministerial calling and tasks today? This is indeed a complex and many-sided question. But let us seek the guidance of the Scripture read for today from 2 Tim 4:1-5. We are led to believe that an elderly Paul is writing to Timothy, foremost among Paul's protégés in ministry, to give advice about the tasks and temptations of ministerial leadership, of engaging in the *diakonia* of the church.

Much of what he says in this epistle, and in this particular passage, pivots around the conviction that the church has its most basic identity in being called by the Gospel of Jesus Christ to witness in word and deed to the living triune God for the benefit of the world. Witnessing to God is the heart of being the church. And this witnessing is in words and deeds, in discourses and practices; and where this witnessing is lacking, there the people of the church are smothering and neglecting their own identity and calling.

Now, if witnessing is essential to the church, then that witnessing must have some distinctive *content* that keeps it focused, faithful, and true. As Paul says, "in view of Christ Jesus and his appearing and his kingdom, I solemnly urge you to proclaim the message." There is a message, a Gospel, that is central to the church's witness, and according to Paul that message is wrapped up in the life, death, and resurrection of Jesus of

Nazareth. Take Jesus away or neglect his centrality, and the witness to God goes astray.

The Greek word Paul uses here for "message" is *logos*, a term so rich in connotations that we are still trying to unpack how the New Testament writers use it. But clearly it is related to what Paul later in this passage calls "sound doctrine" (or if we stumble over the term 'doctrine', we can try 'sound teaching'). The content of Christian witness has some characteristic *teachings* about God, about Jesus, about human beings, and what they are to become in the light of the Gospel. Hence, if sound teachings are important, it seems clear, according to Paul, that there can also be unsound teachings or even confusion in the church about what the teachings are.

It is a further implication of Paul's point about the message that it is not something the people of the world already possess. It is not a knowledge or teaching that they inherently or innately already have. They need to receive the teaching, to learn it, to have their lives shaped by it. Paul does not seem to be asking folk to look within themselves to discover a gospel already hiddenly evident there. To proclaim the Gospel means to give people some knowledge, some understanding, some teaching that they do not already have, and that knowledge is focused around the God of Israel and Jesus Christ.

For our purposes today, we need to understand that for Paul there is no distinction between being a teacher of the faith and being a preacher of the faith. Proclaiming the Gospel means teaching the faith. It does not mean captivating people with one's attractive personality. It does not mean being well-liked by all, though that might be desirable. So let us acknowledge that Paul is saying to us today that *teaching the faith*—which means making sound doctrine accessible and intelligible and vivid to folk—is central to the sort of leadership to which we are ordaining Susan.

But Paul is also advising Timothy about the situation in the church and in the world of his time. I wonder if that might apply to us today as well. Let us listen to Paul: "the time is coming when people will not put up with sound doctrine, but having itching ears, they will accumulate for themselves teachers to suit their own desires, and will turn away from listening to the truth and wander away to myths." These are indeed chilling words. For the sake of Susan's ordination and her understanding of her calling and for our own sake as the church of Jesus Christ, let us explore what Paul is saying.

179

Apparently Paul thinks sound doctrine is in for a hard time in which people—and here we must assume he means people both within and beyond the church—will not put up with sound doctrine. Will not put up with? Other translations have it as "will not tolerate," "will not stand," and "will not accept" sound doctrine or sound teaching. How does it, then, happen that people become so intolerant of such Gospel teaching? In pithy and salty metaphoric language, Paul says this happens because people have "itching ears"! What does it mean to have itching ears? And why do the ears of some folk itch? What sort of scratching of itching ears leads people astray?

If we follow along with Paul, people's ears become itchy when they hear teachings that do not fit their desires. Surely all of us know about ourselves that we are a veritable cauldron of desires, and Paul thinks that maybe we get itchy ears and do not want to hear the Gospel teachings when our desires are not flattered by what the Gospel commends and commands. Now we understand that to have itchy ears is to want to hear something that suits us and our given and restless desires.

So what are people inclined to do who have itchy ears? They scratch their ears by "accumulating teachers" that will suit them and satisfy their desires. They reject the sound doctrine that is intended to build them up in the faith and nurture them in the truth. And they look endlessly for those teachers that will flatter their already existing desires, passions, and inclinations. Other translators say itchy-eared folk look for those who will "tickle their fancy," or who will teach "according to their own tastes." Would this be a fair way of putting Paul's point? *Itchy-eared people are consumers looking desperately for that teacher and those teachings that will give them a gospel on their own terms, on the terms of their own raw desires, their own tastes, their own fancy, their own preferences.*

We can pause now and listen to those voices in our minds saying that this sound doctrine idea is too elusive and dangerous. Haven't there been some doctrines in the church's past that have been harmful to folk and even demonic? Let us forget about doctrines and simply live according to love and justice. So some will say. But are there teachings about what love and justice are and does the whole world agree with those teachings? It is hard to escape teachings of some sort, and it is a *real illusion in the church to suppose that we can get along without doctrines and teachings.*

Of course, we Disciples are leery of doctrines and definite teachings. They divide people, we say. I have even heard some Disciples say, "we have no creed but Christ," and then they whisper that it really does not matter what you believe about Christ. It is like what the beloved Dwight Eisenhower said: "I think everyone should have faith, and I do not care faith in what." Such language would appear to concede the world to folk with itching ears: believe whatever suits your fancy.

I know it must be a comfort to Susan to realize that she will not have to deal with such itchy-eared people in her ministry as teacher. Who in church and world today is stalked by these itching ears, and who flits about in a desperate search to find some teaching that will justify their way of life and assuage their haunting guilt and nervous grasping for self-esteem? Surely itching ears do not want to hear of a Jewish Savior who died on a brutal cross for the sins of the whole world and who gives life free from the clutches of selfishness and self-absorption and who calls folk to live in love at the side of the least of these in the world.

But for the sake of a shorter sermon and for learning some more from Paul, let us imagine that S might indeed be cast as a teacher in a situation strikingly similar to what Paul has described. What would it mean for her to be *a teacher of the faith*?

Having affirmed the overarching task of proclaiming the message, Paul counsels Susan to be persistent. He could also have said, "be constant and not fickle" or "be not daunted by itching ears!" She is to persist in faithfulness to a Gospel that is wonderful good news for those who have ears to hear, but that good news does not sanction our desires in their messy randomness and givenness. And, of course, she could not persist in her teaching without constant prayer, seeking the guidance and upbuilding of the Holy Spirit. We are ordaining Susan to persist in teaching the faith and being accountable to the Gospel of Jesus Christ.

Let us herein grant what seems implicit in Paul's words: discerning sound doctrine is not an easy task. It is indeed arduous work to discern and teach those teachings that are essential to the Gospel. But Susan is to persist in the task of discerning the Gospel message and of teaching the Gospel.

Paul also wants Susan, as such a teacher of the Gospel, to perform skillfully some recognizable teaching practices. She should try to persuade, to address real questions with convincing responses, even to advance arguments, though perhaps knowing full well that few people will give up their itching ears because of good arguments. In short, Paul wants Susan to know her way around in the teachings of the faith, to know how to articulate those teachings in a faithful and fetching way, to show how the teachings shape life and give hope for the future. She is to help folk understand who God is and what they are to become before God. Susan is to be a practitioner of discerning the true from the false, the sound from the unsound, the authentic from the counterfeit, the permanent from the passing whim.

In the midst of such teaching, Paul does not rule out rebuking and reproof. Paul would be dismayed if Susan never became prophetic and even judgmental, as though she wanted everyone to be content and undisturbed. But Susan is not being asked to reprimand from some general moral consensus in the larger social world, but from the gravity of the judgment in the cross of Jesus Christ. She should know that such rebuke is always for the sake of folk hearing the Gospel and not for the sake of her own angry loathing of what is wrong with the world.

Further, Paul wants Susan always to be encouraging, which elsewhere he calls being *upbuilding*. Argument, rebuke, and teaching are for the sake of encouraging people to receive new possibilities and a life far beyond their own small imaginings and for the sake of encouraging folk to trust in God, to have their terrible fear cast out, to have the morrow look like a time of meeting God's grace and having the power to live on behalf of the neighbor, even on behalf of the enemy. A Christian teacher aims to encourage people in the faith and its passionate life.

All these phases of teaching the faith, according to Paul, will require patience on the part of Susan. Of course, she cannot be patient in the right way if she is not also hopeful that the Spirit of God is there with her in her teaching activities. She will be patient because she knows that God will win hearts by loving persuasion and not by coercion. Patience does not mean making room for and accommodating the false and the random desires and passions of itching ears. But it does mean she will patiently strive to understand those itching ears we have and our proneness to embrace the myths of our contemporary world. Such patience will also alert her to her own penchant for itching ears.

But let us reflect further about desire and passion. Desire and passion as such are not bad or shameful. They are the great engines of human life.

But the human problem is that our given desires and passions are often so unruly, destructive, and confusing to us. They pull us this way and that, without constancy of direction. We seem to desire that which cannot confer human fulfillment and peace. Teaching the faith is not a mere intellectual exercise. It involves the patient *use of the teachings to reorder and reshape our desires and passions* such that we learn how to live more abundantly and graciously and thereby more obediently to the God who created us and who intends to redeem us.

There is much more Paul says about ministry and the church in other places, and much more that we might emphasize, but this is an agenda of calling and tasks that can keep Susan inspired for a lifetime of ministerial leadership. She will not be the only teacher in the congregation; there will be wise and competent others among the laity. But she cannot escape the injunction to teach sound doctrine, to witness to the reality of God's grace in Jesus Christ for the benefit of the world.

Is Susan ready to be that teacher of the faith? Are we ready to be the church that has that faith and rejoices in it and seeks every way in which to witness to the love of God for the benefit of the world? I will let you answer the church question for yourselves. But if we are not ready to support teachers such as Paul commends, do we really understand what we are doing today in this ordination?

But I can vouch for Susan. She has the intelligence, the skills of language, and the compassion to teach the faith with insight and empowering persuasion. She has the learning in the faith—from the study of Scripture and other books, from disciplined courses, from writing essays and taking exams, from ardent and engaged conversations, from the many ministerial leaders in her life, from the concerned laypersons in family and church who have counseled her, and from her own devout living of the faith. If there are any itching ears around her, she will know how to scratch them graciously with the Gospel of Jesus Christ.

Let us rejoice that this young woman from our midst wants to give leadership to the church and to embrace boldly the task of witnessing to the Gospel through teaching the faith and vivifying sound doctrine. In ordaining her today, we must also promise to keep her in our prayers that she be not overwhelmed by the temptations of itching ears.

All this, dear friends, I have dared to preach in the name of the Father, the Son, and the Holy Spirit, One God, Mother of us all. Amen.

15

Of Human Longing and the Gospel of Jesus Christ

Romans 8:18-27

This sermon was preached in the Distinguished Pulpit Series at Mayflower United Church of Christ in Oklahoma City on August 4, 2002.

It is indeed a special pleasure to be with you in worship this morning, as it is a privilege to be chosen to preach in the Mayflower Distinguished Pulpit Series. The reputation of this series and the years of faithful witness of this fine congregation bestow an honor on my work and life that is, to be honest, richly undeserved. Thank you.

But there is a sermon here to preach, and we must begin by looking at the text of Holy Scripture from Paul's epistle to the church in Rome. Paul stands as a great proclaimer of the Gospel of Jesus Christ, which is to say, as the one who rings the theological bells on the significance of Jesus' life, death, and resurrection as the works of the grace of God on behalf of a repeatedly rebellious, unceasingly violent, and often bewildered and lost humanity.

In this eighth chapter Paul gathers up the Gospel of Jesus Christ into the full drama of the whole creation, as it too, along with humans, waits with eager longing to be set free from the bondage to decay and death.

We can feel within ourselves that the whole creation is groaning in labor pains, pointing to a birthing of freedom and hope that is all-inclusive and overwhelming. It is In this hope that we are to be saved.

But even this astonishing apostle of grace and hope admits that, in his and in our human weakness and longing, we often do not know how to pray and therefore how to be fully hopeful in God. Our words of desperate prayer can often become astonishing guttural groans and sighs of longing without clarity of vision and hope. But, Paul assures us, the Spirit of God does and will intercede for us in our weakness, empowering us to say and understand what might otherwise elude us. Let us pray that it will be so this morning as we wrestle with Paul's epistle.

It is to this many-sided and complex set of phenomena of what I call *human longing* that I first want us to attend. How are we to interpret the many dimensions of these phenomena? Does everyone, do we, truly understand what this longing signals about human life? Notice how, in our own experience, it seems to encompass a sense of loss and incompleteness, as though one's life has been careening along unfulfilled and running on empty. Notice how our longing vacillates about the future: with a sense of emptiness or loss in the present, the future seems to taunt us between despair and hope. Precisely when we seem so disenchanted with the shape and conditions of our past and present lives and death seems so unavoidable, our longing emerges.

Does not this longing of the human spirit come to expression in the great music of the past and in the many forms of contemporary musical expression? Consider the pathos of longing in country music, in the bitter protests of rap, in the thunderous poundings of rock, in the heartbreak of romantic love gone awry or unrequited. What is "written on the wind" in Bob Dylan's song but the fleeting answers to our human longing for what might have been and for what might yet be?

And does not human longing fuel so much of our great art, especially in its poetic and prose written forms? Who can forget the disarming words of T. S. Eliot? "[H]ollow men . . . shape without form, shade without color . . . [who] wait without hope . . . wait without love . . . wait without thought."

When that often profound but self-destructive playwright Tennessee Williams converted to Roman Catholicism, he said, "I wanted my goodness back." Was this not a longing to repossess what seems to have gotten lost in the mad shuffle of human life in its often self-defeating endeavors to flourish and truly to live? Williams wanted to achieve a sense that his life was good and justified.

It is about this longing that we can consider the rightly insightful construal of Saint Augustine: "O God, our hearts are restless until they find their rest in thee." Restless, homeless, lost; *longing for what might have been and for what might yet be*. Consider also the hymn of Charles Wesley: "Come thou long expected Jesus: Dear desire of every nation, joy of every longing heart." Is not Wesley making the extraordinary claim that the longings and desires of every nation and of every human heart are somehow addressed and answered and illuminated by what God was doing in the life, the death, and the resurrection of Jesus of Nazareth?

Obviously, these phenomena of human longing have other construals and explanations in our contemporary world. In fact, Christian construals of these phenomena are in the distinct minority of views relative to the other construals that dominate our present American world, indeed dominate our lives. Among such other construals are these: 1) human longing is simply the refusal to face the present hard realities of life, to accept that we are finite and animalic, born into a brutish world of evolving chaos and conflicting struggles to survive; it is dog eat dog, so look out for number one and cease longing for some other world than this. Or, 2) human longing is simply the refusal to be the human who takes responsibility for her own autonomous life, but who longs incessantly and self-deceptively for what might have been or what might yet be. Or, 3) human longing is simply that tragic sense of life as doomed to violence and death and meaninglessness.

These are, it seems to me, some of the deep and practical construals of human longing that sometimes *possess* us and thereby *shape* how we actually live. When I say "actually live," I am assuming that for some of us there is a distinction between how we think or pretend we live and how we do in fact live in our emotions and actions.

But we are a Christian community this morning, gathered in worship and tied together, I hope, by some profound convictions and construals of who God is, what it means to be human, and what the Gospel of Jesus Christ is. I want, therefore, briefly to identify some of these Christian construals and how they might bear on our understanding of human longing.

The first construal is the centerpiece of Christian faith and life: that in Jesus of Nazareth, a first century Jew—in his life, death, and resurrection—the Creator of all things has in freedom and love acted to save the world from its self-enacted but false and hopeless destiny. Christian faith pivots around this construal of life and human destiny. Drop Jesus out as no more than an interesting, even arresting teacher, and we have no more than a few moral teachings seeking their grounding somewhere else; and maybe we just ground them in our liberal democratic theories of justice and human autonomy. But given that *God has acted incarnately in Jesus* for the salvation of the world, the world then looks differently to Christians. How differently?

That brings us to the second construal, namely, that the God we know in Jesus is the Creator of all things and of all human beings. As Creative Spirit, God creates humans in God's own image as the sort of creatures that are intended for fellowship with God and for fellowship with other humans. Put more strongly, *humans are capacitated for and summoned by the Spirit of God into fellowship with God and with other humans.*

But, and here we have the third construal, in utter absurdity and irrationality, *humans repress and subjugate this being so created for fellowship*; they live concretely and practically as though this is not so. They live precisely in rebellion against this fellowship with God and with their neighbor. Hence, there arises much evil, much enmity and hostility, much violence and murder, much lying, much fear, much retaliation and revenge, and much longing for what seems to have been lost or forgotten or forsaken. In the midst of such evil and enmity our longing expresses a wistful and regretful sense of brokenness.

Whence this irrational repression of being created for fellowship with God and for fellowship with the neighbor who can appear before us as stranger and even enemy? With few exceptions, Christians have refused to explain this repression and rebelliousness as though it were a necessity of human creatureliness. We have named this rebellion "sin," and we have assumed that it is freely ingested into the human heart through the social traditions of human life. It is as though these traditions, for whatever might be their fleeting grandeur and timely achievements, have repeatedly inculcated into the human heart an *unbelief* that leads to ways of living and construing that are other than that way intended by God in creating us.

It is here that I want to focus on the concept of the *human heart* in order to understand our sin and longing. What is the human heart, Christianly understood? In good biblical and common sense usage, I propose to you that the heart is comprised of the dominant desires and passions of the human spirit and these desires and passions dispose us toward those feelings and actions that shape most decisively how we actually live. It is here in the struggle and dynamics of the human heart that we humans confront the questions of character and meaning. How we put together our desires and passions expresses who we actually think we are.

By *desires* I refer to the way in which we humans have objects to which we are attracted and which we want to possess. To desire something is to want that something. Such objects of desire are, of course, infinite in their variety, from the seemingly harmless desire to see our team win to the many ways in which we are attracted to other persons. Think of how a desire might seem to befall us, to overtake us, to overwhelm us and pull us in its wake into the future. The paradox here is that such desires always presuppose that this is 'what I want and I will be fulfilled and satisfied when I possess what I want.' Strong desires, we feel, are earnestly 'good-for-me.' And these strong desires dispose us to feelings and actions consistent with and necessary to the possession of the object of desire.

It is not accidental that these several generations of Americans gathered at the turning of the century have been characterized as the ones longing for instant gratification of whatever desire or itch seems to have compellingly arisen in their hearts. Since none of us is able to escape completely from the powers of media advertising, and since the advertisers are scientifically acute about human desire, it is not surprising that many of our most compelling desires are stirred within us precisely by those media powers. Over and over, as consumers of recommended goods and values, we are told what is so desirable and so good that our lives will surely be incomplete if we do not possess that advertised object or some valued style of life.

Look briefly now at the concept of *passion*. We all have, in ordinary language, concerns and cares. These are quite simply those matters about which we are concerned. A concern or care is more than a fleeting interest in something; it is rather a giving of sustained attention to something that requires a pattern of actions and feelings. We would not say Fred is concerned about the moral evil of the death penalty if he had never expressed any opinion about it. But if he had argued long and hard in many contexts against the death penalty, perhaps at great personal sacrifice, we could say that Fred has a concern for this issue.

Those concerns of a person's life that are strong and dominant over some phase of her life I am calling 'passions.' Here I mean by 'passion' that one has a compelling and dominating concern about a matter that shapes one's behavior and emotions. Passions also dispose us to feelings and actions consistent with the attending to the concern. Consider: Sharon has a passion to retain her fleeting youth and beauty; George has a passion to make money and exercise power over other people; Priscilla has a passion for seeing to the feeding of the hungry. We would not say that Harold has a passion for the life of the church if Harold seldom came to church or gave of his time and money and person to the church.

In practical terms, the strong desires and passions of the human person are what comprise her heart and their objects are the spirits that occupy her heart and shape her living. It is in those peculiar narratives of each of our lives that we might see expressed what truly are the desires and passions that have pulled us willy-nilly into the future and in which we have sought some sense of fulfillment and meaning or have been haunted by regret and longing.

What is the problem here? Our longings pose the question of what desires and passions lead to and confer blessing and true flourishing on human life. The human heart repeatedly has desires and passions that seem to aim at flourishing or some state of being satisfied. But the human heart seems so insatiable and unsatisfied, in great flux over time, shifting about from one desire to another, consumed by one passion or another, or even worse, without any consuming passion for anything. Think of how greed is never satisfied with whatever amount of money one might possess; it always needs more and is haunted by the fear that it will lose what it has.

It is in this concrete flux of life that humans repeatedly aim at a flourishing that is without fellowship with God and without fellowship with the neighbor. The *pathos* of our hearts is that we are, in bewildering ways, formed by spirits other than the Holy Spirit of God.

O God, our hearts are restless until they find their rest in thee.

It is this very human heart that Christian faith is concerned to heal and reshape by the Holy Spirit, by that Spirit who alone can bring authentic flourishing. It may not be a flourishing that the world thinks it wants, but it is a flourishing that can heal, reconcile, and redeem human life. It is this flourishing toward which our human longing points.

The model for what it means to be occupied by the Holy Spirit is the life, death, and resurrection of Jesus of Nazareth. This life, in its salutary preaching and acting, proclaims a *way of life* that is called the impingement of the Kingdom of God, in which love of God and love of neighbor include even the stranger and the enemy. It is an alternative way of living to the typical ways of the world in which fear, suspicion, protection against the stranger and the enemy, and willingness to slay them in justified self-defense are often the very fragile reasons for our social solidarity.

Jesus is hanged high on the cross in deadly *collision* with these predictable and ordinary desires and passions of the human heart. That this same Jesus is raised from the dead is the Godly confirmation that what humans seem to be most passionate about are just those values that are in conflict with being created in God's image and being called to flourishing in a distinctive way of life.

It is as though the followers of Jesus have awakened from a deep slumber in which they have been haunted by the signals of a longing for that which might bring peace, joy, a pure heart, and a flourishing that is not dependent on how the world treats you or mistreats you. When Charles Wesley, gathering up some Scriptural passages, affirms that Jesus is the deep desire of every human heart and of every society, he means to say that Jesus enacts our hidden and subjugated desire for reunion with God, to be at home with God in which love of God and love of neighbor are pulsating arteries of the human heart and the linchpins of a flourishing human character.

Karl Barth, a Swiss theologian of some stature in the last century, used the following poignant language to describe Jesus Christ: Jesus is the divine Son of God going into the *far country* of human longing, estrangement, and conflict and enacting the Kingdom of God; Jesus is the human Son of God forsaken and hanged on the cross of human rebellion and his resurrection from the dead is the *homecoming* of the Son as the One who fulfills human life and points us to our destiny to be healed and redeemed by God.

Put another way, *Jesus is God lovingly, graciously, and mercifully coming in search of us, being with us and being for us in life and death, giving us forgiveness and hope beyond our sin and deserts.* The Spirit and the hope that are in his life are the Spirit and hope that intercede for us with sighs and groans too deep for words, heal our hearts from the desires and passions that lead only to the kingdom of death and disarray, and empower our hearts to new hopes and new desires and passions for a Kingdom of life that has no end and knows no final defeat.

Friends in Christ, I admit that this language is odd and demanding, even as it is gracious and inviting. It is not the familiar language of the world. The language of Christian faith is so odd that persons who have their passions and desires shaped by it are often those ordinary saints who can give their lives for others in such a way that they know only blessing and gain. The language of *gain and loss* in Christian faith is different from the language of gain and loss in the various kingdoms and worlds that have dominated the flow of human history.

Pointing to that deep and profoundly human longing that overtakes us from time to time—a longing about what might have been and what might yet be—and pointing to Jesus Christ as the good news of God's redemptive work, the Christian believes that the almighty power and love embodied in Jesus Christ is that power and love that is truly sovereign in the world, will eternally be triumphant, and will confer a flourishing that will surprisingly satisfy and free even the most hardened, the most restless, and the most broken human heart.

O God, our hearts are restless until they find their rest in thee.

All this, dear friends in Christ, I have dared to preach in the name of the Father, the Son, and the Holy Spirit, one God, Mother of us all. Amen.

16

Old and New Habits of Mind and Heart

Colossians 3:1-17

A sermon preached at St. Paul United Methodist Church in Muskogee, Oklahoma on December 28, 2003.

I once knew a man named Tom who was really quite ordinary; even his quirks were ordinary. Tom knew the English language quite well and could even be eloquent on occasion. But he had one flaw that seemed to bedevil him and his friends on numerous occasions. As with any English-language speaker, Tom could utter the words "I promise," but he could not, in saying those words, *perform the act of promising*. He would regularly say these words or their virtual equivalents—"I will be there"; "You can count on me"; "I will do it"—but he never acted so as to keep his promises. His friends soon came to realize that no matter what Tom said, he could not be relied upon to keep his word.

What do we make of this all too common phenomenon? At least it means that Tom used the language of promising in an empty way. His words were meaningless because he never stood behind them; he was never present in his words. We could say that Tom never *inhabited* the language and practice of promise-making and promise-keeping.

Søren Kierkegaard, a nineteenth-century Danish philosopher and theologian, was critical of his fellow Danes—most of whom claimed to be good Lutheran Christians. He charged that they used the rich language of the faith—such as claiming they were justified by grace, that they had a Savior in Jesus Christ, and that they were the Body of Christ in the world—but they did not inhabit the language. He meant that the language of grace and sin and having a Savior was used repeatedly by folk who did not seem to live as though they were sinners who needed a Savior. The language and practices of the church did not seem actually to form the lives they lived. They were formed by the language and practices of their bourgeois Danish/European culture. That was the language in terms of which they understood themselves and thought about life and death and made decisions.

Were we to ask these folk if they were Christians, the answer would be an offended "of course, we are Lutherans aren't we?" Yes, they thought of themselves as Christian and even of their nation as a Christian nation.

These two stories should focus for us the question of how do we come to inhabit the language and practices we do. When we *inhabit a language*, then it is that language and its practices that form and shape our lives. It is in and through our language and practices that we construct a world and have patterns of living and thinking and desiring. These deep patterns I am calling the *habits of mind and heart* in terms of which we understand ourselves and others and have desires and passions. A *habit* is a disposition to think or act or feel in a definite way on repeated occasions, and habits of mind and heart are, then, those pervasive patterns of living that form us.

But if we examine carefully these stories about Tom and Denmark, we might discern a flaw that haunts our lives and our understanding and confuses our hearts. People often speak words and feign practices without actually inhabiting the words and without faithfully performing the practices.

I propose to you *there is a distinctive Christian language and distinctive Christian practices that are necessary for living the Christian life*. There are folk in the church today who think that Christian language needs to be continually updated and kept in step with our modern inclinations and patterns of mind and heart. I intend to dispel and subvert that basic assumption. The problem for the church today is not that its distinctive discourses and practices need to be updated to fit modern habits of mind and heart. Rather, the problem is that most of us who think of ourselves as Christians do not seem to be formed and shaped by distinctive Christian language and practices. The discourses and practices of Christian faith are designed to change us from our worldly inclinations to fit the patterns of mind and heart that we find in the Colossians scripture read for today.

In order to understand this Colossian passage, it might be helpful to remember that most of the folk in the New Testament who became followers of Jesus were keenly aware that such following of Jesus stood in stark contrast with the ways in which they used to live. They were themselves aware of being caught up in a new pattern of life in which they were giving up old habits of mind and heart in exchange for the *new habits of mind and heart* that came with confessing Jesus as the Christ of the God of Israel and the Lord of their lives.

This *contrast pattern* between the old way of life—the old habits of mind and heart— and the new way of life in Christ—with its new habits of mind and heart—runs throughout the New Testament. Yet, it is not as though the new pattern of life came easy and that the old habits gave way to the new without a struggle. Old habits of mind and habits of heart do not flee without much struggle and disciplined living. It is wrenching to change old habits, just as it is wrenching to have your life transformed.

My question today is whether we in the contemporary Protestant church in America have lost a sense for just how radical it is to be a follower of Jesus in these times. When I say *radical*, I mean it in the original sense as that which "goes to the root of something." Jesus meant to transform and redeem human lives and thereby go to the root of what it means to be a human being created by God and living before God's impinging Kingdom. I worry that we are more inclined to be formed in our everyday living by these facts about us: our socio-economic status, our consumer habits of mind, and the worldly desires and passions—which we pick up by imitating the significant persons in our lives—that shape our actual living. We may give lip service to being a follower of Jesus Christ, but it seems more likely that we are profoundly shaped by what the New Testament calls the *principalities and powers of the world*. These are the powers that tell us who we are, what we should desire, and how we should live.

What then are these habits of mind and habits of heart that seem so powerful in shaping us that we hardly notice that we have the habit? Let me say it plainly: *habits of mind* are those habits we adopt that shape how we construe ourselves, construe other persons, and construe the world in which we live. *Habits of heart* are those deep desires and passions that shape the values we think are desirable and will confer on us meaning and fulfillment. Habits of mind and habits of heart are tightly intertwined in the actual ways in which anyone of us lives out our everyday life.

Consider these habits of mind that can grip us like an iron vice: "Everyone does it, so it is all right if I do it"; "nobody likes me"; "you cannot trust anyone"; "people who are different scare me"; "my country, right or wrong"; "the poor are poor because they lack ambition and prefer to live that way"; "I deserve all my financial resources and assets because I have earned them by my own independent labor"; "Everyone should do his own thing and be true to himself"; "my property is mine to do with as I please." These habits of mind, and many others with which we are personally acquainted within ourselves, can have a powerful hold on how we think, feel, and live.

Who has not sympathized with the dreadful sorrow of persons who have had loved ones murdered or seriously abused? And we are touched when they then cry out for "an eye for an eye and a tooth for a tooth," as though that simply is the divine law for human life. It is habit of mind that demands *retribution* for every criminal or immoral act. This is a powerful and deep habit that shapes our understanding and our passions.

To speak of a contrast pattern in the NT that transforms our old habits of mind and heart and makes us new and different than we were is to remember the explicit words of Jesus that call for a new habit of mind and heart. In Matt 5:38-42, Jesus is represented as saying:

> You have heard that it was said, 'An eye for an eye and a tooth for a tooth.' But I say to you, Do not resist an evildoer with violence. But if anyone strikes you on the right cheek, turn the other also; and if anyone wants to sue you and take your coat, give your cloak as well; and if anyone forces you to go one mile, go also the second mile. Give to everyone who begs from you, and do not refuse anyone who wants to borrow from you.

I suppose that when Jesus says such things as this, he is sketching for us just what sort of habit of mind and heart he expects his followers to have. It is in this context that I want us now to look at the Scripture for today from Col 3.

Paul is writing to the church in Colossae, which is comprised of folk who think of themselves as followers of Jesus. Paul well knows that being a follower is difficult and demanding, and he admonishes them to remember that they have been "raised with Christ" and therefore must "seek the things that are above." What does he mean by "above"? He says that above is "where Christ is," and I suppose this means that *those raised with Christ are called to live as Christ lived*.

To live in the way of Christ is to be seen in contrast with earlier ways of living in which "fornication, impurity, destructive passion, evil desire, and greed" seemed to thrive. It would take several sermons fully to explore these habits of mind and heart that Paul demands we give up.

But I want to focus briefly on greed. Paul says astonishingly that greed is "idolatry." That seems rather stiff and condemnatory, for isn't a certain measure of greed what makes the capitalist economy hum? But what is this greed, then, that is considered idolatrous? I propose that it is that habit of mind and heart that is never satisfied with what is at hand but always wants to possess and acquire more. The greedy person is never quite content and feels compelled and quite justified in possessing more and more. This habit of unsatisfied possessiveness is idolatry because the object of the greed displaces God and becomes the deepest passion of one's life. Greedy folk are centered only and exclusively in the satisfaction of their own desires to the exclusion of all other values. Of course, greed says to itself that it will be satisfied when it gets enough, but it never is able to admit when enough is enough. *Greed is a habit of the mind and the heart.*

Paul goes on to say that the old way of living includes such habits as anger, malice, slander, filthy language, and lying to others. According to Paul, Christians formerly had the habit of letting their anger burgeon into bitterness and hatred. They formerly had hearts full of malice for those regarded as enemies. They formerly had an inclination to fudge on the truth and to misconstrue the truth when it served and advanced their selfish interests. Well, let us say it bluntly: Paul claims we used to tell lots of lies.

Paul admonishes us Christians "to get rid of such" bad practices. To refer to these habits as *practices* is to teach us that these actions and affections are not just occasional episodes but are repeated over and over again in our living. They are the deep ruts in terms of which we live. They are practices that constitute our living. They are how we actually live.

We are to give up those old practices and put on "the new self" we have been given in Christ Jesus. When we do that, we will be living in conformity with the fact that we were created in the image of God. When we give up those habits, we will adopt the habits of mind and heart that constitute following Jesus and being raised with Jesus.

What sort of habits of mind and heart does this new self that is raised in Christ Jesus have? That new self has, for example, the habits of compassion, of kindness, of humility, of meekness, and of patience. They "bear with one another," and they practice forgiveness of one another. In short, they practice loving other persons and seeking harmony with others. They admonish one another, when such is needed, and in all things they are grateful.

Further, they have that habit of singing "psalms, hymns, and spiritual songs to God." They do not sing in order to be admired, but neither do they remain silent because they cannot carry a tune. They sing as a disposition of a heart full of gratitude. They sing to God.

Paul ends this passage with the following invitation: "whatever you do, in word and deed, do everything in the name of the Lord Jesus, giving thanks to God the Father through him." This is admittedly astonishing. Do everything, whether in word or deed, in the name of the Lord Jesus? Is not this a strange habit to be cultivated? Isn't it profoundly at odds with the typical words and deeds the world teaches us and that are deeply ingrained in us?

I do not know about you, but I find these words of Paul sobering. We all claim to be Christians, but honesty forces us to admit that we do not seem imbued with the spirit of living about which Paul is talking. Who among us does everything in the name of the Lord Jesus? Surely this is an impossible recipe for living.

Yes, it is impossible if we are simply left to our own determination and strength of will. It is impossible if we think of ourselves as autonomous, independent persons who do not really need other persons in order to be

Christian. But we are not left to our own devices—there is a gracious Savior for us.

So, let us think through again what this *Christian pattern of life* is.

First, Christians are those folk who know themselves raised in Christ and forgiven in him. It is impossible to know yourself forgiven until you learn how profoundly you are a sinner and how deeply and passionately you have been living in ways rebellious to the ways of God. We do not even begin to grasp the power and wonder of Christ's forgiveness and grace until we learn to be *truthful about our own sinfulness*. Without the grace and forgiveness of God, the Christian life is impossible.

Second, we are not led by Paul to believe that becoming a new self in Christ is something that magically befalls us, from which all virtue seamlessly flows. It is a strenuous transition to throw off the old practices and switch to some new practices that will empower us to learn how to be faithful and in conformity to Christ. It takes time—even a lifetime—to develop those new habits of mind and heart that are reconciling and redemptive.

Third, it takes discipline to *learn how* to be a follower of Jesus, and the place where we can learn how to be such a follower is the church. It is in the *church* that we find the practices that can discipline us into a new way of living. It is in the church that we learn how to love, how to worship God and sing praises to God, how to read the Bible as Holy Scripture, how to understand enemies in such a way that we can love them and make peace with them. This is why the distinctive language and practices of Christian faith are simply essential to and precious to the life of the church. We cannot be Christian as the lonely stranger who can do it all by himself.

Fourth, it is in the *language of the church* that we will learn to overcome and throw off those habits of mind and heart that are so detrimental to our own salvation and the well-being of others. It is not as though we could learn on our own that Jesus is our Savior and pattern of life to us, that self-giving is expected. It is in the church, when it is richly grateful for the Gospel of Jesus Christ, that we learn we have a Savior who forgives our sin and will endow us with a courage that every tyrant and every liar fears.

In short, it is the disciplined life that finally knows just how much we need grace and how regularly we must feast at the Lord's Table as gracious nourishment for our needy souls. It is in the church that we will learn

198

how to pray and what to pray for. It is one of the great absurdities of worldly language that we all already know, without tutelage and practice, how to pray. Did not Jesus' disciples ask him to teach them how to pray!

The virtues of love and patience and courage grow exponentially as they are practiced repeatedly. We cannot love, as a habit of the mind and heart, without the discipline of loving others, and those others include the stranger and the enemy.

When the church itself is alive and well, then its members are those who inhabit the distinctive language and practices of the Christian faith. *When they so inhabit the language and practices, they come to have habits of mind and heart that renew human life and create truthful, faithful, and reconciling human communities.*

So may all of us be transformed in our habits such that we might learn how to do everything in the name of the Lord. It is indeed a narrow and harrowing way if we are left to our own devices. But by the power of the Holy Spirit working within us and through the language and practices of the church, we can grow—and struggle to grow—into that truth of life and death that we call the Gospel of Jesus Christ.

All this, dear friends, I have dared to proclaim in the name of the Father, the Son, and the Holy Spirit, One God, Mother of us all. Amen.

Notes: The theme of the desires and passions of the heart, and its habits, is central to my understanding of human existence and the Christian life. In GCF, 307–12, 318–19, 362–63, 543–45, 585–86. On the principalities and powers of the world and the related concept of force fields, see GCF, 256, 281–82, 318–19, 350, 354, 359, 535, 548, 572, 630–31, 704, 732.

Of course, modern psychotherapy pivots around practices of transforming and reordering those deep habits of mind and heart that seem to thwart human fulfillment and happiness. However, the various therapeutic practices are often guided by models of human fulfillment and happiness that are seriously at odds with a Christian understanding. See the engaging discussion of these issues by Robert C. Roberts, *Taking the Word to Heart: Self and Other in an Age of Therapies* (Grand Rapids: Eerdmans, 1993) and *Limning the Psyche: Explorations in Christian Psychology*, eds. Robert C. Roberts and Mark Talbot (Grand Rapids: Eerdmans, 1997).

For an insightful study of those habits of mind and heart that remain powerful in American life, see Robert N. Bellah, Richard Madsen, William M. Sullivan, Ann Swidler, and Steven M. Tipton, *Habits of the Heart: Individualism and Commitment in American Life* (Berkeley: University of California Press, 1985).

17

Freedom

Freedom from What? Freedom for What?

Galatians 5:1,6,13-26
"For freedom Christ has set us free."

A slightly revised sermon preached on July 4, 2004, at St. Paul United Methodist Church, Muskogee, Oklahoma.

In this passage from Galatians we have one of the great Christian testimonies about freedom in Christ. And it seems a happy coincidence that we are reading and meditating on this passage on the precise day, the Fourth of July, when our nation celebrates its Declaration of Independence from the rule of the King and Parliament of England. The leaders of the bedraggled colonies had found the governance by England to be a great restraint on their lives, so they declared their freedom from the rule of that nation from which so many of the colonists had emigrated.

It is right and proper that this day should be celebrated in our nation, for an experiment in democratic government was being launched that has had enormous influence on the modern world. Surely each of us has enjoyed freedoms as Americans that might not have been present in other times and places. Not the least of the freedoms the revolutionaries gained was the freedom for religious practice unrestrained by the government.

But should Independence Day be heralded in the church as a high water mark in the history of Christian faith? Surely all of us know that throughout the history of the church it has found itself serving the interests of the powerful in whatever nation or society it happened to be located. Surely we must wince when we remember from the past—and hear even today—that this revolutionary America was and is the New Jerusalem, the light set upon a hill to be a light to the nations, with the moral right and duty to bring freedom to the rest of the world. We wince, surely, because we are indeed Christians whose first loyalty is to the triune God that called the church into existence to witness to the Gospel of Jesus Christ as a saving and freeing light to the world. Surely we do not want to claim that the light of the Gospel is one and the same with the presumed light of the American nation. Were we to do so, we would descend rapidly into idolatry in which the nation becomes the divine Life that we are to serve above all others.

But our task today is not to debate the various virtues or vices of our nation's history, but to meditate on what it means to be *free in Christ*. But no sooner are we launched into that meditation than we realize the word *freedom* is one of the most emotionally powerful words in the modern world, along with that other word, *justice*. Yet both words get up and walk around on us, as they are used in a multitude of differing and often contradictory ways. And surely we know that the last two centuries of human life have experienced the greatest numerical slaughter of humans in recorded history, and much of it was done in the name of someone's freedom and someone's justice.

To facilitate our meditation together on this emotionally powerful word 'freedom,' I recommend that we ask two questions when persons talk of freedom. The first question is *freedom from what?* and the second question is *freedom for what?* All the various uses of the word 'freedom' will have to answer these two questions in order to be intelligible to us.

Let us now explore the first question: *freedom from what?* In its earliest historical usages, *freedom appears in contrast to slavery*. Slaves were persons under the ownership or control of another, and free men were those not owned by any other person but who could own other persons. So, to be free was to be free from slavery. This contrast appears in the earliest traditions of both the Greek world and the Hebrew world.

In the most abstract sense, then, freedom—as freedom from something—can be understood generally as *freedom from some restraint on the willing, choosing, deciding, acting of the human person.* The restraint on freedom can often be understood as some sort of bondage. So, the colonists wanted to be free from the restraints put on their willing and living by the King of England. Later the African slaves, who were not subject to the constitutional freedoms of white males, wanted to be free from their chattel slavery. Even today African Americans want to be free from the lingering prejudices and disadvantages of the institutions of slavery and Jim Crow laws.

Similarly, the prisoner wants to be free from the restraints of the prison. The corporate officers and board of Enron wanted to be free from the restraints on their business activities by an accurate public accounting of those activities; in short, they wanted to be free from the restraints of the law. We have been told the people of Iraq wanted to be free from Saddam Hussein, but now it appears they want even more to be free from American occupation.

Also, in regard to freedom from some restraint on us, we can talk about being free from the anger of others, free from an obsession with food, free from a disease that wracks the body, free from the anxiety that rules our daily living, free from the travails of an unhappy past, free from the fears that prey on us, and so on.

In all these ways of freedom from something, we can see how easily we can substitute *liberation* for the act or activity of being made free from some restraint. We can also see how easily we might understand the restraint upon us as an *oppression.*

Let us attend briefly to the second question about freedom: *freedom for what?* In the world of liberal political theory the most general answer to that question is that humans want to be free—without restraint—*to choose their own preferred forms and styles of happiness.* But no sooner do we say that than we realize persons cannot be happy if they are in continual conflict with each other's pursuit of happiness. To be happy will mean, politically speaking, being willing to accept some restraints on *how* one pursues happiness. We Americans stand in a political tradition in which the pursuit of happiness involves accepting some *covenantal restraints* on our individual actions. We do not have the freedom to kill another, to torture another, to steal from another, and so on. Within some restraints, then, people can pursue their various paths to happiness.

I hope it might seem to you at this point that talk of freedom can often be a dizzying exercise in which we might easily lose our way and become confused. *What sort of freedom persons yearn for has much to do with what they perceive as the most onerous restraints or bondages under which they live and labor.*

For example, the poor are concerned about the restraints of poverty and unaffordable health care, while the rich are concerned about the legal restraints on their capacity to hold and control property and to make money and to spend it as they please. The poor may have the civil freedom to travel to Seattle but their poverty so restrains them that they are not free to pay for such a trip. One of the reasons money is so important to folk is that it seems to empower them to do as they please more readily.

The lesson here is this: *when persons and politicians talk about freedom, we need to ask: freedom from what? freedom for what?* It is hardly credible simply to talk about freedom in general without the important qualifiers regarding what sort of freedom from what sort of restraint.

These reflections should whet our appetite for getting some clarity about what it might mean to be *free in Christ,* to be set free by Christ as though one were previously in bondage. In ways that might surprise you, I should point out that the New Testament has absolutely nothing to say about a presumed *free will* that every person has and that is presupposed by Christ's preaching. Rather, the uniform New Testament assumption is that in a variety of ways *persons are in bondage and unable to free themselves from that bondage by their own will power.*

What then is this bondage or overwhelming restraint under which human beings live and labor? The bottom line is that human beings are everywhere in *bondage to sin and to the consequences of sin.* It is the power of sin to shape and form their lives that humans need to be set free from. And in being set free from sin, they will be set free for living in a way that is peculiar and different from the way in which the world seems to want persons to live. It is a freedom for living a way of life that will confer true flourishing and happiness.

So let us talk about sin, which all of us will agree is an almost forbidden topic in our mainline traditions, in which people want basically to be made to feel good about themselves. Sin-talk seems so negative, and indeed it is. But it is negative for the sake of a higher good, namely, human reconciliation, human redemption, and human flourishing.

We Christians must, however, observe one warning: *sin-talk is first and last talk about ourselves; it is not primarily talk about those 'other people' who are really sinners different from us.*

Sin is that corruption of our human nature in which we live as *practical atheists*: we may profess to believe in some divinity, but we live daily as persons who are in rebellion against the will of God the Creator. We want life on our own terms to will and do as we please. The divinities in our lives are no more than the *means* for us to have life on our own terms. Hence, we human beings are repeatedly self-centered. As rebellious sinners, we tell lies and repeat falsehoods. We are in bondage to the selfish passions of our lives. We live in fear of death and in fear of all those who might do us harm. It is this very fear that generates much hatred, the need for revenge, and violence. In short, we sinners sin and we are sinned against by other sinners.

What then are the *consequences of sin*? In the most general senses, but in deadly practical ways, we sinners live in alienation from God, from our neighbors, and from ourselves. And in our rebellion we humans construct *societies* that install and perpetuate our alienation. These societies, with their huge power over human life, are what some New Testament authors call the "principalities and powers of the world," and what Paul calls here in Galatians "the elemental spirits of the world" (*stoicheia*: 4:3, 9). We humans ingest sin into our hearts as we are ourselves formed by these societies. In so ingesting these powers, we receive from them an identity and presumed destiny.

I know this may sound confusing and obscure, but consider that in the two so-called world wars of this past century persons who called themselves Christians fought on both sides of those bloody conflicts. It was more important to their human identity and therefore to the destiny for which they were willing to fight and to die that they were Germans, Italians, Russians, Americans, French, or English than that they were Christians. Can we conclude anything other than that the Christian identity was itself frail and weak and malleable? The elemental spirits of the world are subtle but fierce in their domination of human life.

I do not mean this to be a condemnation of the ordinary soldiers who fought, killed, and died in these terrible wars. They were put into warring conflict by the decisions of others to go to war, and they suffered much in their subjugation to such warring. But that the folk in the modern nation-states go to war so often—under the clarion call of 'defending their freedom against a dangerous and demonic enemy'—simply illustrates how powerful the national identities are to the soldiers who do the fighting. In the midst of these nation-states, then, is it possible for Christians to have an identity and destiny that can be differentiated from the state?

When Jesus and the New Testament apostles get down to brass tacks in their talk about sin, the common point is that we humans are in bondage to sin; we are slaves to sin and its power to form how we live our lives. Could anything be more astonishing than that even we Americans, who herald and promote our presumed freedoms around the world, are also *persons in bondage to sin, to human pride and selfishness, to human lying and misrepresentation of others, to human enmity and killing*?

What then might it mean to be "free in Christ"? How does Christ Jesus set us free from sin and its consequences?

In other parts of the letter to the church in Galatia, Paul expounds one of the most difficult beliefs of Christian faith. It is not difficult because the belief is abstract and obscure; it is difficult because it is hard to truly believe. Paul claims that *Christ has set us free from the law*. Of course, Paul has in mind the various forms of the laws of Israel. One function of the law is its moral character—with its details on conduct and attitude—as the key to how to live a *justified life before God*: how to stand morally in the right before God. But Paul worries that the law only condemns and does not set folk free. Why does it only condemn? Because the law is so incessantly demanding that none of us can fully satisfy—in any and all circumstances of our living—its rigorous and unforgiving demands. The law makes it clear just how deeply we are in the grips of sin.

So, if we seek our justification before God through works of the law, we will find ourselves condemned. The law in itself and by itself does not forgive. Were we humans to stand before God simply in terms of our obedience to the law of God, we would stand there condemned. Were we then to think of God's justice only in terms of *just deserts*—of reward and punishment—we would find the tally repeatedly coming up as punishment against us. We would stand there before God's justice in the midst of our alienation from God, of our alienation for the neighbors we were called to love, and of our alienation from our own created nature and goodness.

It is this bondage to sin as revealed through the strictness of the law from which Paul claims Christ has set us free. His claim is that, *while we were yet sinners, Christ died for us and revealed God's gracious forgiveness of our sin.* It is not that God will forgive *if* we ask. Rather, even before we might ask, God has acted in the Jew Jesus of Nazareth to take the sins of the world upon and into the divine Life itself and forgive humans their sin and therefore the necessity of living under the consequences of their sin. *Forgiveness, free grace, the infinite and all-encompassing love of God!* God refuses to judge us according to our sins, instead judging us according to God's own forgiving grace as known in the life, death, and resurrection of Jesus.

Being overwhelmed with *gratitude* is the first response of folk who know that God loves them and has forgiven them. This forgiveness is not something they earned or deserved: it is *free grace.* And in that gratitude, they become *free for* living as persons forgiven and loved by God. Or, as Paul says in this passage of Galatians, they are now free to love the neighbor, which includes the stranger and the enemy. They can give up their bondages and slaveries and can live now without fear. They can be free from that retreat to violence that so enslaves and ruins human lives. They can live with an uncommon courage, trusting in the ultimate victory of God's graciousness toward the world.

The problem is that most folk who hear this good news just do not believe it. They might give lip service to the news, but they go on living their lives as though they really were not sinners in need of God's grace and trying to earn the blessings of the divinities that have already populated their lives.

Also, Paul says there are those who are so uncomprehending of this startling announcement of God's grace in Jesus Christ that they ask with their mouths whether this freedom in Christ means they can now live as they please. Paul is abrupt with these folk, for they think their freedom is the freedom to return to the slavery of wanting to live simply as one pleases. *While we may be set free from the law as the means by which we achieve our justification and salvation before God, obedience to the law of God is still the way in which the Christian and the church live freely in the world.*

People who know they are free in Christ from the destructive consequences of sin know as well they are called to live differently from the hurly burly of people seeking this and that freedom in the world. It is astonishing that this same Paul, often imprisoned by worldly authorities, can consistently maintain that he is nevertheless free in Christ. And it remains the case that such extraordinary Christians as Paul—even though they have renounced violence, which should have made them less worrisome to the tyrant—are nevertheless feared by every tyrant. These Christians do not live in fear of death, which is the fear that every tyrant plays upon to maintain his tyranny. And they have a loyalty to God that no tyrant or state can ever subdue.

Hence, we see clearly through the eyes of Paul that being Christian is being one who lives in the light of the forgiveness given in Christ Jesus. It is possible so to live only through the empowerment of Christ's Spirit, which is the Holy Spirit. The freedom conferred in Christ and empowered through the Spirit is the freedom to live for God's Kingdom. To live in this way is to bear the fruit of the Spirit. Such fruit Paul enumerates as "love, joy, peace, patience, kindness, generosity, faithfulness, gentleness, and self-control" (5:22-23).[1]

To live in the Spirit and to bear the fruit of the Spirit is to live in a way that no national culture or state can confer with their various mores and legal freedoms. Yet those who live in the Spirit will witness to that *freedom that comes from the grace of God and that is freely given by God* to all who have ears to hear and eyes to see. And in this witness it will be their earnest desire that all those slaveries that haunt human lives and their societies will be transformed into kingdoms of mutual respect and love. In such new kingdoms, leaders and citizens will abandon all those stratagems by which humans are ensnared by sin and seek to ensnare others. The freedom Christ confers is therefore a *freedom for service to the neighbor, who is now understood to include the stranger and even the enemy.* And it is herein that we might think afresh about what social freedoms are appropriate to a just political order that will thwart and dismantle the many ways in which we humans sin against each other.

We started this sermon by contrasting freedom to slavery. Is it not amazing that Paul, and other apostles, now talk of a freedom in which

---

[1] See the discerning study of how the fruit of Spirit might be cultivated in the midst of the skewing powers—the *stoicheia*—of the dominant culture in America by Philip D. Kenneson, *Life on the Vine: Cultivating the Fruit of the Spirit in Christian Community* (Downers Grove, Ill.: InterVarsity, 1999).

they are free to be the loving slaves of others, seeking the good of others, and in that way being *slaves to Christ?* To be a slave of Christ is to be set free from all those other slaveries that would alienate us from God, from the neighbors we are to love, and from our own created nature and goodness.

It is wonderful to celebrate and to live the freedom Christ has conferred on us.

All this, dear friends, I have dared to preach in the name of the Father, the Son, and the Holy Spirit, One God, Mother of us all. Amen.

18

A Memorial Homily for Angie

Romans 8:18-27, 31-35, 37-39

This homily was preached on April 10, 2002, in Enid, Oklahoma. Angie was twenty-three years old when she died in a one-car accident on the dark night of April 5.[1]

It is our given human condition that we are born into the world independent of any decision of our own, and we live in a space and time that we did not create and that defines and delimits our life. As creatures of time, we not only have a beginning in time, but we have an ending in time. All creatures great and small will die and cease to exist in space and time.

It is also true that many of us may spend a lifetime trying to escape from or hide from ourselves this unyielding fact of our finitude and

---

[1] Over the years I have urged students and ministers to separate the homily from the eulogy/biography phases of the funeral or memorial service. The narrative character of the eulogy is the place where the deceased's life is properly celebrated and, when appropriate, showered with encomia. The homily, on the other hand, is directed to the gathered community and properly aims at the proclamation of the Gospel as it throws light on the sobering reality of death, grief, bewilderment, and hope. In Angie's service, my wife, Sarah Jones, Angie's school counselor in high school, had previously delivered the eulogy.

vulnerability to death. Nevertheless, the signals of death are ever present in the many ways in which each of us is vulnerable to harm and the fear of being harmed. We are frail creatures whose very lives are continuously vulnerable to the affliction of harm from other creatures, from disease and the decay of our bodies, and from that multitude of self-inflicted harms and injuries about which each of us is all too familiar. If we were our own creator, we might be prone to render ourselves invulnerable to pain, suffering, loss, and death.

Yet this same all too human vulnerability is also the wondrous power of our being open to and affected by others; it places joy, friendship, parenting, love, and self-giving among the amazing possibilities of life. To be utterly invulnerable would mean being closed off to the richness of a genuinely human life with others.

This inescapable vulnerability of life is, however, haunted by the fact of death. Death, thus, stalks us in its many forms and faces, and we know not whence it comes and whither it goes. But the inevitability of death scares us, fills us with fear, and often casts a shadow over our living.

Today we are confronted with the stark realization that Angie has been abruptly and without warning—without preparation and proper goodbyes—taken from us by an untimely and bewildering death. A chill and numbing wind blew through our hearts in the late hours of April 5 and in the dawning of April 6.

Her life in time with us is over and has reached its limit. We find it unbearable that she is no longer present to interact with us, to plan a future with us, to realize all those spoken and unspoken possibilities and hopes we had for her. Our urgent memories may struggle to capture and cherish the past we had with her, but a memory is not a living, interacting presence with a vital future before it.

Dear family and friends of Angie, our loss is great, our suffering, confusion, and our excruciating pain are without relief. In Angie's death an irretrievable loss has been inflicted upon us as well. But, for our own sakes and for the sake of our relationships with Angie, we all need to acknowledge our loss honestly and to learn how to look to a future that has been shaped both by Angie's death and by her life.

This means that this question is before us all: are there possibilities of hope and understanding available to us as we reckon now with her death and our own vulnerabilities? Is there hope either for her or for us?

It should be obvious—but it requires clear acknowledgment now—that this is not a memorial service rooted in some vague and sentimental sense of human immortality and the indestructibility of human love. Today we have read Christian Scriptures and uttered Christian prayers. We do indeed bring to this service a formative understanding of the Christian narrative about God and human life and death. It is in that formative understanding that I hope we will find support, clarity, and strength to face our loss and the future that lies ahead of us.

May we first remember that the Christian trusts in a God who is Creator of all things in heaven and on earth. No creature comes to be without the sovereign action of God's love in bestowing life and being on that creature. However troubling may be some of the conditions under which humans live out their lives, it is central to Christian convictions that we stand before a Creator who loves us and who suffers greatly when we suffer or when we fritter away our lives in self-indulgent neglect of God's love. We are created for fellowship with God and for flourishing. All creatures great and small are loved by God.

But the Christian God who creates all things is not also a god who stands on the sidelines of life, aloof and untouched by the creature's life. While the Creator does not give us life that is invulnerable to harm and the contingencies of living in the midst of other creatures, the Creator does go in search of human life to be a covenant partner in the grand adventure of living.

In search of God's beloved creatures, the Creator liberates and elects Israel to be a special people, to bear a special covenant and to be a light to the nations. It is in this Israel that God does a new thing for humans so vulnerable to the sheer uncertainties of life and their strange and surprising entanglements with death.

In a mighty act of humility and loving resolve, God comes among us humans in the form and life of Jesus, the Jew from Nazareth. This Jesus is God going out to gather the lost sheep, to heal the wounds of life and unfaithful living, to give hope to the hopeless and despairing, to encourage our vulnerability and openness to the lives of others, and to confront the terrible brutalities of the many faces of death that seem so invincible and dominating. Jesus is God's love taking the place of us vulnerable humans who stagger uncertainly under the burdens of accidents, afflictions, despair, and the fear of death.

It is this Jesus that takes death—with its assaulting sting of finality—takes it with him upon the cross and there he undergoes death's most violent exercise of dominion and forsakenness. Jesus dies on the cross and is rendered vulnerable to the powers that appear to the world to confer life and death.

The sting of death has always been its pretense to be what is most real and final about us all. We will all indeed die. Jesus died. No make-believe death here. No immortal soul quickly escaping the body. Body and soul, dead.

But death does not have the last word. This divinely human Jesus is raised bodily from the dead and declares to all who have eyes to see and ears to hear that the last word is God's reconciling love and grace that confers life eternal.

We have just passed through the Easter season, but let us emphatically note what might have become glib and insignificant to us: God in Christ Jesus has taken the sins and vulnerabilities of the world upon Godself and into God's own life and deprived them of being the last and final judgment on any of us. God's love resurrects life in the face and aftermath of death. In Jesus, death is defeated in its power to provoke consuming fear and despair. After Jesus' death and resurrection, it is possible to say: O death where is thy victory? Where is thy sting?

So, dear family and friends, what do we make of this? This Gospel, which Jesus Christ is and proclaims, does not tell us that we will not die; it does not tell us that we are not frail and vulnerable creatures subject to harm and death; it does not tell us that we will never suffer irretrievable loss and broken hearts. It does not tell us to trust in our own resources and strength and to render ourselves invulnerable to life and death.

But it does tell us that we are sustained by the only God there is and that this triune God loves us with a lavishness and excess of grace that is truly redemptive of our living and our dying. In this God we have hope: hope that Angie as she encountered the mystery of her own dying also encountered the almighty love of God and was resurrected by that love to a life bathed in sheer grace and forgiveness. We can let Angie go to that unimaginable glory; we do not have to clutch after her by refusing to admit that she has died.

By admitting our own real loss in not having her near at hand, we too can live courageously and trustingly into the future as that time over which the sting of death has been plucked. We can understand and live as though nothing can separate Angie or us from the love of God in Christ Jesus our Lord

This means as well that we can be grateful for the gift that Angie was to us all. Her life had a beauty and vitality that blessed us all, even when we found her perplexing and singularly herself. Be grateful and celebrate what she has given to us all. It can truly be said that we were marvelously vulnerable to her life with us. We weep so deeply for her passing because our gratitude and delight in her life were such rich blessings.

It is part of the profound grandeur and dignity of human life that we can grieve over our irretrievable losses without being defeated and destroyed by them.

To Angie's parents, may you know the peace of realizing that you do not have to keep Angie alive; she lives eternally in the grace of God. In the midst of your aching grief and loss may you also know the embrace of God's gracious love for yourselves. With your own wounds, misgivings, and the anguish of unfulfilled plans for Angie, may you find strength and solace in your hope and trust in God's triumphant power and grace.

To Angie's brother and to her grandparents and other relatives, hear the pathos and faithfulness of a God who will not let you go, who will not forsake you in your despair and regrets and loss. Trust that, whether you live or whether you die, you are the Lord's.

And to all of us friends, touched by the dancing and unpredictable liveliness of Angie in her scurrying about among us, take delight in the gift of her life. And be comforted by the whispers of the Holy Spirit that build up life and give us courage and thankfulness. This Spirit will give us a joy that will not be overcome by the fragility and vulnerability of life and will not be bullied into fear by death or the threat of death and loss. This is joy in the Lord of Life. This joy casts out fear and bestows hope.

So, with apostle Paul, we can say: "[We are] convinced that neither death, nor life, nor angels, nor rulers, nor thing present, nor things to come, nor powers, nor height, not depth, nor anything else in all creation, will be able to separate us from the love of God in Christ Jesus our Lord."

All this, dear family and friends, I have dared to speak in the name of the Father, the Son, and the Holy Spirit, One God, Mother of us all. Amen.

19
A Memorial Homily for Jerry Bob

Romans 8:18-35, 37-39

This homily was preached at a memorial service in Wagoner, Oklahoma, on December 20, 2003, for Jerry Bob, a dear friend and neighbor whose dying was prolonged but untimely. The homily was preceded in the service by a eulogy that lifted up and celebrated the wonderful particularities of Jerry Bob's life.

We have indeed celebrated the wonderful gift that Jerry Bob's life was to each of us. We have done this before a graceful God. I hope this homily will help all of us to hear the Gospel of Jesus Christ as good news to us— precisely as good news to us amidst that self-examination that death and memorial services inevitably provoke within us.

Even as we have celebrated Jerry Bob's life and expressed our gratitude for his years with us, we must also confess that we grieve his loss deeply. He will no longer interact with our lives nor stand side by side with us amidst life's challenges. We grieve now and we will grieve more in the days ahead, and rightly so. But our grief is an expression of the sobering grandeur of human life that we have the capacity to care so profoundly for others and to miss them so dearly. Yet we must never forget that our grieving is before a merciful God who grieves as well.

The passage from Paul's letter to the church in Rome is so rich that we could hardly exhaust its meaning in this brief homily. But it does address us with a realism and hopefulness that is rare and seldom found on human tongues and in human hearts.

Paul reminds us that we are creatures in relation to a whole cosmos of other creatures and that we and the cosmos are inclined from time to time to *groan* under the burdens of our finitude. We are creatures who have been granted the gift of living among other creatures, but such living is for a limited time. We are bodily creatures, and our bodies are so vulnerable to disease, to decline, to the sufferings of our own destructive living, and to the afflictions of harm from other creatures.

All of us here this day will surely die, and that fact weighs upon us like a heavy burden. It has been said more than once by Christian saints over the centuries that our *fear of death* is at the root of all our other fears and anxieties and our proneness to violence. And it is not only the fear of our own death but of the deaths of those others who are important to us.

Paul sees us as creatures living in time under the summons of God to be obedient to God's commands and to live in peace and love with our neighbors and with our enemies. But Paul also sees us humans—most of the times of our lives—tumbling along, pulled this way and that by our disordered desires, invariably self-centered, prone to the neglect of others we think we love, filled with self-deceptions, and fearful not only of dying but of the truth about ourselves.

Our lives seem so entangled with good intentions unrealized, with hearts full of bitterness and regret, with a suffocating guilt and a haunting despair that our lives do not seem to add up to much. We are prone to brood over past wrongs done to us and over wrongs we have done to others. In short, we face the daily future full of fear and confusion and a gnawing hopelessness. Whence cometh hope for those of us so mired in sin, in pride, and in guilt?

In this and in other passages from Paul, we humans, living out our lives in a limited time and space, find it difficult consistently to will obedience to God's coming Kingdom. We seem more inclined to serve the kingdoms of the world than the Kingdom of God.

But, of course, Paul goes on to say that just for such people as we seem to be, there is a Gospel that is more powerful and truthful than all of our lies, sins, fears, and regrets. It is the *truthfulness of God's forgiving grace in*

Jesus Christ that comes to us through the mysterious working of the Holy Spirit. The God who is our Creator and who knows our hearts better than we do, who in truth knows our shortcomings, is also the God who comes in search of us with a grace that will not let us go nor leave us to our own devices and just deserts.

To be forgiven by God does not mean that we have led a reasonably good life; rather it means that we have much for which to be forgiven, insofar as we have been enmeshed in sin, both as doers of sin and as ones sinned against by others. But the forgiveness of God is a gracious declaration that God does not count our sinful lives against us, does not keep tally on us, but invites us to *live as persons constantly being given new lives and new hearts.*

People who come to accept that new heart given by the grace of God, are people who can speak truthfully the words of Paul:

> If God is for us, who is against us? It is God who justifies. Who is to condemn? It is Christ Jesus who died, yes, who was raised, who is at the right hand of God, who intercedes for us. Who will separate us from the love of Christ? Will hardship, or distress, or persecution, or famine, or nakedness, or peril, or sword? No, in all these things we are more than conquerors through him who loved us. For I am convinced that neither death, nor life, nor angels, nor rulers, nor things present, nor things to come, nor powers, nor height, nor depth, nor anything in all creation will be able to separate us from the love of God in Christ Jesus our Lord.

People who speak and live this way with holy passion know that they do not face death nor the deaths of their loved ones trusting in their own righteousness. Rather they *trust in the forgiving grace of God*, which does, of course, call them to repent and live graciously as well. Those who know themselves forgiven by God know as well that they are called to forgive much and to forgive without ceasing.

People who speak as Paul speaks are people who have had the fear of death and the fear of suffering cast out of their lives. They are a people launched on the great kingdom venture of living with a joy and hopefulness that no possible future, come what may, will be able to separate them from the love of God in Christ. Such people also have the freedom and passion to dance with the Spirit and to be generously open to the lives of others. They take delight in having family and friends to love, and they are compassionately open to the strangers and the enemies who also live in their world.

Those who will be resurrected are not resurrected because of their moral perfection, but because of the powerful grace of God manifested in the life, death, and resurrection of Jesus of Nazareth. It is in the Spirit of Jesus that we trust in the resurrection of Jerry Bob; he has not died unto annihilation, nor has he died unto a condemning wrath of God. Rather, *he has died unto the sheer merciful love and beauty of God.* God did not let Jerry Bob go mercilessly into the night of death, and neither will God let us go without mercy.

So, let us all hear the words of God's forgiving grace as words of life for us. Let us repent of our lives lived in fear, lived in alienation from family and from friends and from enemies, and lived in the silent despair that we can never really be forgiven and that death will surely have the last word about us. Let us gladly and humbly embrace that grace of God that will meet us in death and will beckon us lovingly into life beyond death.

Let us rejoice that God's gifts are many and that Jerry Bob has been a precious gift to us. And let us praise God that God's love is that ultimate and almighty power and word that is the final word about Jerry Bob and about each of us.

All this, dear friends, I have dared to proclaim in the name of the Father, the Son, and the Holy Spirit, One God, Mother of us all. Amen.

20
Prayers in and for the Church

These pastoral prayers were spoken over two years in my occasional duties as a liturgical assistant at St. Paul United Methodist Church in Muskogee, Oklahoma.

First Sunday after Christmas, December 29, 2002

It is with joyous gratitude, O Lord, that we gather this day to worship thy name and thy glorious works of salvation in Jesus Christ. It is with humility and thanksgiving that we remember thy coming to us in Jesus as one born in humble poverty among the least of the persons of the world. It never ceases to utterly surprise us when we grasp how he refused to garb himself in the glories of the world—the glories that even now seem so seductive and attractive to us. As we pray this day, O Lord, we confess we remain uncertain about the full meaning of thy condescension and humility in coming among us in such low estate, and it startles us that you ended up strung out on a cross.

As the Advent and Christmas season fades from us and Epiphany arises before us, we confess that we have often been less joyous, more bedraggled, and more on edge during these receding Advent and Christmas times. We wonder what has sapped the joy from us and plunged us into

218

the helter-skelter of buying what seemed like the necessary gifts. Now give us in the coming days the joy we missed in Advent and Christmas.

Because of thy mercy toward us, O Lord, we are bold to pray for those In our community of faith who are stricken with illness and distress or who have lost loved ones to death. May these friends in Christ know the comfort and challenge of thy love and embrace that hope in thee that is the secret hope of all nations and all humans: to flourish eternally in health and peace with thee and our neighbors.

As our nation and others march grimly toward war and the kingdom of death, O Lord, empower us to heed thy counsels and become peacemakers. We pray for those who have died or even now are dying or will yet die at the violent hands of human hatred, fear, and revenge. We know that thy love will not be defeated by their violent deaths and that thy grace will finally prevail for them. You will surely embrace the dead and the dying by thy tender mercies and transformative life. But O Lord, why do so many have to die, as nations in their violence toward others claim only to be doing what justice requires? Why does such presumed justice seem so tattered and unpromising for establishing a peace commensurate with thy Kingdom?

In praying about these matters of concern, O Lord, we are grateful that thy Word in Christ continues to inform and transform us. Many of these thoughts we might never have had in the absence of thy coming to us in Jesus of Nazareth. Teach us even more how to clutch his Word and be freed from sin and be filled with an uncommon courage and undaunted hope.

In Christ's name we pray. Amen.

February 23, 2003

O triune God, Father, Son, and Holy Spirit, one God, and Mother of us all, we gather as thy people, as the ones who were created by thee in love, as the ones who were reconciled and saved from sin by thy incarnate love in Jesus, and as the ones inspired and formed by thy Holy Spirit. We gather with profound gratitude and thanksgiving for the wonders of thy gracious love. We trust in the ultimate triumph of thy almighty love, even as we face the perils of living in these days and times.

You have beckoned us to come to thee in prayer, without arrogance and without expecting that our will should be done instead of thy will. We come to thee in humility suffused with hope as we lay before thee the concerns that bear heavily on our hearts.

In particular, Lord, we lift up to thee those members of our congregation and their families, who have experienced sickness, injury, consternation, or grief in the preceding days and whom we now name. We pray they might know the comfort of thy love and the hope thy Spirit bestows so abundantly.

Even as we know ourselves called and gathered by thy loving Gospel, we know that we are not the only ones you love and about whom you are concerned. It is a great mystery to us that not all confess the name of Jesus and live in that pattern of life he exemplified. But we surely know that all those beyond thy church have also been blessed in Jesus' name by the redeeming power of his cross and resurrection.

Teach us, O Lord, how to be a blessing to those beyond thy church, how to weep for their miseries, how to work for their liberation from oppression, and how to respect the sheer dignity you have conferred on them as thy beloved creatures. Give us the courage, O Lord, to learn how to live on their behalf; how to hear their sorrows, laments, aspirations, and hopes; how to enfold them in our arms as the tender arms of thy mercy.

We pray, O Lord, for the strength to live by faith in thee, even as we confess our own individual and collective tendencies to live in oblivious self-centeredness. We confess how often and how deeply we want our own self-interested will to be done instead of thy wise and reconciling will. Relieve us from the toxicity of our own desperate desire to have our lives—and the lives of many others—on our own terms, instead of on the terms you have blessedly revealed in Jesus. Relieve us from that vaunted toughness and insularity in which we are willing to set Jesus aside and do what we might think is compellingly necessary for our good and for the good of those we prefer to love—even to be so tough as to will the destruction of those others we judge expendable. Relieve us from the self-justifying need to be the ultimate judge of others.

O Lord, we confess our hearts turn to icy stone when we are dominated by fear, and we confess that faith then flees from our judgments and feelings and actions. It is so hard to give up the fears that stalk us, so we seek in thee that faith that casts out fear and that empowers us to be courageous peacemakers, to be lovers of thy creation and of all those creatures for whom you constantly search and for whom you have never abandoned hope.

The joy of thy grace does still stir our hearts, and it is in earnestness for thy grace in Jesus that we have dared so to pray. Amen.

Easter, April 20, 2003

Dear Lord of all creation, we come this day to celebrate the crowning moment of thy incarnate life with us in Jesus Christ. On this Easter morning, the crucified Jesus was raised from the dead and thy eternal verdict on his life and brutal death was made manifest to his closest disciples.

While we, the people who claim to be the Body of Christ in the world, do indeed marvel at the splendid mystery of Jesus' resurrection, we are also baffled about how we are to take it. We confess that it is not the simple, magical belief that just any dead person came back to life. But it is the resurrection of Jesus, who preached thy coming kingdom and who was brutally slain by the reigning powers of the world. We know that when they crucified him those powers were declaring to Jew and Gentile alike that their power to dominate and impose their will on others was supreme.

Even as the disciples fled the scene of the crucifixion, they were haunted that perhaps the only real power was Rome and they feared Rome. Rome was trying to put an end to that life that had proclaimed thy coming kingdom, in which peace and love of neighbor and enemy were the supreme and defining powers of a new, resurrected world.

We too, Lord, are as bewildered as the fleeing disciples. We too fear the kind of power Rome had, even as we secretly admire the sheer coercive, dominating strength of armies and weapons. We confess that too often we think that Roman power is what is decisive in human history, because we trust that power more than we trust the power of Jesus' way of life. We do not want to be crucified, but we pray that we will not become the crucifiers of others.

221

Yet we cannot escape the testimony of the disciples that Jesus was raised from the dead and declared the real Victor and the final, ultimate power in the world. When you raised Jesus from the dead, you declared that the power of his life and kingdom is the real power in human history.

O Lord of life, we too know that we are in a war, intending to use the supremacy of new precision weapons to impose our will on unruly nations and declared enemies. We are stalked by fear of others, and we have an uncanny pride in the presumed discriminating powers of our weapons. Teach us, O Lord, as thy people, what it might mean to believe in Jesus' resurrection as that way of life that is indeed the Alpha and Omega of all things in heaven and on earth.

As thy people, we pray for soldiers who are commanded by authoritative others to slay and subdue and place themselves in harm's way. Even if you cannot place thy blessings on this war as a just war, we pray for their safekeeping.

We also pray for the people of Iraq, a people strange to us, who seem full of bitterness, fear, hostility, and, hopefully, a desire for a peaceful and free life. We confess that they too are thy creatures and are included in the ones for whom Jesus died and was raised. In the confusion that will engulf them in the days ahead, O Lord, guide their leaders and ours that they might love peace and justice more than the power to impose their wills on others.

As thy Son Jesus is raised from a death at the hands of the world's principalities and powers, then teach us how to have an uncommon faith and hope in him as the true revelation of thy will and the real Lord of history. Teach us how to live the way he lived. Teach us how to hope in the face of death and domination and despair. Confer on us the resurrecting power of vulnerable love that we might be faithful witnesses to thy love in Christ.

It is with hopeful joy that we pray in the name of the raised Jesus. Amen.

Third Sunday of Easter, May 4, 2003

O Lord God, we gather on this third Sunday of Easter, remembering the days in which Jesus was appearing and teaching his astonished disciples and friends. We know that his rising and his appearing to others is the great miracle of thy Life with the world. We are thankful that our gathering today would be inconceivable without the magnificence of Jesus manifesting himself to others in the days following his repudiation of death's tomb. We praise thee that Jesus is not among the dead and that he gives us hope about our lives now and in life beyond death.

It is because of the power and grace of his resurrection that we dare to hope in thy Son Jesus as the hope for the world. It is in that hope that we pray for those among us in this gathered congregation who feel hopeless or who are in desperation because of illness or the death of a loved one or who are in despair about their own possibilities in life or who are in sorrow about the losses of war and conflict in our world today. We pray that they might know thy peace that builds hope. In all these ways we pray for a resurrected future in which thy peace might prevail among the people of thy world.

We especially lift up those brothers and sisters in our nation who are out of work and in despair of finding the sort of work that is meaningful and financially sufficient. We know that these unemployed folk are subject to a terrible fall into self-accusation and feelings of worthlessness. Not many of us, O Lord, understand that the real source of our final worth is in relationship to thee. Empower us, however, to understand clearly and practically that those who cannot find work are those whom Jesus summoned us to love and to whom we can offer our own assets and securities. Save us from the demonic thought that these folk have brought their unemployment on themselves. We pray as well for an economy that values honesty, fidelity, justice, and truthfulness and that is not engendered by greed and selfishness.

We pray for the little ones around the world who lack power over their lives and destiny, who are continually subject to the neglect and oppression by the powerful. Give them power, O Lord, to maintain and assert their own dignity before thee and as our brothers and sisters.

All these words, O Lord, are but our own earnest searching to understand what it means to believe that Jesus is raised from the dead. Teach us how to hope in thee in all things, how to become the sort of folk who raise up and encourage others, how to be the sort of folk consumed by a miraculous generosity, how to become the servants of thy kingdom of grace and life, resisting and thwarting the kingdom of death and death-dealing.

We confess that if Jesus still lives, then we should not live as though he is dead and irrelevant to our actual living. Teach us how to live as he lived and how to hope in the final joy of that sort of resurrecting confidence.

It is in Jesus' name that we have prayed these concerns. Amen.

August 24, 2003

O Lord God, we gather today as thy people, praising thy wondrous works of creation and redemption and giving thanks for thy coming amongst us in Jesus Christ. We seek to be conformed to his life and in that way to be in conformity with thy life.

You have taught us that whether we live or whether we die, we are thy beloved children and friends. We confess that we do not often live as though we believe that. Rather, we know ourselves as inclined to fear death above all things and we are often confused as to how to live. We pray that you will not give up on us in the bitter depths of our failures and in our foolish desires to have life on our own terms.

We are thankful that we can gather as a congregation amidst others who can teach and upbuild us in the faith. We pray that we might be open to the guidance of those wise saints among us and to the guidance of thy Holy Spirit.

We pray for the one sent to pastor us in faith and life, even thy servant Kevin. Give him the courage he will always need to be a faithful and truthful interpreter of thy Word, to be a bold conveyor of thy justice, and to be a resolute proclaimer of thy unfailing grace. Give him that keen vision of the cosmic sweep and grandeur of thy life and works and the almighty power of thy grace. Keep him mindful of his own spiritual needs and preserve him from the peril of trying to run on empty. We also pray for his family that we might be a blessing to them and that they might find friendship and solidarity with us.

And O Lord, save Kevin and save us from that terrible heresy into which he and we are inclined to fall, namely, that he is the one who does the ministering and we are the ones who get ministered unto. Keep us all mindful of our common priesthood and ministry as believers in Christ and witnesses to Christ's Gospel.

Dear Lord, there is much in the world today that distresses us and strikes dismay in our hearts. The world seems so out of control and so full of uncompromising hatred and selfish violence and arrogant exertions of power aimed at domination and subjugation. Keep us from the temptations of either the despair that nothing can be done or the indifference of not caring.

So once again, O Lord, we pray for thy beloved people in Liberia, torn by a chaos created by violent and reckless men. And we pray for our brothers and sisters in Israel and in Palestine as they struggle to rise above the hatred, revenge, and demonic violence that decades of conflict have made into habits shackled in iron. We know that you are always trying to bring good out of the evil that is done by us humans to each other, and so teach us how to find ways to work with thee for good.

O lord we pray for peace, even as we know from thy Word that thy peace can never be achieved down the barrel of a gun.

It is in Christ's name that we have dared to pray so boldly. Amen.

October 5, 2003

O God, merciful giver of all life and blessing, the fount of all goodness, we come gladly and gratefully together to praise thy name, to confess our sins, and to find ourselves addressed by thy judging and forgiving Word.

Even as we praise thy name, we also confess that we have lived largely for ourselves throughout much of this past week and have neglected loving thee and loving our neighbors. Embrace us with thy forgiveness to remind us how we too must be forgiving of those who harm us. Address us in Kevin's sermon with thy Word. Give us ears to hear and hearts to feel and minds to think thy Word as it comes into our lives.

There are many, O Lord, in our community of faith who are stricken with illness or decline or despair. We lift them up to thee as the ones who need thy special care and love and restoration. Move within their lives that they may know thy love and be comforted by thy peace.

O Lord, we especially beseech thee about the violence that seems so rampant on our streets, the easy way death comes into our midst, the frightening consequences of guns too accessible to those of us filled with anger and hate. We pray for those families in our town and state this past week that have had loved ones mindlessly slaughtered on our streets, in our stores, and in our homes. Give those families, in their inconsolable grief, the strength of thy love that they may not become further victims consumed by an unquenchable hatred and lust for retaliation. Teach us that thy justice does not require returning evil with evil.

We pray for our youth, O Lord. Empower us to be faithful and loving parents living lives worthy of imitation by our children. Give us the peace to be patient, the attentive wisdom to know our children well, and the courage to give them direction and support. Relieve us of that self-centered and careless neglect that leaves our children to their own devices.

We pray for this congregation that we might be faithful witnesses to thee and thy grace. Teach us how to be hospitable to each other and to those who come to worship with us but are not yet committed.

Finally, O Lord of all goodness, it is wonderful to be alive in these times, however challenging and confusing they might be. It is wonderful just to have life from thee and before thee and to have a hope in thy unfailing grace and love.

In Christ's name we pray, Amen.

Third Sunday of Advent, December 14, 2003

O Lord of Hosts, we have heard once again the rumblings out of Bethlehem of thy sure invasion of our privacy and our kingdoms. You keep coming after us and disturbing our peace. You will not let us alone and you will not leave us to our own devices. We confess that we often long for a savior who will do our bidding and take up our private and public causes. But these rumblings of advent warn us that you want to disturb our lives and save us on thy own terms for thy Kingdom.

We earnestly pray this third Sunday of Advent that you not take from us the warm sentimentalities of our Santa Claus Christmas. Yes, we know we spend too much, and we purchase the sentiments without glad hearts. But at least this hectic season keeps the economy going, people have work, corporations thrive when we buy. Please, O Lord—the One proclaimed by John the Baptist—do not disturb us with any other news than that the real meaning of Christmas simply is the warm fuzzies of family, the lighted evergreens, the tinsel stars, and the cozy songs that wring tears from our eyes.

Do not disturb us with the thunder of war and destruction that the powerful Herods of the world are wreaking on near and distant battlefields. Soothe us with the thought that these battlefields will bring a better future and will surely protect our freedoms and our right to privacy and our right to live our lives on our own terms.

Please, O God of our own desires, just leave us alone. The last thing we want to hear now is that you are coming toward us out of the midst of stark poverty to be born a poor Jew who will challenge the mighty powers of life and death that we both fear and love. Do not beckon us to any kingdom that calls upon us to repent of our illusions and betrayals, that calls us to lay down our security devices and disband our armies, that calls us to comfort the prisoners among us, that calls us to feed the hungry, that calls us to clothe the naked and forsaken.

O God, we are so afraid of being called to these sacrifices that we will surely strike out in violence at anyone who lays another guilt trip on us. If you really want to do us a favor, forget that stuff about a new kingdom of peace, about death-dealing crosses, about saints who give without restraint. Just leave us to Santa Claus and Wal-Mart and peanut brittle and hot chocolate.

O God of all truth, forgive what we have been praying, even as we admit that these are the honest discourses of our hearts. Teach us how to speak of thy coming Kingdom, of thy mighty power and love in such a way that we might become thy servants following the way of Lord Jesus, the One we crucified. Teach us once again just what thy Kingdom is about and what you want from us and how you want to redeem us. We are really quite lost.

Come, O come, Emmanuel. Do not leave us to our own devices. Do not leave us alone in the darkness of this world of selfish conflict and violence that is of our own making. Come, Emmanuel, shine thy light into the darkness and we will surely repent and change our ways. Amen.

February 15, 2004

O God of supreme power and Creator of all creatures, we humbly come before thee this morning to praise thy name and thy wonderful works on our behalf. We know that what you curse is cursed and rejected from thy blessings and that what you bless is looked upon with thy favor. In spite of our sinful ways, of our self-centeredness, of our cantankerousness, of our slippery tongues that arrogantly condemn others, and of our war-machines that crush enemies, it is a great wonder to us that you still seek to bestow blessings upon us.

Yet, we confess that we are inclined to think that blessings are those sorts of goods that make us successful and safe and hefty in the eyes of the world. We gather this morning, having been jerked awake by thy Gospel words that tell us what is cursed and condemned and frightening and what is blessed and hopeful. Even though we stand cursed in our sin by thee, we cling to the gracious blessings you have given in Christ Jesus, who is the way, the truth, and the life of blessing.

You bless us when you call us into obedience to thy way of life in contrast to the ways of death and death-dealing, when you forgive our sins against thee and against others, when you give us crosses to bear on behalf of thy Kingdom, when you stir our hearts with a joy the world can neither confer nor take away, when you fill us with hope in desperate situations, when your Spirit whispers love songs into our souls bedraggled with doubt, guilt, and shame. We would have no clue about these extraordinary blessings were we not confronted with the sheer awesome and gracious beauty of thy coming among us in the life, death, and resurrection of Jesus of Nazareth.

Because we have breathed deeply of thy gracious Spirit in Jesus, we trust thee with our lives and we come to thee now with our concerns and prayers.

We pray for the sick and dying in our midst; may they know thy tender care and receive hope from thee. We pray for this town of Muskogee that it might find better ways of living together and paying heed to the neglected and impoverished among us, and that it might deal more peacefully with those smitten with addictions and with a seething anger toward the powerful in the town. We pray for those who are lonely, isolated, and friendless and who know no blessings; help us to be-a-blessing to them. We pray for the wealthy among us that they may not be consumed by their own guilt and greed, but may come to know the blessings of being-a-blessing to those in need. We pray for ministers who are burdened with criticism and gossipy rumors that they do not deserve and from which they cannot escape; give them a passionate courage to endure and upbuild thy church in truth.

Teach us, O Lord of all creation, how to live in this world as though it is thy world and not ours. Teach us how to mourn for the sake of righteousness in thy Kingdom. Teach us how to speak the truth in love. Teach us how to discern the blessings of thy Kingdom. Teach us how to give of ourselves boldly, even recklessly. Teach us the ways of thy peacefulness and peace-making that we may learn to rest peacefully in thy arms even in the midst of war.

All this we dare to ask in the name of Jesus, who is thy glorious blessing to us all. Amen.

March 28, 2004

O Lord God, we gladly come before thee on this day of worship. You have invited us to share our concerns with thee, to lay our hearts out before thee, to search our souls for those passions that might give life to us and to others.

We lift up to thee those already mentioned in our bulletin as those who are ill or in special need of comfort and strength. We pray for their endurance and courage in the midst of their distresses.

We pray for those in our midst who are dying, who are slowly slipping away from us. May they know thy presence even in the midst of their uninterruptible decline. Give comfort to their families and friends and shield them and us from that fear of death that betrays thy presence in our lives.

We pray for those in our midst who are unhappy with their aging bodies, who find day to day living painful and distressing, and who are inclined to lament the frailty of their minds and bodies. Remind them gently that we are finite and made from clay, and yet are destined for fellowship with thee.

We pray for the youth in our midst whose bodies are growing rapidly beyond their capacities of understanding and patience. May thy Spirit whisper gently to them that there is wisdom available from those parents and others who, surprisingly enough, once knew the restless passions of new sprouting bodies and restless hearts.

We pray for those in our midst who are disappointed with themselves, with the patterns of their lives, with those self-imposed barriers they seem to butt into every day. Give them the courage to change, to seek thy guidance and to follow it, to cease blaming others for their failures.

We pray for those in our midst who are genuinely confused about what it means to live as a disciple of Jesus. Bring them into contact with those wise others in our midst who might patiently respond to their doubts and questions, and who might shed light on their confused but searching minds.

We pray for those in our midst who are teachers in our schools. Give them intellectual audacity and courage that they might model for their students how joyful it is to inquire, to raise questions, and to learn about thy creation, that they might also model and speak a language that excites and stimulates their students to continue the inquiry on their own. And in all things empower them to be grateful for being a teacher of youth, even though sometimes the youth seem distracted or undisciplined or even ungrateful.

We pray for those in our midst who have broken hearts, who have experienced grievous disappointments about those significant others in their lives and who now seem bewildered about what the future might hold. Mend their hearts and open them to a surprising future of self-giving to others.

We pray for those in our midst who are haunted by their lonely singleness. Give them the courage to be friends of others, to give of themselves to others, and to know friendship from us and the friendship of thy Spirit.

We pray for our pastor in his earnest struggle with thy Word and how to interpret it with faithfulness and verve and truthfulness. We pray for his wife and children that they might know from us how deeply we care about them and how much we appreciate their sharing him with us.

O Lord, we pray that we all might find guidance in how to live before thee and before our neighbors in the world in that inescapable everydayness that rises before us as we awaken in the morning and as dreams occupy our nights. Give us a sturdy faithfulness and boldness of intellect and heart and resoluteness of will that we might live joyfully without illusions.

In Christ's name we have dared so to pray. Amen.

Maundy Thursday Communion Service, April 8, 2004

O Lord Jesus, you lived amongst us, called us to participate in your Father's coming Kingdom of peace and reconciliation, called us to come to thy Passover table to feast on a new forgiveness and to become servants of that impinging Kingdom. But even as we gather now to feast again at thy table of forgiveness, we are in awe—in fear and trembling—of what we know was ahead for thee as Prophet and Priest of the Kingdom. The principalities and powers that ruled the worldly kingdoms struck thee dead with horrendous brutality, announcing to all in their worlds that they were the real rulers who are in charge of order and safety in the world. Yet we know from thy resurrection that *what* you taught about reconciliation and peace and *how* you lived that reconciliation and peace are the true nature of how things are ultimately before thy Father.

We gather tonight to partake of thy feast of goodness and hope, even as we know in our hearts that we too have crosses to bear if we are to become thy disciples. We pray for courage and faithfulness as we—like Peter—are tested as to whether we will follow thy way of truth and peace or the way of those who rule by killing, by the brutal exercises of power and armaments.

We pray these things quite simply as people who feel threatened by enemies and by military saviors and the calls to hatred and revenge. We are burdened indeed as just the people we are here in Muskogee, bewildered by war. As we partake of thy bread and thy blood, teach us how to trust thee and to hope in thee in all that we do and live.

We have so prayed as the ones invited by thee to the table of forgiveness and hope. Amen.

Mother's Day, May 9, 2004

O Lord God, Giver of all mercy and everlasting Lover of us all, we gladly come together this morning to sing praises to thee, to celebrate the gift of motherhood and mothers, to pray for those among us in need, and to pray for peace in thy world. We are grateful that you have invited us to pray the concerns and passions of our hearts, and our hearts are indeed full this morning.

There are many of our church family that we lift up to thee for safekeeping. Some dwell in such pain and decline that it darkens their souls. We pray for their healing and that they might know thy presence and that their families might learn to trust in thee even more deeply. Do not leave them to their own wits and resources.

We come before thee remembering that each of us was born from the womb of a mother. We rejoice in our births and that a particular woman endured our birthing with all its attendant pains, fears, and hopes. Many of us were nursed and lovingly and wisely nudged patiently but firmly into adulthood by marvelous mothers, and we remain grateful for the many gifts they conveyed to us. Yet we also know that some of us were hurt in childhood by mothers absent or unskilled in mothering, and we bear the scars of that neglect. And there are mothers among us this day who have suffered the disappointments of ill health, of estrangement, and of early or tragic deaths of their children.

We are not sentimental and foolish that all mothering has been a blessing to the mothers or to their children. Just so, we do not indulge the falsehood that all fathers are kind, strong, attentive, reliable, and loving. We mostly know the frailty of our own lives, the frailty of our parents, and the frailty of our own parenting. But in the mystery of thy creating, we are thankful for our mothers in bearing the gift of life to us. And many are the mothers among us who are grateful for the sheer beauty, blessing, and grace of bearing and raising their children.

O Lord God, as we pray to thee, we know that you are in dismay at the suffering and blindness of thy children who war incessantly, who have constructed societies that celebrate conflict and breed superiority over others and who need enemies in order to induce their own social solidarity. Many are thy children who have constructed religions to do their own bidding and meet their own twisted desires. We know that many of thy children ask for victory in war and the death of their enemies. We know that many leaders of nations and peoples seek their own power and betray their people. We know the world stands on the brink of cascading violence and enmity that will poison human life for decades to come.

Our worship of thee this day, O Lord, would be pagan and unfaithful if we did not pray for peace on thy terms and not on our own terms. And we earnestly pray, O Lord, that you will teach and lead each of us in the paths of forgiving justice and truth-telling in the days ahead. Disabuse us of our illusions and falsehoods and throw thy loving light upon us that we might be faithful to thy Kingdom in the days ahead, in the months to come, and in the remaining years we have to live. Teach us the special disciplines and joys of being lovers of thy Kingdom and followers of Jesus.

All this O Lord, we have prayed in the name of Jesus Christ, who also taught us well how to pray. Amen.

Father's Day, June 20, 2004

O Lord God, Father of us all, the One who sent Jesus the Son into the far country of human goodness and rebellion, of human beauty and ugliness, of human grandeur and misery, we come together this morning to praise thy name and to remember thy ways among thy creatures. You are the One who called thy church into being as those summoned to follow Jesus and his way of life and to witness to new possibilities of living lovingly and peacefully with neighbors, with strangers, with enemies.

We come to thee this day as just those people who have heard Jesus' summons. But we confess that we are weak and that we often stand on the sidelines of faith, unwilling to live as he lived, unwilling to love thee before all the other idols that claim our loyalties, unwilling to care passionately about thy peace. We pray for the strength, courage, and grace to refuse to live amidst the wastelands of self-centeredness, of idolatry, of wanting to be and act as the final judge of those about us who seem to threaten us.

Many of us this day are fathers who have bred children from the loins of our bodies. And some of us have been fatherly to our children as you have taught us to be, and some of us have been absent, neglectful, and even hateful in repudiation of the gift of being-a-father. Those among us who had good, wise, and dependable fathers are grateful for their loving care, and those among us who had less dependable fathers seek from thee that forgiving heart about which Jesus taught.

Yet we pray that we might learn how, without lies and delusions, to honor our fathers just because they bore life to us and upon them we are forever dependent as the agents of thy bringing us into the world. And O

233

Lord, we fathers, now with children of all ages, pray that we might find ways in which to upbuild our children with many acts of tender mercy and wise counsel. Teach us fathers how to teach thy ways to our children by daily acts of faithfulness, of love, and of justice.

Many are they, O Lord, among us this day who are filled with gratitude by the abundance of life they have experienced this past week. May you know in this prayer of ours how profoundly grateful they are. And many are they, O Lord, among us this day who are filled with doubt, remorse, unbridled anger, sick and deteriorating bodies, and languishing souls. May they know the transforming comfort of thy love. And may we all know the burning depths of thy gracious truth about us—each and every one of us in the particularity of our lives—for it is a truth that destroys arrogance and slothfulness and yet gives strength and hope. Great is our wonder at your everlasting mercy, upon which we are learning how to depend.

All this we have dared to pray in the name of Jesus, who taught us in our hesitations and confusions how to pray. Amen.

August 1, 2004

O Lord God, we rejoice this morning as we are called together by thy Gospel. It is thy Word in Jesus Christ that has changed our lives and called us to live in ways different from the ways of the world. It is thy Word that conveys thy abundant grace to us, calls us to attention, and gives us direction into the future. It is thy Word that has taught us how to think about ourselves, about the meaning of life, about thy power and love. Without thy Word in Jesus Christ we would still be enthralled to idols, we would be pagans full of fear and violence, we would be barbaric warriors among the peoples of the world. But with thy Word we have become cross-bearers who love peace and who put the good of others above our own appetites and inclinations.

Because we are a changed people with an absolute loyalty to thee above all else, we lift up to thee those individuals and families in our congregation who suffer disease, who find themselves with declining bodies, who are stalked by depressed and confused minds, who bear an anger so deep that it poisons their hearts. We pray that all of these may know the light of thy powerful Word and Grace and the comfort of thy unwavering mercy.

O Lord, we ask for guidance as we are plunged into the midst of presidential politics. Even as we gather this day, there are some among us who admire one candidate as savior of us all and there are others among us who admire the other candidate as savior of us all. It would seem that we are looking for a savior who would do our bidding, keep us safe from harm, lower our taxes, and make us the mightiest and most feared nation on thy earth. Forgive us, O Lord, if we act and sound as though we have no savior, as though our loyalty to thee is second in line to the candidate we think is the righteous savior, the everlasting truth-teller, the most just of all the nations' leaders. Forgive us when we act like pagans, creating idols that serve our own selfish interests and refusing to trust in thee.

The weather this past week has been a delight. The rains have been cooling, the sun has been soothingly bright. Teach us, O Lord, how to enjoy thy creation without destroying it, how to live gratefully amidst the lilies of the fields and the foxes and the coyotes of the forests, and even the armadillos of the night that dig up our lawns. We want to live well and honestly, O Lord, even as you have taught us a new way to live as a people who forgive, who love earnestly, and who refuse to slay others out of fear and hatred.

All this we ask in the name of Jesus, thy Word made flesh, thy Word spoken to us in words and actions. Amen.

September 12, 2004

O Lord God, Creator of all things in heaven and on earth, the One in whose image all humans were made, and the One who came searching for us in Christ Jesus, we come this day with our hearts and minds full of the sounds of disarray in our world. We pray this day as the people of thy church, confessing Jesus as Lord and Savior. But we also pray as Oklahomans and Americans who still live under the haunting spell of the frightening crimes of what we now simply call "9/11." And we confess we sometimes do not know whether we are first disciples of Jesus or disciples of our nation and its present government. We are torn and we are frightened and we are often confused.

As Christians, O Lord, we are truly dismayed why others of thy human creation find us Americans so hateful and dreadful, why they should take delight in killing us. We think, as Americans, that we do not want to dominate the world; we just want to live in peace and that we never go to war without a just cause. Are we deluded in that, O Lord? Are our skirts really so clean? Give us guidance here. We confess that we are not inclined to love these enemies and that we do want to return evil for evil, we do want revenge and to protect ourselves whatever the cost. Do you look kindly, O Lord, on these thoughts and actions of ours? Is the sword what you are summoning us to draw out and use? What, O Lord, we want to know, does it mean in these times to take up the cross and follow thee?

Even as we pray this day for guidance and illumination in the midst of our fear, anger, and pride, we know we must earnestly pray for those who are daily dying in this project many call "The War on Terror." The families of our fallen and wounded soldiers are suffering grave losses, and their grief is not easily consoled. We lift them up to thee for comfort and hope. The families of the fallen Iraqis and other Arabs cry long and sobering laments as well. O Lord, it is only in thee that we and they might find a grace that gives hope. We pray as well for the families of those civilians slain by wayward shells. We pray that the illuminating light of thy peaceful Spirit might cover the Middle East and bring all together in a reunion of peace and hope.

We lift up the families of those who were killed or wounded on the dark day of 9/11. We see some of them on television and it breaks our hearts that ones they loved met such horrendous deaths. We pray thy Spirit might fall upon them and comfort them in a hope not dependent on revenge. We pray as well that they might all know that firm hope for themselves and their dead loved ones that you have disclosed in the resurrection of Christ Jesus: that he is the ultimate gracious Lord who contends eternally with death and all forms of violence.

To pray, O Lord, with such directness and pathos exhausts us. We want to run and hide or we want to kill without restraint the ones we call evildoers. But we know you call us to raise our heads and hearts to thy truth and to thy eternal Gospel. We pray for release from the fear, anger, and hatred that imprisons our hearts. O Lord, give us and our enemies peace and much grace.

In Christ we pray. Amen.

Sunday before Election Day, October 31, 2004

O Lord God, giver of all life and goodness, we come this morning rejoicing in thy great gifts of love to us in Christ Jesus and in the saints of the church over the centuries. While we were yet sinners, you did not count our sins against us. Instead, unlike us—who hate enemies and are reluctant to forgive harm done to us—you came among us in Jesus, forgiving our sins even before we asked and calling us to love thee and thy Kingdom above all else. We confess before thee this day that we struggle with thy calling and with thy forgiveness. We struggle with being thy people who seek in all ways to be reconcilers and peacemakers in thy world. We confess that we have used many excuses to avoid being such reconciling peacemakers.

But, O Lord, we come before thee this day seeking thy guidance in these perilous and threatening times. We are coming to the conclusion of a long and bitter public election at all levels of our civic life. We feel quite beaten up with the sound and fury of incessant ads, of lies, of obfuscations, of evasive and poisonous sound-bites, and of unrelieved mendacity. We have found it difficult to sort through the issues and to find a firm perspective and truth from which to vote—especially to vote in such a way that we reflect the imperatives of thy Gospel as made known to us in Jesus. We confess that we are haunted by fears: fears of a malevolent enemy threatening our lives; fears that our preferred candidates might lose; fears that we might descend into a whirlwind of endless war, staggering debts, and vicious conflicts among the people.

We worry that we are a divided people, both in thy church and in this nation. We are beset with anger toward those with whom we disagree. We are inclined to think those who disagree with us are selfish, stupid, mischievous, and just plain evil. O Lord, we are inclined to demonize those who oppose us and disagree with us, and we are drowning in a sea of bitterness and suspicion.

In short, God, we need thy help. Guide us to do what is acceptable in thy sight. Give us the courage to think deeply and honestly and to vote without rancor. We want to be thy people called to manifest thy love and grace in a world that seems bereft of grace and love and mercy. We want to be thy people called to care for the least of thy children that are largely neglected by the world. We want to be thy people who do not simply seek our own selfish interests and look for candidates and referenda that support our privileges and our wealth.

We pray, O Lord, that we might simply know thee as the Creator, Reconciler, and Redeemer of the whole world and the One before whom we all stand in judgment and grace when we step into the voting booth.

We also pray, O Lord, that when the votes are counted and the winners announced, we might seek reconciliation among the people and find hope for a time of peace and justice for all. We also pray, O Lord, that we might have the courage after the elections to continue to be thy people, full of mercy and grace, and full of hope in thee as the Final Merciful Judge of us all. May we all be winners as we trust in thy mercy to heal our wounds and disappointments and to empower us with new hopes.

In Christ's name we have dared so to pray. Amen.

Second Sunday of Advent, December 5, 2004

O God of fierce judgment and unlimited mercy, we gladly come this second Sunday of Advent to praise thy name and to remember again that you came among us in humility and great determination. As we gather now, we pray that this season of Advent might be a time of solemn preparation and unrestrained joy and that we might not fall into the trap of confusing the mythical coming of an overweight Santa Claus with the coming of Jesus the radical prophet.

We pray that we may take delight in the giving and receiving of gifts, remembering how you have given life and hope to us and remembering that "it is more blessed to give than to receive." Yet, O Lord, empower us to be grateful and humble when others—family, friends, and strangers— give generously to us. Overwhelm us with the simple joy of giving and receiving without expectation of repayment or exchange.

Even as we remember that the baby Jesus grew into that sort of divine prophet that ended up crucified by the powerful leaders of his day, so too let us remember those who live in terror in the midst of battles, guns, and the dreadful fear of sudden death. We pray that soldiers might be safe from harm and that they might not be called upon to do harm. We pray that our brothers and sisters in Islamic lands might lay down their swords and fears of us and join Christians around the world in praying and acting for peace and justice.

We know, O Lord, that many among us in this congregation are entering into Advent in the midst of illness, decline, sorrow, confusion, and unrelieved anxiety. May they know the comfort of thy sustaining love and Spirit, even as their bodies and spirits are healed and infused with hope in the finality of thy Incarnate love in Jesus.

We pray in gratitude for our pastor and his family. May they all know the tenderness of our concern for them and may they know the blessings of receiving our earnest prayers for their well-being.

All this, O Lord, we have dared to pray in the name of Jesus. Amen.